TOPICS IN SAFETY

3rd EDITION

The Association for Science Education

The Editorial Committee

This edition of Topics in Safety began with a conference of individuals representing many of the organisations in the UK with an interest in health and safety in secondary science. Those individuals who wrote the topics are identified in italics, but all the members of the committee contributed ideas, and commented on the text in its various draft stages.

Peter Borrows   ASE Safeguards in Science Committee, Director of CLEAPSS

Phil Bunyan   Editor of this edition, Chair ASE Safeguards in Science Committee

Allen Cochrane ASE Safeguards in Science Committee, SSERC

Martin Elliott   DfEE

John Grainger Reading University School of Animal and Microbiological Sciences

Joe Jefferies   ASE Safeguards in Science Committee

John Lawrence ASE Safeguards in Science Committee, Deputy Chief Executive ASE

Mike Lexton   ASE Safeguards in Science Committee

Dick Orton   Independent consultant, formerly CLEAPSS

Colin Osborne Royal Society of Chemistry

Richard Price   Science and Plants for Schools (SAPS)

Phil Stone   ASE Safeguards in Science Committee

John Tranter   ASE Safeguards in Science Committee, CLEAPSS

Ray Vincent   ASE Safeguards in Science Committee

Mary Wood   Institute of Physics

Bob Worley   CLEAPSS

In addition, the following also wrote some or all of a topic:

Gill Halton   Manchester Metropolitan University Education department

Roger Delpech Haberdashers' Aske School

Dean Madden   National Centre for Biotechnology Education (NCBE)

TOPICS IN SAFETY

3rd EDITION

The Association for Science Education

Published by the Association for Science Education,
College Lane, Hatfield, Herts AL20 9AA

First edition   1982
Second edition 1988
Third edition   2001
© The Association for Science Education

Printed by the Black Bear Press, Cambridge, UK
Designed and typeset by Paul and Hendrina Ellis

ISBN 0 86357 316 9

CONTENTS

INTRODUCTION

This is the third edition of a publication which first appeared in 1982 and was updated in 1988. Since then there have been a number of significant changes in the health and safety regulations which apply to science education in schools and colleges, and, therefore, a need to update advice. The science curriculum has also changed over the period. Activities which were common are no longer often done, to be replaced by others which were previously rare. Given all this, it was an appropriate time for a fresh look at this book.

Topics in Safety is not, and never was, a comprehensive health and safety manual for secondary school science. Many other excellent publications provide brief but comprehensive advice on laboratory safety: the ASE's *Safeguards in the School Laboratory*, the DfEE *Safety in Science Education,* and the collected publications from CLEAPSS and SSERC, are examples. *Topics in Safety* is intended to be a reference book: a collection of health and safety-related essays on issues which are important, current, complex and perhaps contentious. Emphasising that it is a collection, the book does not have chapters but individual Topics. Each Topic provides a level of detail and background information which allows those involved in secondary science education to understand issues before making decisions on behalf of their employer, or to provide suitable advice to influence decision-making. The Topics are written as far as possible to stand alone, although there are cross references for linked ideas and definitions, e.g. that for employers, which occur in several places. Virtually all of the Topics make reference to advice and publications from the ASE, CLEAPSS and SSERC so, for convenience, full details of these organisations are given at the end of this Introduction.

There has also been a change in emphasis from previous editions. Although it was always the intention to support practical activities in science, a general view has grown over the years that health and safety impose restrictions on the activities which can be done and the materials and equipment which can be used. In the previous edition the 'Notes to Readers' stated that '*safety considerations are not intended to restrict practical work but simply to make it safer to carry it out*'. However, this message did not come through as clearly as was hoped. In this edition we have set out to inform the reader of what can be done and how to do it. Wherever possible authors have drawn attention to the process of making a risk assessment. They have shown how knowledge of the factors that are considered in assessing risk enables activities to be modified, with equipment or substances substituted, so that work can still be carried out with as much fun and educational validity as before – but with acceptable levels of safety. The authors and editorial team are committed to practical science in schools and colleges.

This edition is larger than the previous two. There are more Topics, some derived from earlier editions, others completely new. Among the latter are Topics on teaching health and safety through science, technicians, manual handling, allergies and asthma, living organisms, working with DNA, and lasers, infrared, ultraviolet and visible radiation. However, readers will find the contents of Topics which appeared in earlier editions have often been much modified to bring them up-to-date. As always with health and safety, we could have waited a few months for some impending regulations to be finalised and published. This is particularly true of ionising radiations and working with DNA. However, we could not wait indefinitely. All the authors have consulted widely, drawing on expertise from the editorial team and beyond. We are confident, therefore, that the advice given is sensible and conforms to both existing regulations and the spirit of those which are expected.

Note to readers

Readers must remember that the recommendations made in these topics have no legal status and are only the best advice which is available at the time of publication. **Teachers and technicians have a duty under the Health and Safety at Work Act to comply with any safety instructions given them by their employer** (see Topic 1 for a definition of employer). There may well be cases where the employer's advice is more restrictive than that given here, e.g. it may ban the use of a chemical allowed in a Topic. In this case the teacher or technician has a duty to follow the employer's instructions. However, they are perfectly at liberty to challenge the reasoning behind the instruction and to seek to get the local regulation modified.

Science teachers should also bear in mind that the advice given in these Topics is based on an estimate of the possible situation in the school and the likely experience of the students at a particular stage in their school career.

It must be remembered that teachers know best the capabilities of their students and that teachers and technicians know best their circumstances. They must be allowed a certain amount of professional judgement in adjusting the risk assessments given.

Extract from *COSSH: Guidance for Schools*, Health and Safety Commission; Education Services Advisory Committee, HMSO, 1989, ISBN 0 11 885511 5.

> 7 *In order to help those undertaking these responsibilities (risk assessments), a number of general assessments have already been developed for most of the substances and experiments found in school science. Examples are included in the second edition of the Association for Science Education's (ASE's) Topics in Safety...*
>
> 8 *For science subjects, employers have the choice of:*
>
> *(a) adopting and if necessary adapting to particular circumstances such well researched and established general assessments for school science work;...*

The Editorial Committee

This edition of *Topics in Safety* began with a conference of individuals representing many of the organisations in the UK with an interest in health and safety in secondary science. A few have been involved since the first and second editions, others have been asked to contribute to the new topic areas of this edition. The Committee and other contributors are listed on page (ii).

Acknowledgements

The committee wishes to thank others who helped with this publication. These include the HSE, Quadeer Khan, OBE (formerly head of the South Yorkshire Waste Regulation Authority) for advice on Topic 11, J. R. Carlton for the original paper which became Topic 8, and John Richardson, Jim Jamieson (both of SSERC) and numerous other colleagues for comments on the draft text.

This edition has been prepared with the kind support of Esso UK plc, through the offices of Martin Tims (Manager Education and Environment Programmes).

The following organisations are frequently referred to throughout this book as sources of further advice or publications.

The Association for Science Education (ASE)

College Lane, Hatfield, Herts, AL10 9AA.
Tel: 01707 283000, fax: 01707 266532
E-mail: membership@ase.org.uk
Website: www.ase.org.uk
Membership is open to anyone but especially teachers.

The CLEAPSS School Science Service

Brunel University, Uxbridge, UB8 3PH.
Tel: 01895 251496, fax: 01895 814372
E-mail: science@cleapss.org.uk
Website: www.cleapss.org.uk
Membership open to education authorities, and hence all of their schools throughout the UK (not Scotland). Independent schools and teacher training establishments may join as associate members.

SSERC

St Mary's Building, 23 Holyrood Road, Edinburgh EH8 8AE.
Tel: 0131 558 8180, fax: 0131 558 8191
E-mail: sts@sserc.org.uk
Website: www.sserc.org.uk
Membership is open to education authorities, and hence all of their schools in Scotland. Independent establishments may also subscribe.

Health and Safety Executive (HSE)

General enquiries should be addressed or faxed to the Sheffield Information Centre, Health and Safety Laboratory, Broad Lane, Sheffield S3 7HQ.
Fax: 0114 289 2333

The public enquiry point telephone numbers are: 0541 545 500 and 08701 545 500
Website: www.hse.gov.uk

MANAGING HEALTH AND SAFETY

This Topic replaces Chapter 1 'Organizing for safety' in the second edition of Topics in Safety.

1 Introduction

The Management of Health and Safety at Work Regulations 1999[1] (Management Regulations) make explicit some requirements of employers in terms of managing health and safety. These are:

■ to assess the risks to health and safety to which employees and others are exposed (the significant findings of the assessments must be recorded);

■ to make arrangements for the effective planning, control, monitoring and review of safety measures, which should be recorded;

■ to provide comprehensive and relevant information to employees on risks, specific safety measures, procedures to be taken in the event of serious and imminent danger, and to identify those responsible for implementing such procedures;

■ to appoint a competent person or persons, to assist the employer in complying with its legal duties. Employers are encouraged to appoint such competent persons from amongst their own employees.

A head of science is expected to be a competent person as described in the last of the above points. S/he will be expected to manage health and safety within the science department in order to support the employer in fulfilling its duties.

Rather than reiterate many of the existing detailed requirements, helpful checklists and model procedures for management of health and safety in science, the reader will be referred to information commonly available in other standard science health and safety texts. This Topic will concentrate on the significant management principles such as the need to make arrangements for the effective planning, organisation, control, monitoring and review of preventative and protective measures. Within this Topic these principles are discussed under the following headings:

■ Organisation – who does what.

■ The need for training.

■ The need for monitoring.

2 Science is safe

It is important in the management of health and safety within a science department to recognise that, in schools, science is extremely safe. However, this observation does not provide an opportunity for complacency, rather the opposite. It does provide a context for implementation of practices and procedures which will ensure that the present safety record is maintained, and even improved.

The most recent suitable data from the Health and Safety Executive (1996/7) (HSE) show that, in schools, the majority of reported accidents to students occur during sporting activities and in playgrounds. Only 2.3% of reportable incidents occur in a science lab. The proportion of such incidents resulting in significant injury in science labs is even less, at around 0.8%. A comment from a Health and Safety Inspector endorsed this by stating that the number of accidents in school science is vanishingly small. Such a record reflects the knowledge and understanding which science teachers and technicians have of the risks associated with their work and the care taken to minimise them. However, a few of the accidents are very serious and there continues to be a number of minor accidents such as chemical splashes on skin and in eyes, cuts from glass and sharp scalpels, and burns and scalds. The aim is to reduce or eliminate these as well as ensure that the more obvious and significant risks continue to be controlled.

3 Employers and employees

The Health and Safety at Work (HSW) Act (1974) places duties on employers and on employees. The employer is the body with whom the employee has a written contract of employment. In education this may be:

■ local education authorities in England and Wales (for community and voluntary controlled schools);

---

[1] Management of Health and Safety at Work Regulations, 1999. SI No. 1999/3242. Stationery Office. Also HSE (2000) *Approved Code of Practice and Guidance L21: Management of Health and Safety at Work.* HSE. ISBN 0 7176 2488 9.

- governing bodies in England and Wales (for foundation and voluntary aided schools, CTCs and post-16 colleges, etc.);

- education authorities in Scotland;

- education and library boards (in Northern Ireland);

- governing bodies, charitable trusts or proprietors, as appropriate (in independent schools).

A head of department and all the staff working in the department are employees. Students and visitors are referred to as 'others', who are covered by the general duty of care.

The term 'head of science' is generic and is taken to mean any person who has some management responsibility for science in a school or college. This could be a head of department or faculty, the principal teacher or director of science; a head of biology, physics or chemistry; or teacher in charge of a key stage. The term 'staff' is taken to mean any employee who works within science, full or part time. This may include teachers, technicians, non-science teachers covering lessons or tutor periods; support assistants, other adults working in science; supply teachers or agency technicians.

The HSW Act gives employers the duty:

- to provide safe and healthy working conditions for employees and others;

- to provide information, instruction, and training about health and safety;

- to prepare a written health and safety policy which must be brought to the attention of employees.

Employees have the duty:

- to take reasonable care for their own and others' health and safety;

- to cooperate with their employers over health and safety matters;

- to not interfere with or misuse items provided for health and safety.

This last provision also applies to non-employees.

The Management Regulations additionally require employees:

- to carry out activities in accordance with training and instructions;

- to inform the employer of any serious risk and failure in health and safety arrangements.

Delegation of tasks by the employer is made through the governors (or from the governors where they are the employer, e.g. in independent schools) and the headteacher to the head of science.

The head of science will therefore need to have systems to plan for and manage health and safety within science, to ensure staff within the department are kept up-to-date and given training as appropriate, and to monitor and review the effective working of the systems.

It is important to note that although tasks have been delegated to the head of science, the responsibility for ensuring health and safety still ultimately rests with the employer. The employer is required to provide information, instruction and training in order that a competent person remains competent. The full working of the health and safety legislation is founded on the principle that the employer identifies the hazards and risks, sets up health and safety management systems, trains or appoints employees to carry out tasks, and monitors the successful working of the system. As long as a suitably trained employee does not wilfully or negligently disregard advice or instruction, and does take reasonable care for his/her own and others' health and safety, the responsibility, in the event of an accident, rests with the employer.

The management structure (next page) illustrates one possible way of organising a science department in order to fulfil the requirements of the Management Regulations. Functions are allocated to individuals to illustrate how the system might work. Remember, however, it is not the precise details which are important but the structure which ensures that the department can plan for, manage and monitor the health and safety systems needed.

4 The need for training

Under the HSW Act, reinforced by the Management Regulations, there is a requirement to provide training for all staff: teachers, technicians and others who work in the department. Such training is required:

- when new staff are recruited (i.e. induction);

- if staff roles change (e.g. a physicist starting to teach chemistry or a PE teacher helping out in the science department);

- in the use of particularly hazardous equipment or materials;

- when new equipment or materials are introduced;

- in emergency procedures.

This training must be repeated periodically, must take place during working hours, and must take account of the needs of part-time staff. To prevent the spread of misinformation it must also be authoritative, using trainers or materials that are known to be accurate and up-to-date.

A head of science is often required to ensure that the above training requirements are met for the science

Table 1 Example of possible allocation of health and safety duties in a science department.

Head of science (who happens to be a biologist)

In overall charge of health and safety in the department; specifically in charge of ensuring risk assessments for post-16 biology are present; also for providing risk assessment information for 11–16 courses; is in charge of GCSE and therefore for ensuring risk assessments are in place in these course(s). Produces annual health and safety report for headteacher and governors.

Second in charge of department (who happens to be the senior chemist) and is responsible for KS3 science

In overall charge of ensuring risk assessments for lower school course are in place and that appropriate input is made by specialist colleagues; in charge of risk assessment in post-16 chemistry course; in charge of updating department on health and safety issues to do with chemicals; oversees health and safety implications of chemicals including their storage. Reports termly to head of science.

Senior physics teacher

In charge of risk assessment in post-16 physics courses and for providing risk assessment information and advice for 11–16 courses; in charge of safe storage and monitoring of radioactive sources and materials. Reports on these annually to head of science.

AN Other science teacher (a biologist of 5+ years experience)

Agreed, as part of professional development, to be in charge of newly-qualified teachers, including their health and safety induction and monitoring, reports termly on this to the head of science; also, as the most experienced microbiologist, is in charge of risk assessments to do with microbiology and with ensuring microbiological equipment and procedures are in place, suitable and up-to-date.

Senior technician (10+ years experience)

In charge of technicians' health and safety; reports health and safety issues which arise to appropriate staff, e.g. difficulties with chemical storage to senior chemist; in charge of (because of training) annual inspection of fume cupboard (but not for repair work, nor responsible for any subsequent failure), and in charge of seeing that inspection of portable electrical appliances takes place (but not for doing this). Reports formally, termly, to head of science on health and safety matters and, informally, very much more frequently.

Technician (part time, shared with technology department)

Because of training and agreed job description carries out the inspection of portable electrical appliances. Reports health and safety issues arising from these, and other aspects of work, to senior technician.

Other teachers and technicians

Responsible for personal health and safety.

---

department. Often the appropriate training is most easily and appropriately provided within the department itself, using suitably experienced teachers or technicians. Discussions at department meetings will constitute training. So also would the chemistry teacher giving a demonstration to the rest of the staff on how to conduct, for example, the thermit reaction safely. A new, but experienced, member of staff may only need to be given the department health and safety policy with an appropriate commentary identifying specific ways of working within the department. A newly-qualified teacher requires a more thorough and systematic induction, which is likely to include more wide-ranging themes than just how the department works.

Trainee teachers (ITT students) need closer and more detailed training and scrutiny. Health and safety issues should feature prominently in lesson planning and should be checked carefully by the teacher mentor.

There should be regular and frequent discussion about lesson plans, where there is doubt about a trainee teacher's experience in carrying out a procedure safely, then specific training should be provided. The regular teacher should be present for the first few lessons until s/he is satisfied that the trainee teacher can be left alone with the class. Even then an experienced teacher should always be within earshot and should check from time to time that all is well.

Occasional attendance at a training course is useful for every individual. The head of science or an aspiring head of science could attend one of the management of health and safety courses available through the ASE or others (such as CLEAPSS or SSERC, see 'Introduction' page 2). Such training is most useful if the person trained is later required to report significant issues and details back to a meeting of the whole department.

The ASE has produced an INSET pack[2], *Safe and exciting science*, that enables a department to train itself. The flexibility of the pack allows training over a short period or, using occasional department meetings, to complete the programme over a couple of years. As well as being economical, the flexibility allows a department to tailor its training to meet its individual requirements.

Non-science staff such as form tutors, supply teachers and classroom assistants also require training if they are working in a laboratory. Usually such training can be brief and limited to some do's and don't's (e.g. do not leave the class unsupervised) that can be summarised in a simple handout. The training need only take a few minutes as long as there are no practical activities involved. If supply teachers or classroom assistants undertake practical work then more substantial training is required. This is also the case if a non-science specialist is required, for timetable reasons, to teach science regularly.

It is essential that technicians are included in all staff training, including that which is undertaken at department meetings. In addition, technicians often need more substantial training as they can act as an important source of health and safety information for teaching staff. The extent of training will depend on the experience and qualifications of the technician and much can be undertaken in-house. However, enabling a technician to attend occasional good quality local or national training courses is often cost-effective, particularly if this includes planned feedback to the rest of the department.

All members of the department need training in emergency procedures such as using eye-wash facilities. Training of this sort generally involves practising the procedures that are already well documented in several safety publications. Training for other emergency remedial action, such as dealing with cuts or possibly resuscitation techniques, requires specialist input. The school nurse or first-aider will be able to offer such training or suggest someone who can. This kind of training ought to be repeated every few years to ensure it remains fresh in staff minds. The ASE INSET pack provides a suitable resource.

As part of continuing training it is important that department staff have access to correct as well as up-to-date information. Ways of bringing this about are given below but on all occasions where new information is discussed, it is essential that the source of the information is specified and, if necessary, checked. It is inappropriate for a member of the department to report a health and safety item that was relayed from a colleague perhaps in a different school that was in turn brought back from a training course by a further colleague. Like

Chinese whispers, such information gains much in the re-telling, often becoming educationally harmful rather than anything else. It should be a criterion for all health and safety information that the documentary source and/ or information route is known and recognised as informed and trustworthy. If there is any doubt, a telephone call to the ASE, CLEAPSS or SSERC (see Introduction) will quickly establish the accuracy or otherwise of any information.

One of the simplest and most effective ways of ensuring all staff keep up to date is to have health and safety as a standing item on the agenda of all science department meetings. That way, if there is anything to note, it can be raised and discussed. Encourage staff to report near-misses and examples of potentially unsafe practice. If there are no issues then the meeting passes on to the next agenda item. Having health and safety as a standing item ensures that it is regularly considered and never overlooked. A 'Hazard Book' hanging in the prep room may encourage reporting, as long as it is routinely checked.

Important health and safety documents often need to be read in full or in part by all members of the department. These include health and safety circulars, education authority-produced summary documents, articles in ASE journals, newsletters from CLEAPPS and SSERC and occasionally new health and safety reference texts. Such documents should be circulated systematically through the department with a staff list attached and a reasonable timescale for individual reading given. A date for final return to the head of department should also help to ensure that the document does not become irretrievably lost.

Short articles can be easily read by all. New books, however, present more of an obstacle because of the quantity of material in them. It would help if the head of department annotates the staff list with suggestions as to which parts of the book are most appropriate for each member of staff. In this way all staff become familiar with the book without the burden of believing it must be read from cover to cover. Individuals are more likely to read one or two relevant chapters, particularly if there is a requirement to report back to a department meeting on any significant issues. By sharing information tasks in this way, the burden of keeping up with developments is much reduced, and keeping up to date with health and safety becomes more fully integrated into the thinking of the department.

---

2 ASE (1999) *Safe and exciting science*. ISBN 0 86357 295 2.

5 Students with special needs

The range of special needs in the school population is now very large and strategies for teaching health and safety in science must take account of the diversity of special needs in educational institutions. The support given by the teacher or a helper to students with learning disabilities, for example, will obviously need to be much closer than that required by other students. If there are students in the class with reading difficulties, help that is given verbally is often more effective than that which is text-based. Where reading is a problem, the use of graphic rather than textual material in point-of-use texts or worksheets is likely to be helpful.

Risk assessments and risk control measures will often need to be modified for some students with special needs, perhaps because there is an increased risk in a practical activity that is attempted by a student with a disability. For a fuller discussion see ASE *Safety reprints*[3].

6 The need for monitoring

Once appropriate systems and practices are in place, the head of science is required to monitor that they are working as planned. Monitoring is not the same as checking everything – a representative sample is enough. The head of department does not personally have to check all aspects of health and safety in the department. Some checking can be delegated to those members of staff who have responsibility for specific elements of the curriculum. Planned health and safety discussions with those staff will enable the head of science to monitor the outcomes of those checks.

Monitoring of procedures and equipment can use checklists such as those in Appendices 1 and 2 at the end of this Topic. There should be a programmed time each year when the checklists are used and signed to confirm that all is well. The timing of this monitoring could usefully coincide with a brief annual written report on health and safety within the department to the headteacher and/or governors.

Trainee teachers can be monitored against department laboratory rules and accepted ways of working (such as the wearing of eye protection). Such monitoring is primarily the task of the individual science teacher but the head of science should sample lessons to see that the rules are being followed.

Monitoring of teachers' and technicians' practice is less simple but no less important. Discussions at department meetings will identify much about health and safety practice. Occasional observation of lessons, or even brief visits to classes, can confirm whether, for example, risk assessments are leading to safe practice and whether students are generally working safely. Occasional scrutiny of technicians' requisition sheets will indicate whether risk assessment procedures are being followed. The department's 'accident record' will identify whether there are any patterns to accidents and incidents, although these will usually emerge much more quickly through regular discussion.

Newly-qualified and less-experienced teachers will require closer monitoring than more experienced colleagues. However, beware also the 'creative' teacher or technician or any who are unwilling to change long-established practices. Monitoring is best set in the context of verifying lesson planning and occasional paired working in the lab to observe practice. It would be inappropriate for monitoring of a new colleague to be heavy handed even where health and safety matters are being checked. More experienced staff teaching an area of the curriculum for the first time may also require more sensitive handling but this is no reason to assume that the health and safety of their practice should not be verified.

Schemes of work, their associated risk assessments and the department health and safety policy will establish acceptable practice. Monitoring can be used to ensure all staff follow guidelines but it is generally more effective if, through department meetings, staff understand they are expected to follow the guidance. Subsequent monitoring can then be of a 'lighter touch' except where there is reasonable cause to believe that guidelines are not being followed.

A science department should maintain a health and safety monitoring log to record outcomes of monitoring, and which can act as a cross check that monitoring has taken place. Such a log may be kept within a department diary or even an exercise book. A record is kept of the date a monitoring activity or discussion took place and a note of any significant outcomes if these are not recorded elsewhere. For example, following a brief discussion with the senior physics teacher, an entry in the log could read: 'radioactive sources and procedures checked and confirmed, details in ionising radiation folder and log'. In the case of a newly-qualified teacher the entry would indicate whether or not health and safety issues were successfully managed, e.g. in a lesson observed, and whether, in addition to ensuring students follow safe practice, any notable advice or instructions were given.

---

[3] ASE (1996) *Safety reprints*. ISBN 0 86357 246 4.

Appendix 1 Timetable for significant regular safety checks

Check	Frequency	Legal status
Fume cupboards (see Topic 7)	At least every 14 months	Specific requirement under COSHH Regulations
Contamination of radium sources Damage to any sealed radioactive sources (in Scotland, leakage of all sealed sources) (see Topic 19)	Visual check every time used Formal check as per regulations but annual may be more practicable	Specific requirement under Administrative Memorandum 1/92 The Use of Ionising Radiations in Educational Establishments in England and Wales. And in SOED (now SEED) (1987) Circular 1166
Portable mains-operated electrical equipment (see Topic 17)	Dependent on use, items used frequently such as lab packs should be checked termly	Specific requirement under Electricity at Work Regulations
Autoclaves, model steam engines and pressure cookers	As specified in the written Scheme of Examination drawn up by a competent person	Specific requirement under Pressure Systems Safety Regulations
Chemicals with a short safe shelf-life	Annual	General duties under HSW Act
General laboratory fixtures and fittings, equipment, etc.	A checklist should be used for items to be checked daily, weekly, termly or annually	General duties under HSW Act

Appendix 2 Summary health and safety checklist for heads of science

1 Health and safety policy document

If required by the employer, is there an up-to-date and appropriate science health and safety policy?   yes ❑ no ❑

2 Health and safety check logbook or file

Does the department have a file or logbook, showing when various checks/tests were carried out, by whom, and with what outcome?   yes ❑ no ❑

3 Functions of named persons

Do named individuals have health and safety functions related to particular courses, for the induction of new staff, etc?   yes ❑ no ❑

List the names and their functions (on the back, if necessary):

4 Risk assessments (for the COSHH Regulations, the Management Regulations, etc.)

Are there clear procedures for risk assessment and for alerting staff to the outcomes?   yes ❑ no ❑

5 Health and safety guidance, training and communication

Are there appropriate rules for students, suitable guidance and training for staff and an effective mechanism for communication and dissemination of health and safety information?   yes ❑ no ❑

6 Fume cupboard testing

Is the testing of fume cupboards in accordance with the COSHH Regulations?   yes ❑ no ❑

7 Pressure vessels

Is the testing and checking of pressure vessels in accordance with the requirements of the Pressure Vessels Safety Regulations?   yes ❑ no ❑

8 Radioactive substances and ionising radiations

Are the legal requirements fully met?   yes ❑ no ❑

9 Portable electrical appliance testing

If portable electrical appliance testing is a task delegated to the science department, does the testing meet the employer's requirements?   yes ❑ no ❑

10 Fire extinguishers

Are fire extinguishers checked annually?   yes ❑ no ❑

11 Chemicals

Are chemicals date-stamped on arrival, clearly labelled, and the condition of those liable to deteriorate checked regularly?   yes ❑ no ❑

12 Personal protective equipment and other health and safety equipment

Are eye protection and other protective equipment readily available, in good condition, and used whenever the risk assessment requires them?   yes ❑ no ❑

13 Condition of laboratories, store rooms and preparation rooms

Is the condition of the science accommodation (including appropriate health and safety signs) subject to regular systematic checks?   yes ❑ no ❑

14 Employer's local rules or codes of practice

If required by the employer, are any local rules/codes of practice known and adhered to?   yes ❑ no ❑

15 External health and safety audit

Has there been any health and safety audit by someone external to the school, with recommendations being acted upon?   yes ❑ no ❑

TEACHING HEALTH AND SAFETY THROUGH SCIENCE

This is a new Topic, which was not included in the first or second editions of Topics in Safety.

1 Introduction

Experimental and investigative work has been a statutory entitlement for all school students for some time. This means that schools must offer practical approaches to science that not only develop students' problem-solving skills and deepen their knowledge and understanding but are also *healthy* and *safe* for them to carry out. The use of practical approaches in the science curriculum demands a commensurate effort in teaching and learning about health and safety issues.

The requirement for health and safety in the laboratory or classroom is sometimes misconstrued as an obstacle to developing practical approaches to science in schools and colleges. However, the ability to recognise hazards, assess risks and work safely are important skills not only in the school laboratory but also at home and at work. They contribute to the general health and safety education of the school population. No less importantly, such skills also allow students to carry out in safety the kind of experimental and investigative science that they often enjoy. The aim of this topic is to discuss some of the approaches to health and safety teaching that make practical work in school science both safe and exciting.

2 General issues

2.1 Leading by example

It is important that students are *shown* how to work safely. A short demonstration is often the most effective way of teaching safe methods of working and of reducing the risk to students when they begin a practical activity. Safety during heating operations, for example, is dependent on correct technique that must be carefully demonstrated by the teacher and there must be frequent reminders. Do not simply give commands, ensure students understand the reasons for them.

An important role of the head of department/head of subject is to disseminate and monitor healthy and safe laboratory practice in his/her department or subject area. It is particularly important that newly-qualified teachers, student teachers and colleagues who may be teaching outside their own specialisms are given an appropriate level of support and are confident about teaching the scheme of work, including all aspects of health and safety education.

If the science department's health and safety guidelines are to be credible, every science teacher must take care to show students that his/her own practice is consistent with them. This requires the teacher as well as the students to wear eye protection if the activity demands it. Or, since drinks are not allowed in the laboratory, the teacher must refrain from taking his/her morning beverage there!

2.2 Ground rules

The development of health and safety awareness that should accompany progress by students through school needs to be underpinned by some ground rules for the conduct of practical activities in the laboratory or classroom. If developed through negotiation with the students, these rules would probably be better understood and would give students a sense of ownership. Alternatively, a set of laboratory rules, such as those in *Safeguards in the school laboratory*[1] (ASE) can be adapted to suit local circumstances and issued to the students. The principles that underpin healthy and safe laboratory practice should be taught early on, for example when students begin a new school or stage, and reference should be made to them at every opportunity until they are assimilated.

3 Building on experience

Approaches to teaching health and safety in the secondary school must build on the experiences and prior knowledge that students bring from their primary schools. By the time they enter secondary school it is likely that some students will have developed the ability to *assess* the risks from particular hazards and may be able to take simple steps to control them. Health and safety teaching in secondary school should seek to build on this. It must broaden experience of hazardous substances and procedures while developing the student's ability to assess risk and implement control measures.

---

[1] ASE (1996) *Safeguards in the school laboratory*. 10th edn. ISBN 0 86357 250 2.

3.1 Primary education

In England, Wales and Northern Ireland, the National Curricula have provided a framework for the development of health and safety education in science. Most students entering secondary school will recognise that chemicals, including some of those used at home, can be a source of hazard. Although in primary schools hazardous substances are encountered only very rarely, most students will have come across products used in and around the home that carry a hazard warning sign. By the end of the primary phase, students will have learned how to respond to symbols that alert them to chemical hazards and take action themselves, with the close support of their teacher, to reduce the risks that any hazardous substances may present.

In Scotland, guidelines for Environmental Studies 5–14 offer the following targets for health and safety education.

Students will:

■ *answer questions about simple rules for safety and hygiene during activities;*

■ *suggest suitable safety and hygiene procedures;*

■ *use simple apparatus and techniques simply to collect information;*

■ *undertake practical tasks to seek answers with attention to safety and hygiene;*

■ *use equipment safely;*

■ *identify constraints affecting environments and their effects on people's health and lifestyle in design and making;*

■ *demonstrate effective and safe use of materials;*

■ *explore views about local environmental, health and safety problems;*

■ *appreciate and enjoy the benefits of safe and responsible care of living things and the use of energy.*

3.2 Secondary education

In order to build on their grounding in health and safety in primary science, students entering secondary school should be encouraged to take more responsibility for the safe conduct of their practical work in science. The National Curriculum Orders for both England and Wales require that students should be taught in their science lessons:

(a) about hazards, risks and risk control;

(b) to recognize hazards, assess consequent risks and take steps to control the risks to themselves and others;

(c) to use information to assess risks, both immediate and cumulative;

(d) to manage their environment to ensure the health and safety of others;

(e) to explain the steps they take to control risks.

Before they can meet these requirements in science, students will need to have experienced a wide range of practical activities and have been taught at every opportunity how simple control measures can be used to minimise risks in basic laboratory work. Table 1 shows how hazards are identified, risks are assessed and control measures implemented in some science activities in the school in which the author teaches.

Appropriate information sources written for students that help them to assess risks from hazardous substances can be found in the CLEAPSS *Student Safety Sheets*[2]. This resource is written in student-friendly language and avoids the need for students to use very detailed sources of hazard information. Activities that give students practice in assessing risks in their practical work also appear in the *Student Safety Sheets* series.

Further progression can be achieved by giving older (15- and 16-year-old) students opportunities to recognise hazards and assess risk in *unfamiliar* situations. Here again the *Student Safety Sheets* will prove valuable, as well as the SATIS units on Health and Safety in *The World of Science*[3]. The latter deal with the principles of risk assessment and control and provide further practice for students in thinking through and documenting their own risk assessments.

By 16, most students will have had some experience of risk assessment, in that planning for safety must be incorporated into the design of investigations. The latter should provide some scope for students to assess risks in unfamiliar situations although students should have met the basic operations earlier and be familiar with most of the hazards in their investigations. The use of information sources to assess the risk of the unfamiliar will also offer students opportunities to gain coursework marks for obtaining relevant information from secondary sources.

3.3 Post-16 education

In September 2000, the procedural skills of planning, obtaining evidence, analysing and evaluating that give structure to investigative and experimental work at GCSE will be a formal requirement of all new post-16 specifications in the science curriculum of England and Wales. All students following post-16 science courses will therefore be expected to demonstrate competence at appropriate levels in the same kind of investigative and

[2] CLEAPSS (1997/2000) *Student Safety Sheets*. CLEAPSS School Science Service.
[3] Whitehouse, M. (ed) (1997) *The World of Science (New SATIS 14–16)*. John Murray. ISBN 0 7195 7411 0.

Table 1 Controlling risks in some basic laboratory work carried out by 11-year-old students.

Activity	Hazard(s)	Risk	Control measure(s)
Finding boiling point of water/ investigating changes of state	Beaker of boiling water on tripod and gauze	Scalding if beaker topples	Ensure gauze is flat; before beaker is heated, carefully clamp in position partially immersed thermometer; wear eye protection; ensure pupils stand to carry out experiment.
Measuring friction between load and lubricated surfaces	Oil, small polystyrene beads	Slipping on floor after spills of oil or beads	Avoid pouring lubricants and use them in a container
Measuring breaking strength of plastic bags	Falling masses	Injury from falling masses when breaking load is used	Ensure that drop height of masses is minimal or allow masses to fall into a suitable container
Comparing the energy values of fuels	Flammable liquid (methylated spirits)	Uncontrolled combustion	Appropriate volume of fuel to be dispensed by teacher or technician; wear eye protection
Testing a leaf for starch	Flammable liquid (ethanol/methylated spirits)	Uncontrolled combustion	Use electric kettle or extinguish Bunsen burners before ethanol is distributed by teacher or technician; wear eye protection
Solubility of copper sulfate	Copper sulfate (harmful)	Skin contact with crystals or solution; splashingsolution into eyes	Avoid skin contact and wear eye protection; use stoppered tube when shaking up solution
Simple apparatus for distillation of ink	Heated apparatus containing liquid (water-based ink) at boiling point	Scalding if distillation vessel falls; cuts from broken glass	Clamp vessel being heated; wear eye protection
	Suck back	Breaking glass	Disconnect apparatus once heating has ended. Do not distil to dryness
Chemical changes	Reaction mixture containing dilute acid and carbonate	Acid spray	Use eye protection; ensure that quantity of carbonate added does not cause excessive frothing

experimental skills as those that they learned at GCSE. The emphasis on planning and obtaining evidence in many new 16+ courses is likely to increase the need for teaching and learning healthy and safe practical approaches in experimental and investigative science.

In post-16 courses, it is much more likely that students will encounter hazardous substances and procedures and it is appropriate at this level that the students should play a more proactive role in identifying those hazards and in assessing risks. To do this, the students will need access to appropriate health and safety literature, as well as the close support of their supervising teachers, with whom responsibility for student health and safety remains.

In Scotland, candidates for the Advanced Higher Grade examination must carry out an assessment of the hazards and risks that accompany their project work. In cases where procedures or substances are not covered by model (general) assessments, the necessary risk is assessed and documented by the students using the procedures in SSERC *Preparing COSHH risk assessments for project work in schools*[4]. Risk assessment forms are then submitted by the students to the teacher for checking before the project is attempted, modified or abandoned. In this way, the students think through for themselves the health and safety implications of their planning instead of being directed to follow detailed safety procedures that may be poorly understood.

In cases where model risk assessments in the health and safety literature do not cover the experimental or investigative work that is planned and there is doubt about possible hazards, a request may be made to the CLEAPSS *Helpline* or in Scotland to SSERC for a Special Risk Assessment.

---

[4] SSERC (1991) *Preparing COSHH risk assessments for project work in schools.*

4 Students with special needs

Risk assessments and risk control measures will often need to be modified for some students with special needs. For a fuller discussion see ASE *Safety reprints*[5]. Where possible, the students themselves should be involved in any revision. For example, the risk of spills is obviously increased if a dyspraxic student or one for whom physical coordination is difficult is transferring liquids between laboratory glassware. In this case, the student might be asked to consider how a different choice of glassware might reduce the risk of spills or how the effect of any spills might be mitigated.

5 The importance of planning

Teachers' planning needs to identify opportunities for teaching about health and safety. Although schemes of work usually give warnings about health and safety issues that might arise in practical work they rarely suggest that this should be exploited. The use of sodium hydroxide solution in a science lesson, for example, is an opportunity to discuss with students the hazard it presents, the risk of injury, particularly to the eyes, how the hazard varies with the concentration of the solution and the control measures that are necessary to reduce the risks. This might include consideration of the risks to technicians when clearing away after practical work. The discussion could be broadened to include the handling of substances used at home in which sodium hydroxide or other hazardous chemicals are present.

Health and safety references in the scheme of work should provide pointers to the contexts in which students can learn about hazards and the control of risk while they develop experimental and investigative skills and acquire knowledge and understanding. An example is given in Appendix 1. Embedding health and safety issues in the scheme of work provides a natural context in which they can be taught and helps to establish health and safety education as a pervasive theme in the science curriculum.

Appendix 1   An example of safety notes incorporated into a scheme of work

3   *Class*: Year 11   *Syllabus section*: 8.4 Elements and the Periodic Table

Content	Hrs	Teaching approaches (Safety notes italicised)	Resources/ICT/ Reference to GCSE Chemistry	Assessment questions for homework underlined	Learning outcomes (*Use of Key Skills italicised*) Pupils should:
The alkali metals	1	Remind pupils of electronic structures of alkali metals and link to position in PT. Demonstrate reactions of K and Na with *cold* water with *pupils at a safe distance.* *Use eye protection and safety screens, check condition of potassium for signs of deterioration.* Show that alkali is formed and discuss evidence that hydrogen is a product. Predict likely reaction of Li with water and establish reactivity trend. *See Hazcards for potassium and sodium.* Discuss with students why each of the following control measures was necessary: safety screen, students sitting 2–3 m away, eye protection, small pieces of metal.	Alkali metals, and handling equipment; water trough, indicator, safety screen. CD-ROM, *The Chemistry Set.* Spread 3.18	<u>HW (3) in Section 8.4 of pupil notes</u>	■ Know the elements in Group 1 are reactive metals. ■ Know the alkali metals react with water releasing hydrogen and forming hydroxides which dissolve in water giving alkaline solutions. ■ Understand that the metals in Group I become more reactive and easier to melt as the Group is descended. ■ *Be able to write word/symbol equations for the reactions of the alkali metals with water.* ■ Recognise the hazards and consequent risks associated with alkali metals, their hydroxides and hydrogen. ■ Be able to explain the steps taken to control the risks when using alkali metals.

---

[5] ASE (1996) *Safety reprints*. ISBN 0 86357 246 4.

3 SCIENCE TECHNICIANS

This is a new Topic, not included in the first or second editions of Topics in Safety.

1 Introduction

The science team comprises the head of science, teachers **and technicians,** all of whom have a role in health and safety. Communications among team members are vital but not always simple. A department needs communication systems which enable all views to be equally heard and valued.

Technicians often deal with larger quantities of materials and, usually, heavier loads than teachers or students. Their health and safety can be at risk if they rush their work, suffer constant interruptions and work in cramped conditions.

2 Communication

2.1 General

Technicians should have access to the employer's and departmental health and safety policies. They should also be provided with information concerning relevant health, safety and welfare issues that the department and teachers receive from employers and professional bodies such the ASE, CLEAPSS or SSERC (see 'Introduction', page 2).

Technicians should be given access to and taught how to use both model (general) and any special risk assessments endorsed by their employer.

Technicians should be given the relevant training to work safely in accordance with health and safety policies.

2.2 The technician at departmental meetings

Technicians should be encouraged to be present at departmental meetings[1] (see Topic 1) especially when the health and safety policy or particular health and safety matters are discussed. If meetings are after the technician's day ends, heads of department should consider a flexible working hours arrangement or

perhaps even arrange paid overtime. Minutes of meetings should be available for those technicians who are not present.

Heads of department should try to arrange departmental meetings when **all** members of the department can attend. If this is not possible, any items which are of specific concern to technicians should be dealt with when they can be available. Technicians should feel that they can be proactive in these meetings, and if they have any items of concern these should be included on the agenda, not relegated to any other business at the end of the meeting. When a new course with new practicals is being planned, the involvement of technicians can be invaluable in highlighting areas where health and safety issues may arise for themselves, students and other staff, on the availability of resources and the need for any further training. Items that involve health and safety to which technicians can contribute in departmental meetings are listed below.

- How proposed alterations to the departmental health and safety policy could affect them.

- Ways in which in experimental procedures can be altered to solve practical problems.

- Effects on technicians' safe-working practices brought about by alteration to the timetable.

- Accidents and dangerous occurrences.

- Incidents that could have resulted in an accident or a dangerous incident which a technician has witnessed.

- Problems in the day-to-day working of the department which may affect a technician's health and safety such as late requests or laboratories left in a hazardous condition.

- Resourcing a new course, syllabus or teaching scheme.

- State of equipment (e.g. safety spectacles) and materials in the laboratories.

- Updates on loss of equipment (e.g. scissors) and materials (e.g. magnesium ribbon) through theft.

---

[1] DfEE (1996) *Safety in science education*, paragraph 3.2.1. Stationery Office. ISBN 0 11270 915 X.

2.3 Technician issues that a head of department should be aware of

(a) Technicians must have access to personal protective equipment (see Topic 5). This should include:

■ comfortable eye protection[2];

■ appropriate protective gloves for dealing with corrosive liquids, hot objects, microbiological samples;

■ laboratory coats for dealing with radioactive or microbiological material; and when handling and dispensing large volumes (e.g. 2.5 litres) of hazardous solutions;

■ a face shield;

■ a face mask of the appropriate standard if deemed necessary (e.g. dealing with spores or fine wood dusts).

(b) Heads of department should be aware that technicians are put in a difficult position if they are given instructions which, in their view, may affect their personal health and safety, such as being asked to monitor classes or look after individual students. The latter can occur during lunch times when technicians are particularly busy. The head of department may have to act as an arbitrator if a technician has to say 'no' to a teacher for reasons of health and safety.

(c) Technicians should have a clean, healthy and safe working environment. They are entitled to take breaks as stated in their contracts.

(d) Technicians should have regular appraisal/review meetings to discuss their continuing professional development and training needs to ensure that they are fully up-to-date on health and safety. The head of department should ensure that technicians receive the relevant training.

e) Teaching staff should make it clear to students that instructions involving health and safety from a technician carry the same weight as from a teacher. For example, a technician, seeing a student not wearing eye protection, may ask the student to wear the protective equipment correctly.

2.4 The new technician

An induction programme must be in place so that a new technician is integrated quickly into the department and is fully aware of all health and safety procedures. A departmental technicians' file[3], which should include items as listed below, could be used to ascertain the training needs of the technician.

■ Reference to the employer's health and safety policy.

■ Departmental health and safety policy (which includes emergency procedures).

■ Job description – which should detail what is expected of a technician.

■ Line management structure.

■ Lines of communication.

■ Preparative procedures.

■ Procedures within the department.

New technicians need to work under supervision until they have demonstrated their competence at various procedures.

3 Risk assessment and technicians

3.1 General

Teachers should not assume that all technicians have the knowledge or skills for preparing the materials for particular activities. When requesting practicals, instructions with risk assessments should be provided or referred to for the preparation, removal and possible disposal of material.

Technicians should be able to access model risk assessments endorsed by their employer. Special risk assessments should be obtained for any procedure not covered by model risk assessments. Technicians should have easy access to copies of the schemes of work, practical worksheets and any published teacher/ technician guides.

It would be good practice for technicians to write up those procedures which they use on a regular basis to avoid repeatedly looking up information. A portfolio (technicians' file) of useful information could be assembled and updated or amended as new information becomes available. Time should be made available to complete these tasks.

3.2 Lone working

Lone working occurs when there is no other employee present in the same building or even on the same floor as the working technician. With technician numbers reducing, this is an increasing problem. Occasions when technicians find themselves working alone can be:

■ at the very beginning and end of the day;

■ during school holidays;

■ during lunch times;

■ when teaching staff are occupied away from the department.

---

2 Safety spectacles with prescription lenses may be desirable. A face shield will give legally required protection.
3 *The Prep-Room Organiser* (ASE, 1997) is useful in this situation. ISBN 0 86357 283 9.

Table 1 Technician activities with large quantities of materials.

Operation	Notes of particular importance for technicians
Disposal of hazardous materials	Technicians may be required to dispose of the combined waste of several experiments carried out during the day. The disposal of hazardous chemicals and biological materials should follow the guidelines of the employer's policy. See Topic 11 for advice. Help should be obtained when confronted with unusual chemical names or bottles in poor condition. The technician should be made aware of any hazards that might occur during the cleaning of equipment at the end of the class practicals or demonstrations.
Handling of hazardous gases, liquids and solids	Technicians may be required to prepare, for example, 2.5 litres of dilute acid, or several gas jars of chlorine. Full use should be made of personal protective equipment as indicated in the employer's risk assessments. See Topic 5 for advice. Technicians should seek advice and instruction if such procedures are being carried out for the first time.
Handling of pressurised gas cylinders	Technicians may be required to move and handle cylinders of various gases. Instruction should be undertaken when using a gas cylinder for the first time.
Transporting heavy equipment, books, etc.	Technicians may be required to carry, for example, a 2.5-litre bottle of concentrated acid, or several large pieces of equipment, from one area to another (possibly up and down stairs). Full use should be made of specific procedures and mechanical aids as indicated in the employer's risk assessments. See Topic 4 for advice. Technicians should seek training in manual handling techniques.

Laboratory procedures and manual handling operations that should **not** be carried out during these periods should be proscribed, e.g. the dilution of concentrated sulfuric acid or moving heavy objects from one floor to another. Accidents can and do happen even to experienced technicians and in such circumstances they must have rapid access to help. Outside doors, which may be locked to prevent intruders, could delay assistance reaching the technician.

3.3 The handling of heavy items and large quantities of materials

During much of their work, technicians, unlike teachers, often have to cope with heavy and bulky materials. Table 1 highlights areas that are of concern and need to be addressed through discussion and training. Manual handling issues are fully dealt with in Topic 4.

3.4 Dealing with requests for equipment and materials

It should be departmental policy that requests for materials from teachers are given to technicians as early as possible and normally no later than two working days before the activity. This allows the technician time to organise visits to local shops to collect material and/or carry out time-consuming preparative procedures.

Although a technician may understand that a late request from a teacher can sometimes happen, it should not be a common occurrence.

Teachers should always pay attention to the health and safety implication of any requests they make of a technician. In particular, when considering making requests at short notice, or asking for jobs which are not really the technician's primary role, remember that both will put pressure on time and compromise health and safety. Teachers should ask themselves the following questions.

- If the technician does this job, what will he/she have to leave to do it? e.g. disruption of other classes.

- If the job the technician has to leave has to be rushed, could this cause an increase in risk to his/her health and safety?

- Is the job I am asking the technician to do more important than the job he/she is presently doing irrespective of who has asked him/her to do it?

- Is the job I am asking the technician to do really a technician job?

- Has the technician the qualifications/experience to do the job safely?

If the risk assessment and procedure indicate that to carry out a requested procedure in the time available would constitute an unnecessary risk, the technician would have to say 'no'. In this case, teachers should respect this right.

3.5 Tidying up

Practicals which may present little risk in setting up can present more serious risks to the technician when being cleared away. Teachers should deal with hazardous residues where possible or ensure that technicians are well aware of any hazards before clearing up. Practical worksheets used by students should, if appropriate, have

Table 2 Examples of problems encountered in clearing up students' practical work.

Activity or equipment	Problems encountered	Control measures
Activities involving heating	Burns when handling hot equipment.	Technician to be informed if any equipment is hot (e.g. beakers, tripods, soldering irons). Use heat-proof gloves if waiting for the items to cool is impossible.
Demonstrations with alkali metals	Washing equipment with water may produce fire and/or explosions.	Staff to ensure the complete reaction of any metals on knives, tiles, etc., by placing these in water after their use.
Glassware	Students mixing broken glass with other waste. Technicians or cleaners can be cut.	Students should be aware of the hazard of broken glass and encouraged to report any breakages. The teacher or technician should deal with breakages as quickly as possible by placing broken glass in a separate bin.
High-voltage equipment	Items could be left charged, e.g. van de Graaff generators. A static discharge can be given to the technician.	Staff to discharge the equipment before leaving the apparatus.
Microbiological experiments	Contaminated equipment in normal washing trays.	Staff should ensure that correct procedures are used by students. Technician must wear suitable protective clothing and equipment (gloves).
Open-ended activities	Reactions between chemicals during washing up, producing harmful or toxic gases.	Teachers should be aware of these situations and provide suitable information if equipment or materials are left out overnight or require washing or disposal.
Returning class sets of scalpels, syringes or other hazardous equipment	Technicians can receive cuts from sharp objects.	Teachers should ensure that all hazardous equipment is returned to the correct containers.
Use of concentrated chemicals	Chemical burns. Toxic effects.	Students to follow the established procedures for clearing away contaminated glassware. Technician should wear adequate eye protection and, if necessary, gloves when clearing away chemicals.

a section on clearing up procedures. Some examples of problems that technicians encounter are given in Table 2.

Both technicians and teachers have a duty of care to the cleaners, whose health and safety should not be put at risk by leaving broken glass or other hazardous materials in rooms or waste baskets which are cleaned or emptied every evening.

Any equipment that needs to be left out overnight should be suitably labelled if it presents a hazard.

3.6 Trying out or researching practical activities

When asked to trial new practicals or solve practical problems that teachers are experiencing, the technician should discuss the risk assessments with the teacher. If the practical is unusual in any way, then expert advice is available from various organisations such as the ASE, CLEAPSS and SSERC. Technicians should record any further unanticipated hazards they encounter whilst conducting the practical, and communicate their findings back to the teacher.

4 Technicians in the classroom

4.1 Working with students in the laboratory

If the head of department considers that a technician is required to be in the laboratory during a practical session, clear guidelines should be given as to what is required in terms of input, e.g. showing how to use the equipment, but not helping with worksheets. Technicians should not be expected to run practical sessions in a laboratory on their own.

Students should respond to safety instructions from a technician in the same way as they would from a teacher.

4.2 Demonstrating during lessons

Technicians are sometimes asked to demonstrate to students procedures such as aseptic technique for plant tissue culture, titrations, use of microscopes and balances, particular chemical reactions, data collection, etc. A risk assessment, if required, should be provided before the demonstration takes place. Technicians should only demonstrate to students with a member of science staff present and if they have rehearsed the procedure.

5 Health and safety in the prep room

5.1 Introduction

Technicians work in the prep room for the majority of their time. It should be not only a healthy and safe place for themselves but also for visitors. Teachers might enter the prep room to discuss various issues and possibly carry out their own practical work (if laboratories are otherwise occupied and the prep room is large) but, if at all possible, it should not be used as a staff meeting room (unless the room is very large). Students may visit the prep room to collect material for a teacher but they should not be encouraged to enter the room. On display may be expensive balances and hazardous chemicals which may be a future target for theft. The practice of leaving students in the prep room to complete an exam or class test with only a technician in attendance should be discouraged.

5.2 Space

A recommended area for a prep room and storage space is given by the formula[4]:

$$\text{Area of prep room and storage area} = \frac{\text{number of student places in the}}{\text{science rooms}} \times (0.4 \text{ to } 0.5) \text{ m}^2$$

(For a school with six laboratories each holding 30 students, 72 to 90 m^2 of prep room and storage space are needed.)

There should be adequate and appropriate storage for chemicals, glassware, other equipment, books (related to the technician's work) and space for both prepared and returned practicals. The aim is to avoid obstacles preventing free movement about the room. Bench height should reflect the fact that adults work in this room and not students. In addition, technicians should not be expected to work at sinks in a stooping posture for long periods. (See Topic 6 on laboratory and prep room design for health and safety.)

5.3 Environmental issues

The prep room should be warm enough during cold weather, cool during the summer and well illuminated. As volatile chemicals may be handled, there should be adequate ventilation which could be provided either by a fume cupboard[5] (see Topic 7) or an air-extracting unit

fitted in an outside wall or window, providing at least five air changes an hour. If there is no fume cupboard present, then there should be easy access to one in an adjoining laboratory. Teachers in these rooms should accept that technicians may have to interrupt lessons to carry out certain operations which demand the use of a fume cupboard. There should be a clear space for dealing with all the paperwork and the prep room computer and telephone, preferably not near a wet area.

Prep rooms should ideally have two sinks: one for washing equipment and disposing of chemicals and the other for washing hands and possibly eyes in case of an accident. Eating, drinking, smoking and applying cosmetics should not take place in the prep room.

6 Equipment safety testing

Technicians are often required by their employer to carry out tests on equipment. They should be suitably trained before carrying out this activity and given adequate time. There should be no attempt to repair any faults found by testing unless the technician has the relevant experience and/or qualifications. Faults (and any subsequent repairs) should be reported in writing to the relevant line manager.

If technicians can demonstrate that they have carried out the testing procedure required by their employer in accordance with training, they are not responsible for any future faults that may occur. Any person subsequently using specialist equipment should visually check that it is working satisfactorily before using it, e.g. that the fume cupboard does indeed work before making chlorine.

Testing of portable appliances, fume cupboards and pressure vessels is mandatory and can be carried out by a trained technician, if the employer considers him/her to be competent. Examples of other routine inspections which are generally required of technicians are detailed in Table 3.

7 Maintenance of resources

Part of the technician's job is to maintain the resources of the department. Health and safety considerations are outlined in Table 4.

Technicians will often carry out simple maintenance of the laboratory, for example, cleaning sinks and sink traps. These may contain sharp objects, unpleasant materials and strong odours. Water should be flushed through before starting. Suitable gloves, eye protection (and old clothing) should be worn and the room should be well ventilated.

---

4   DfEE (revised 1999) *Science accommodation in secondary schools, a Design Guide,* Building Bulletin 80, Paragraph 3.2. Stationery Office. ISBN 0 11271039 5.

5   DfEE (1998) *Fume cupboards in schools,* Building Bulletin 88, Paragraph 2.8. Stationery Office. ISBN 0 11271027 1.

Table 3 Examples of visual inspection of equipment to be carried out by technicians.

Tests	Frequency	Comments
Apparatus containing mercury	Yearly	Carefully inspect any flexible tubing for signs of cracking and fit properly. Apparatus should stand in trays.
Bunsen burner tubing	Yearly	Look for damaged surfaces, pinholes or loose butt-ends.
Gas cylinder regulators	Yearly	Look for damage.
Gas cylinders	Before use	Check valves to ensure that they turn readily.
Gas taps and fittings	Termly	The fittings should be firmly fixed. The taps should turn easily and not leak. Faults and leaks require a specialist to repair them but the technician may remove temporary blockages if this does not cause damage.
Lifting beams, rings and hoists	Before use	Look for signs of corroding metal, cracked plaster or frayed ropes.
Old equipment	When required	Examine carefully old equipment not used for some years (e.g. frayed rubber connections) before use.
Workshop tools	Yearly	Inspect for firmness of mounting and correct operation of switches.

Table 4 Maintenance of materials, livestock and equipment.

Animals	The treatment of livestock kept by the school should be discussed with the senior biologist. Looking after animals during holidays is a particular problem. Signs of sensitivity or allergies developing in a technician should be reported to the senior biologist. Hygiene is very important.
Blocked gas taps	Gas taps may be unblocked as long as it is impossible to damage the installation.
Budgeting	Priority should be given to the safety and suitability of the equipment. For example, soda-glass tubing is inexpensive but does not withstand heat stress or careless use. It can break and give rise to cuts; borosilicate tubing is more expensive but safer to use. Advice on the safety of suitable equipment can be obtained from organisations such as CLEAPSS and SSERC (see 'Introduction' page 2).
Chemical stocktaking	Some chemicals pose storage hazards. For example, bottles, such as those containing '880' ammonia and 100 'vol' hydrogen peroxide solution can become pressurised. For safety reasons, these should be checked whilst stocktaking. Stocktaking is best carried out when the technician is unlikely to be disturbed as omissions can easily be made when there are constant interruptions.
Equipment stocktaking	This is normally carried out once a year and is best tackled when there is likely to be the least interruption. Non-electrical equipment should be visually checked to see if it appears safe and, if not, replaced or repaired. For example, rubber tubing connected to glass tubing may be weakening due to attack by corrosive gases or uv light; if not replaced, rubber tubing may leak when being used.
Mains electrical equipment	Only a technician who has experience or received relevant training and deemed competent by the employer should maintain such equipment. Advice can be obtained from organisations such as CLEAPSS and SSERC (see 'Introduction' page 2).
Microbial cultures	The subculturing of microbial cultures should be carried out at regular intervals to maintain viability.
Plants	The variety of plants ordered and their care should be discussed with the senior biologist. Signs of sensitivity or allergies developing should be reported to the senior biologist. Hygiene is very important.

MANUAL HANDLING

This is a new Topic.

1 Introduction

The term 'manual handling operations' means 'any transportation or supporting of a load (including the lifting, putting down, pushing, pulling, carrying or moving thereof) by hand or bodily force'[1].

Both employers and employees often dismiss the problems caused by manual handling operations as not relevant to education because it does not appear to involve continuous heavy manual labour as seen in heavy industry. However, manual handling activities are responsible for over 40% of RIDDOR[2]-reported injuries amongst employees in education, against 0.5% for accidents in laboratories and chemical handling[3]. The consequences of injuries caused by manual handling operations going wrong are expensive both in time and money to the science team and the employer (e.g. in employing supply staff).

A legal case may be brought against the employer, either through prosecution or civil action. A 60-year-old injured her back lifting a 10 kg bucket of water out of a sink, resting it on the sink edge and lowering it to the floor. Compensation of £7920 was awarded[4] because a risk assessment would have revealed that the lifting process could have been avoided by the use of a hose. In another case, damages of £384 497 were awarded to an office worker who suffered severe back injuries when forced to carry boxes of stationery up staircases. The employer had failed to carry out a suitable risk assessment and provide training[5]. Both these activities are carried out by technicians or teachers.

Risk assessment for manual handling operations does not involve just the mass of the load. It needs to examine the nature of the task, the environment in which the task takes place and the individual's capability. The study of work operations is known as **ergonomics** and the aim of the assessment is to fit the operation to the individual, rather than the other way round.

2 What the law requires

2.1 ... of the employer

In schools, manual handling operations are best assessed by a team including senior management, health and safety representatives, teachers, technicians (who have direct experience of the problems) and other ancillary staff working together to provide recorded guidance to other members of staff. At such meetings staff will find that most of the tasks they carry out (e.g. moving piles of textbooks) are common to many workers in education, and model risk assessments already provided by the employer will apply. Information, assessment reviews, training sessions and keeping accurate records of accidents are important aspects of the team's work. Special tasks (e.g. asking the technicians to clear laboratories for redecoration) need particular attention and last-minute risk assessments are unlikely to be 'suitable and sufficient'.

The Manual Handling Regulations demand that, as far as is reasonably practicable, employees should avoid carrying out hazardous manual handling operations. In the first place, this should be done by redesigning the task, if possible. For instance, if an activity requires moving fifteen 7 kg microscopes down a flight of stairs to another laboratory, moving the students to the room where the microscopes are kept reduces risk of injury to the technician. A reluctance to move by teachers because 'it is not my room' is a poor excuse; the over-riding concern is for health and safety, although student behaviour may be an issue.

A second stage is to examine whether any mechanical aids can be introduced. Schools should seriously examine the provision of hoists (especially when designing new laboratories or refurbishing old buildings) for moving material between floors and supplying suitably robust trolleys.

If avoidance of the task is impossible then the employer has a duty to see that suitable risk assessments are prepared and from these deduce the

---

[1] HSE (1998) L23 *Manual Handling: Guidance on Regulations 1992.* HSE Books. ISBN 0 71762415 3.
[2] HSE (1999) L73 *A guide to the Reporting of Injuries, Diseases and Dangerous Occurrences Regulations.* HSE Books. ISBN 0 71762431 5.
[3] HSE reported statistics for 1996/7.
[4] Warren *v* Harlow DC (1997), *Health and Safety Briefing,* No 166. Croner.
[5] Clark *v* Metropolitan Police *Safety Management,* October 1999. British Safety Council.

steps required to reduce the risk of injury to the employee so far as is reasonably practicable.

The term 'reasonably practicable' has financial implications. The code of practice indicates that the employer has to show that 'the cost of any further preventative steps would be *grossly* (ASE italics) disproportionate to the further benefit from their introduction'.

Just as hazardous chemicals are labelled 'CORROSIVE', 'TOXIC', etc., to inform the user that control measures are required, so a particularly heavy load should be labelled with its mass, and, if the load's centre of gravity is not positioned centrally, then this should be indicated too. Items which are particularly heavy include vacuum pumps, autoclaves, water baths, overhead projectors, TV monitors, low-voltage supply units, ramps, fire extinguishers, gas-cylinders, large containers of distilled water, weights, rocks, microscopes and 2.5 litre bottles of chemicals. However, it should not be forgotten that small items can be piled up into a particularly heavy load. Five reams of A4 paper can weigh over 13 kg and a pile of textbooks can be even heavier!

2.2 ... of the employee

There is a duty in the Manual Handling Regulations to make 'full and proper use' of any equipment or control measures set in place by the risk assessments carried out by the employer. If trolleys, step ladders or bottle carriers are provided by the employer, members of staff should use them!

2.3 Assessing the risk in manual handling activities

How do people with responsibility for examining manual handling in schools and colleges know when a risk assessment is required? It is necessary to filter out the tasks which present a minimal risk from those that could cause injury. For each recognised activity, Table 1 should be checked. If the answer is 'yes' to any of the statements, then a more detailed risk assessment needs to be carried out, initially using the employer's risk assessments which then may be adapted to the school environment and personnel. Failing this, a special risk assessment with more detailed control measures needs to be obtained and adopted.

Table 1 Manual handling tasks likely to require a risk assessment.

Task	Load	Environment	Individual capability
The load has to be held away from the trunk (1).	The load is heavy (6).	There are constraints on posture (9).	The load requires exceptional strength.
Twisting is involved.	The load is bulky (7).	There are poor floors (10).	The load is a hazard to those with a health problem.
Stooping is involved.	The load has a large surface area (8).	There are stairs.	The load is a hazard to those who are pregnant.
Reaching upwards is involved.	The load is difficult to grasp.	There is poor lighting.	There is a need for special training.
The load is carried through a large vertical distance (2).	The load has sharp edges.	The load is taken outside the building during inclement weather conditions.	
The load is carried over a long distance (3).	The load is unevenly distributed.	It is a windy day (11).	
Frequent handling operations are involved (4).	The load is continually moving inside the container.	There are students in the vicinity (12).	
There is insufficient rest or recovery (5).	The load is toxic or corrosive.		

Notes

(1) Not keeping a load close to the body increases stress to the spine and to the stomach muscles.

(2) Lifting from floor to shoulder height will involve a change of grip. Lifts from the floor should finish at waist height.

(3) If a load is carried more than 10 m, then the physical demands of the task could cause distress.

(4) Frequent means the operation is repeated within two minutes.

(5) Two minutes recovery time is a reasonable guide.

(6) See section 3.

(7) If the dimension of a load exceeds 75 cm in any direction, then it could pose a risk.

(8) For example, poster boards and sheets of hardboard.

(9) Low work surfaces, low headroom or obstacles may lead to twisting, stooping or other poor postures.

(10) Wet floors are a particular hazard in laboratories.

(11) Crossing playgrounds can be a particular problem.

(12) Students create a number of obstacles, especially on stairs.

3 Assessment of a person's individual capability

3.1 Introduction

Design of the workplace is usually more important than the manual handling capability of individual staff. However, there are some important facts to consider about those involved in manual handling operations.

- The lifting strength of women is generally less than that of men.

- An individual's capability generally increases until the early 20s and declines in the mid-40s. Those in their teens and the over-50s generally have similar capabilities.

- General fitness is important. Pregnancy seriously affects a woman's manual handling capability. Hormonal changes and posture problems (especially in the last three months of pregnancy) further reduce capability. It must not be forgotten that time is required after giving birth for full fitness to return.

- The individual may have a disability or other health problem that affects his or her manual handling capability.

3.2 Guidelines for lifting, lowering and carrying loads over a short distance

Figure 1 gives the masses of loads in various positions, relative to the body, that can be safely lifted or lowered, for which it is felt that detailed risk assessments are **not** required unless environmental factors exist (see Table 1). The guideline figures are for infrequent lifting and lowering tasks. A fit man of average height/mass can cradle in his arms a load of 25 kg close to his body and carry it a distance of 10 m. A fit woman can carry a bucket, in each hand, each containing 6.5 kg (i.e. a total of 13 kg) a distance of 10 m. The capability of carrying a load decreases the further the load is held away from the body. Those who are over-50 or under-20 should multiply the data in Figure 1 by 0.7. Those who are pregnant, disabled or have any other health condition should obtain medical advice as to what tasks they should not tackle which involve manual handling.

People who take regular exercise and are very fit may be able to cope with heavier loads than those given in Figure 1, but even these individuals, working under good conditions, should not attempt loads more than twice as heavy as those shown. Injuries have been known to occur when far heavier loads have been lifted in order to impress others.

Students up to 16 years old have an even lower capacity to carry loads and are not classed as employees. The use of students as gang-labour should be resisted. It has also been established that students who repeatedly carry heavy books (and science books can be heavy) and equipment to and from school and between lessons may show signs of spinal injuries.

Sensible shoes and clothing should be worn for these operations. Also, if the weather is hot, more breaks between tasks should be taken and plenty of water should be drunk.

If a risk assessment requires two people to lift the object as a team then they should not attempt to lift a load which is greater than two thirds of the sum of their individual capabilities. The team members should be of similar build and physical capability. If the load is uneven, the strongest member of the group should cope with the heavier end.

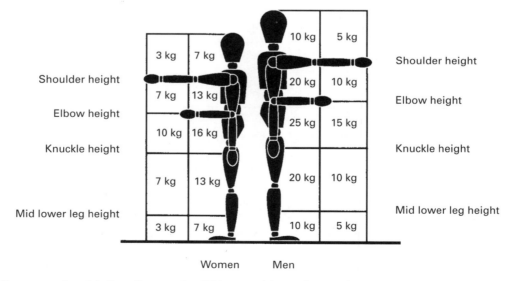

Figure 1 Suggested guideline figures for lifting and lowering tasks.

(From HSE (1998) L23 *Manual Handling: Guidance on Regulations 1992*. HSE Books. ISBN 0 7176 2415 3. Reproduced with permission of the Controller of HMSO.)

3.3 Guidelines for pushing and pulling trolleys

The knuckle-height values (in Figure 1) can be used as a guideline for the force required to move a trolley. If it is thought that a trolley is particularly difficult to move or a fire door requires a lot of effort to open, a Newton meter can be attached to a handle to check the force required to initiate movement. This should be no more than 250 N for men and 160 N for women. The force required to keep the load in motion should be less than 100 N for men and 70 N for women.

Trolleys should be used for the work they are designed to do. A shelf trolley with small wheels is unsuitable for pushing over rough ground between sites. For this work, materials and apparatus may have to be placed in boxes and transferred on sack trolleys, which have larger wheels and can cope with rough terrain. Trolleys should be regularly maintained (e.g. axles should be oiled).

4 Model risk assessments

Many tasks that are carried out in schools are very similar, so much so that a list of control measures can be produced after only a few minutes consideration. Naturally, as each establishment is different in layout, uses different apparatus and the capabilities of the personnel will vary, the control measures should be tailored and customised further. A list similar to Table 2 can be developed for the departmental health and safety policy. (It may also serve as a blueprint for other departments and ancillary staff.)

5 Special risk assessments

If the initial assessment of the task raises issues not covered in Table 2, a special risk assessment should be obtained, the findings of which should be circulated to all involved. Some activities which might precipitate such action are listed below.

■ Laboratories are relocated to new buildings.

■ Laboratories are being stripped down for redecoration.

■ Rooms are being cleaned up after a serious fire.

■ Timetable changes result in more practical periods being taught, resulting in more heavy loads to be moved about.

■ The number of hours worked by technicians is reduced. Help for certain tasks will be less available and technicians may carry heavier loads to attempt to make up time.

■ There are medical reasons for restricting the tasks being carried out.

6 Training

Training is an important part of the employer's duties. Training should be organised on a regular basis, and when new staff join the department. It is also a suitable time to label heavy objects with their masses and review existing practices. Often it is only by doing a task that new and safer work practices can be established. Techniques to practice include general lifting techniques and team-lifting. The senior biology teacher could provide basic information about the spine and muscles and the senior physics teacher could provide information about mass and forces. Local authority health and safety advisers can sometimes provide suitable training (see Figure 2).

There are eight general steps to follow:

1 Stop, think and test the load by rocking it gently from side to side. Some loads are heavier than expected and some bulky loads may be lighter. If the load is beyond your capabilities, don't move it, seek help.

2 Place the feet apart, with one leg further forward than the other.

3 Adopt a good posture, bending the knees and keeping the spine in an upright position (tucking the chin in helps). It may be necessary to lean forward over the load. Stooping should be avoided.

4 Grip the object firmly.

5 Lift the object smoothly using the thigh muscles, raising the chin in the process.

6 Do not twist the body but move the feet if required.

7 The load should be held with straight arms but as close to the body as possible.

8 Place the object on the table and then slide it to the correct position.

Figure 2 The general technique of lifting from floor level to bench height.

(From HSE (1998) L23 *Manual Handling: Guidance on Regulations 1992*. HSE Books. ISBN 0 7176 2415 3. Reproduced with permission of the Controller of HMSO.)

Table 2 Control measures for manual handling operations.

Hazardous situation	Control measures
Carrying equipment and materials to and from outside stores and laboratories	Avoid times when there may be ice on the pathway or high winds. Trolleys for outdoor use should have large robust wheels but not be used if the surface is very uneven.
Carrying large bottles of chemicals	Use special bottle carriers.
Carrying loads up and down stairs	Classes where possible should be moved to laboratories where the special equipment is kept. *In the short term*, make sure that the load does not obscure one's view of the steps, the steps are in good condition and free of obstacles. Avoid busy times. *In the long term*, purchase additional sets of regularly used equipment so that movement up and down stairs is no longer necessary.
Cluttered floors	Before the task begins, all clutter from prep room and laboratory floors should be removed. Doorways should be kept clear. Make sure laboratories have designated places for students' bags.
Congestion in corridors, etc.	Items should not be moved between laboratories and prep rooms at change of lesson times, when substantial numbers of students are moving around. Another person could accompany the carrier to clear a path.
Damaged floors	Damaged floors, which increase the risk of slipping or tripping, should be reported in writing to the manager.
Moving equipment through heavy fire doors	Fire doors with magnetic catches that release in the event of fire are available. Check the force required to open fire doors with a Newton meter to see if they need adjusting. Forces required should be less than those quoted for pushing and pulling trolleys (see Figure 1). Another person could accompany the carrier to open doors. However, if alone, use wedges to keep doors open temporarily while the task is carried out. If fire doors have to be wedged open, the risk assessment should record the judgement that manual handling injury is a greater risk than fire. Place small tables near doors to limit the amount of lowering and lifting being done.
Lifting awkwardly-shaped objects including vacuum pumps, large autoclaves, piles of textbooks, etc.	A two-person lift may be required. Particular care and extra help or guidance will be required if using stairs. Students should not lift heavy objects.
Lifting heavy objects	If possible, the mass of the load should be written on these objects. Consider taking heavy objects apart and make extra trips (e.g. separate a pile of textbooks).
Lifting objects from high-level storage	Store heavy frequently-used items at waist level so they can be moved sideways to a trolley. If rarely-used items need to be stored at a high level, use a suitable step ladder to reach them. Do not store one item behind another on high shelves.
Moving gas cylinders between laboratories and prep rooms	Cylinder trolleys should be used. Cylinders should never be rolled along the floor. Moving medium-sized cylinders up and down stairs will involve more than one person. Larger cylinders are not recommended for school use.
Moving general equipment between laboratories and prep rooms	Equipment trolleys should be used whenever possible. Trolleys should not be used for the temporary storage of exercise books, etc. The need for security, i.e. locking the store or prep room after removing equipment, requires the possibility of placing a heavy object on the floor. Small tables could be placed near doors to limit the amount of lowering and lifting being done.
Moving general equipment up and down stairs	A hoist is recommended especially in new and refurbished laboratories. Do not attempt to carry heavy objects (e.g. TVs) on one's own; classes should swap rooms instead. Any procedure involving stairs has a medium to high risk of injury. Special stair-trolleys are available but are not easy to use.
Moving general equipment along the same floor but with variations in levels	Consideration should be given to placing gentle slopes to avoid steps, thus allowing trolleys to move over a greater distance without being unloaded.
Wet floors	Before the task, ensure spills are mopped up quickly until dry.

EYE PROTECTION AND OTHER PERSONAL PROTECTIVE EQUIPMENT

This Topic extends and replaces Chapter 2 in the second edition of Topics in Safety.

1 Introduction

The Personal Protective Equipment at Work Regulations (1992)[1] require employers to provide their employees with the personal protective equipment (PPE) which is deemed necessary as a result of an appropriate risk assessment. The general duty of care for others (i.e. students and visitors) in the Health and Safety at Work Act means that the employer must also look after the safety of others using the premises. This means that where PPE is deemed necessary in science teaching, it must be provided and correctly worn by staff, students and others. Although the duty rests with the employer, in practice the provision of PPE in science is delegated to the head of science, and the requirement to ensure it is correctly worn is delegated to individual science teachers in their lessons.

The form of PPE most commonly used in science teaching is eye protection. Most laboratories are equipped with a class set of safety goggles or spectacles and prep rooms are likely to need one or more face shields. It is now well established that eye protection is routinely worn in science lessons because of the risks to the eyes from handling hazardous chemicals, heating liquids and some solids, grinding solids, some dissection work, etc. Evidence suggests that despite this, eye injuries are still quite common. They occur when:

■ students remove their own eye protection at the end of their practical whilst others around are still working;

■ students fail to wear eye protection correctly;

■ teachers (or students), believing a substance to be low hazard (e.g. limewater), do not ensure eye protection is worn;

■ spilled crystals and liquids are inadvertently rubbed into an eye on fingers contaminated from the bench;

■ occasionally one student deliberately squirts a hazardous liquid at another.

The only other PPEs which might be considered necessary in science lessons are gloves, aprons, lab coats or some means of tying back long hair. It is possible to envisage a situation where wellington boots might be needed (see section 5). It must be remembered that PPE should not be the first line of defence. Any activity should be queried in which the risk assessment identifies that some significant item of PPE (other than the usual items) is required. Are there safer alternative procedures? Can the quantity or concentration be reduced? Will a fume cupboard or safety screen reduce the risk? Can students simply be kept out of the way? Is the activity educationally valid?

The two questions with regard to PPE are:

■ what kind of PPE should be worn?

■ when should PPE be worn?

These are considered separately, first for eye protection and then for other forms of PPE.

2 Teacher's responsibility for students wearing PPE

If the risk assessment for an activity deems that PPE (usually eye protection) is needed, the class teacher is responsible for ensuring that it is worn. Many published texts now include eye protection symbols or words near to activities requiring its use. Departments are encouraged to use a similar approach with locally-produced worksheets or workbooks. These are very helpful and act as a regular reminder to students. However, it is not sufficient to rely on students noticing them and putting on their eye protection. The teacher has to instruct the students that the eye protection is needed and to remind them during the lesson on several occasions if the eye protection is not being worn appropriately. Do not ignore transgressions. It is also important that the teacher sets a good example by wearing his or her own eye protection and insisting that any others in the room (technicians or inspectors) do the same. Some departments display the blue and white circular eye protection safety sign (see Topic 9). Strictly speaking this is a mandatory sign and means eye protection must always be worn by anyone in the room,

---

[1] HSE (1992) L25 *Personal Protective Equipment at Work. Guidance on Regulations: Personal Protective Equipment at Work Regulations 1992.* HSE Books. ISBN 0 71760415 2.

which is clearly not the case in all science lessons (see also Topic 9). In addition, such permanent signs quickly cease to have any impact. If a department wishes to make use of the safety sign then it is best used temporarily, for example, by sticking the sign to a magnetic board.

Following the above procedure will not guarantee that all students will always wear their eye protection correctly, but nothing will. However, it would indicate that the teacher had taken reasonable and appropriate steps to ensure students wear eye protection, or indeed any other kind of PPE.

3 Eye protection: what kind should be worn?

3.1 General points

Science departments tend to make eye protection last as long as possible, often well beyond its effective and useful life. Students are notoriously careless in the way they handle and put down their eye protection, so that lenses can quickly become scratched, ear pieces of safety spectacles can become broken and vents are removed from goggles so that they are no longer liquid-proof. It is necessary, therefore, for a science department to ensure that part of the annual budget is set aside for routine replacement. It is sometimes possible to purchase lenses separately so that scratched lenses can be replaced. However, replacing a lens is not necessarily easy and may actually invalidate the manufacturer's guarantee of security. In the main it is probably simpler

and easier all round to buy new than to repair, although it is quite simple to replace the elastic straps of safety goggles.

Despite the general infrequency of cleaning, there is no evidence that infectious organisms can be transferred from one person to another through sharing eye protection. We are assured that viable head lice cannot be transmitted by headwear. However since cleaning is easy (any washing-up liquid will do) it would seem sensible to aim to wash eye protection termly to ensure lenses remain clean and to enable staff to check its condition and the need for replacement.

3.2 European standards for eye protection

Formerly, British Standards were used to define different levels of protection offered. (The basic standard was BS2092 with the addition of an extra number to denote higher levels of impact protection, a 'c' to denote liquid-proof, or other letters for higher levels of penetration protection.) Nowadays the European Standard is used, the basic being 'EN166' (often written as BSEN 166). It is important to realise that eye protection which is marked with the older British Standards is still perfectly adequate for use.

The level of protection offered is stamped on the frame of the eye protection. Markings are as follows:

- The first mark is the manufacturer's symbol.

- The second is 'EN166'. All newly-purchased eye protection used in schools must be marked with this.

Table 1 Eye protection European standard codes and British Standard equivalent.

Symbol	Explanation	BS equivalent
None	Basic protection against low level hazards (e.g. harmful/irritant substances) and general mechanical hazards.	BS2092
3	Protects against liquid droplets and/or splashes.	BS2092 C
4	Protects against large dust particles, i.e. >5 µm.	BS2092 D
5	Protects against toxic and corrosive gases, vapours, sprays, smoke and dusts < 5 µm.	BS2092 G
8	Protects against short-circuit in electrical equipment.	None
9	Protects against splashes of molten metals and penetration of hot solids.	BS2092 M
F	Low-energy impact; can be applied to all types of eye protection. This level of protection is adequate for virtually all activities carried out by students in laboratories.	BS2092
B	Medium energy impact; applies to goggle or face shield only.	BS2092 1
A	High-energy impact; applies only to specialised face shields.	None

- The third is one or more numbers to represent the correct application for the eye protection. Safety spectacles, which offer basic protection, carry no number.

- The fourth is a letter preceded by -, and denotes the resistance to the impact of high-speed particles.

- Finally there may be a certification mark (e.g. the kitemark) which is optional and can be used only when the eye protection has been independently tested and its properties confirmed. The British Standards Institute is one such independent testing organisation and it awards the kitemark.

Table 1 explains the European Standard number and letter codes and their equivalent British Standard[2].

The lens may have the manufacturer's mark, a number representing the optical class (usually 1, the best) and the mechanical strength (F, B, A, see Table 1).

3.3 Acceptable kinds of eye protection

There are three kinds of eye protection acceptable for use in school science.

- **Spectacles**, which should conform to the basic standard. They are often the easiest to wear but they do not offer full protection against splashes. Many examples now have wide side pieces for sideways protection and fit close to the face to reduce the possibility of splashes entering the eye.

- **Goggles**, which should offer full protection against liquid splashes and basic protection for other hazards. Safety goggles must not be confused with other goggles such as those used in workshops which do not generally give splash protection and skiing goggles, which are generally unlikely to offer even the basic levels of protection required.

- **Face shields,** which are designed to protect the whole face.

Teachers and technicians should have a personal set of eye protection which they find comfortable and which accommodates any need for prescription spectacles. It is possible to have prescription spectacles with impact resistant lenses but these are expensive and will be of little advantage if the style means the lenses are smaller than those generally fitted to safety spectacles. As well, there ought to be one or more face shields available in the prep room for teachers or technicians to use.

Table 2 lists the advantages and disadvantages of each type of eye protection.

Table 2 Advantages and disadvantages of different kinds of eye protection.

	Advantages	Disadvantages
Spectacles	Comfortable Little restriction of vision (when clean and not scratched) Easy to wash Easiest to store Students wear them more readily	Only offer partial protection Do not generally fit over prescription spectacles Frames do not always protect the lenses from becoming scratched when spectacles put down
Goggles	Offer greater protection than spectacles Often large enough to fit over prescription spectacles Rim protects lenses from scratching to some extent Elastic straps adjustable for different size heads	Some models very uncomfortable More restricted vision than spectacles Tend to mist up Not always readily worn by students Surplus elastic sometimes a nuisance, and occasionally a fire hazard Slightly more expensive than spectacles
Face shields	Maximum protection for face and head Very wide angle of vision Will fit easily over prescription spectacles Visor can be replaced separately	Careful adjustment needed for secure fit Speech muffled and hearing may be slightly impaired Relatively expensive Some tendency to mist up Visor can, in some models, be flipped up which can be a minor hazard Very awkward to store

[2] Adapted from CLEAPSS guide R135 (April 1998) on eye and face protection. (See 'Introduction' page 2.)

4 When should eye protection be worn?

4.1 When are the eyes at risk?

Clearly eye protection should be worn whenever there is any foreseeable risk to the eyes, no matter what the practical work. A student's (and teacher's) eyes can be at risk:

- during teacher demonstrations;

- during student practical work;

- when the student has finished his/her practical work but neighbours are still doing it;

- during clearing away and washing up.

Consideration should always be given to reducing risk to the eyes by changing the method of working. There is considerable scope for this in much practical work: e.g. heating liquids such as Benedict's reagent in a water bath; putting a **loose** ceramic wool plug in test-tubes before heating solids; keeping students at a safe distance during demonstrations. Safety screens, which protect more than the eyes, should be used whenever there is a risk of explosion, splashing or, as with alkali metals and water, where the reaction is well known to be vigorous and can lead to materials spitting.

Technicians would be wise to wear eye protection when clearing away apparatus containing reagents or their reaction products which are known to be hazardous or are unknown.

4.2 What eye protection is needed for particular jobs?

It is difficult to give precise guidelines as to which type of eye protection should be used in particular circumstances. However, it is important for a science department to have a consistent policy based on an assessment of the circumstances of the school and department. The HSE has agreed that in school science:

- spectacles are suitable for most operations;

- a set of goggles is available and worn where there is a particular risk;

- a face shield is worn when large quantities of chemicals are dispensed, or cleared up after a spill.

This advice is a sensible compromise. We have found that the balance of advantage and disadvantage in many lessons falls in favour of spectacles because students wear these correctly most readily. However, where the danger presented by hazardous (by their nature, concentration or temperature) liquids is significant then goggles must be worn. Employers sometimes insist that only goggles are acceptable in science, but this is not the case and may actually be less safe. Students often find goggles less comfortable to wear and are tempted to remove then as soon as possible, irrespective of whether those around are still carrying out practical work.

4.3 Need for detailed local rules

Teachers and technicians must follow any rules laid down by their employer. However, choice of which type of eye protection to wear may be left to departments or individual teachers exercising their professional judgement. The following rough guide may help.

A   Goggles are needed when handling:

- corrosive solids or liquids, including alkali solutions ≥ 0.5 M and most acid solutions ≥ 0.5 M;

- toxic chemicals;

- cryogenic liquids.

B   Spectacles: except for substances classified in A spectacles are adequate for:

- heating chemicals (including cases where the heat comes from the reaction itself);

- shaking liquids in a separating funnel;

- grinding solids with pestle and mortar (but not oxidising agents);

- dispensing small volumes of liquids;

- dispensing solids;

- heating partially sealed vessels (e.g. in gas preparations, passing gases over solids etc);

- handling –
  organic liquids
  oxidising agents
  dilute acids and alkalis (less than 0.5 M);

- glass working;

- breaking rocks during geological studies;

- stretching metal wires or plastic cords;

- metalwork in the prep room;

- dissection of material containing cartilage or bone;

- any other operation likely to give rise to flying splinters.

C   Face shields should be worn when:

- dispensing large volumes of concentrated acids, alkalis (including ammonia) or other corrosive substances;

- opening and dispensing from storage containers that may be under pressure (e.g. '880' ammonia, hydrogen peroxide, silicon tetrachloride, etc.).

D Eye protection is not needed when using:

■ class 2 lasers (see Topic 18);

■ ultraviolet radiation – instead arrange the equipment so that the uv radiation cannot reach the eyes.

4.4 Other eye protection issues

1 Misting up

Misting up is a problem of both the outside and inside of lenses, mainly of goggles. Anti-mist sprays can be purchased and used and some goggles can be purchased as anti-mist. The tendency to mist up is one reason why students find goggles less easy to wear. Ventilated goggles are intended to allow moisture out but often fail. They have ventilation holes, which are covered by splash-proof caps. Note that some workshop goggles are vented directly, i.e. they simply have holes in. These do not give adquate splash protection and are therefore little better than safety spectacles.

2 Contact lenses

Contact lenses can be a problem in the event of an eye accident because they can be difficult to remove. Concerns that they impose a greater risk to the eyes in the event of an accident by hindering the washing out of chemicals have proved unfounded by research. Staff and students who wear contact lenses should wear eye protection of the same sort and at the same time as the rest of the class.

3 Prescription spectacles

As stated before, these will not offer any recognised level of protection. Neither staff nor students should be allowed to avoid wearing proper eye protection because they wear prescription spectacles. The department should ensure that an adequate supply of eye protection which fits over prescription spectacles is always available.

4 Eye washing

The simplest and most practical form of eye wash is a short length of rubber tubing attached to a suitable laboratory-type tap. The advantage of this is the availability of copious clean water for extended eye washing. Departments overcome the temptation of students to abuse the system by having the length of tube in a clear plastic bag pinned up very close to the tap and labelled 'Eye-Wash Station' or similar.

Filled eye-wash bottles are available but are less desirable because they contain only a small volume of water and are relatively expensive.

In the event that alkali gets into the eye then continuous irrigation is required. An ambulance should be called and the crew told that the contaminant is alkali and advised to continue irrigation during the journey to hospital. Do not be tempted to stop irrigation after 10 minutes to take the affected individual to hospital.

Plumbed-in eye-wash stations are probably too expensive for school use except if planned for in new buildings.

5 What other kinds of PPE should be worn, and when?

■ Gloves

Teachers and especially technicians should have access to appropriate gloves. There are times when heat-resistant gloves are necessary but a single pair in the department will usually suffice. Rubber or synthetic gloves may be needed (including, occasionally, by post-16 students) to prevent some chemicals being absorbed by the skin. Kitchen gloves are often satisfactory for this purpose but are not impervious to all solvents and must be removed quickly if they come into contact with concentrated acids or other corrosives[3]. Kitchen gloves may be needed for clearing up after class practicals involving microorganisms or harmful liquids, when the risks are increased because of the quantity of materials or sets of equipment.

Gloves are rarely needed by pre-16 students but if the risk assessment identifies the wearing of gloves, they must be worn. Disposable plastic gloves are quite common in schools and are needed to protect the skin against contamination from radioactive substances. Some departments use such gloves when students are collecting litter or handling plant or animal material. In general, ensuring students wash their hands thoroughly with soap and water after such activities is a simpler and less costly course of action. Cuts and scratches should be covered with waterproof plasters prior to the activity and sometimes wearing gloves may be helpful provided the teacher can ensure the insides of the gloves do not become contaminated. Many students, if offered a choice, will put on disposable gloves in order to stay clean or to avoid touching something thought of as distasteful. This is of course acceptable but is not a safety measure and the gloves cannot in such a case be regarded as PPE. The use of disposable gloves in the lab may increase hazards because, with such gloves on, it is more likely that, for example, a beaker of liquid may be dropped.

■ Laboratory coats

The general purpose of lab coats is to stop an individual's clothes from getting dirty rather than serving as PPE. When properly buttoned up they can

---

[3] Further information on gloves for use at post-16 can be found in section 11 of SSERC (1997) *Hazardous chemicals. A manual for science education* (ISBN 0 95317760 2, also available as CD-ROM, 1998); and in section 20.12 of CLEAPSS *Laboratory Handbook (1992)*.

stop ties or other garments from hanging loose and getting into Bunsen flames or becoming entangled with machinery. Lab coats constitute proper PPE in activities involving radioactive materials or microbiology, where removal of the lab coat removes the contamination, and when handling large volumes of hazardous materials.

Teachers and technicians often wear lab coats and post-16 students are frequently encouraged to do so. This makes sound sense where any individual handles chemicals and other material frequently. However, the lab coat is only effective if its is properly buttoned up and teachers and technicians should set a good example in this. Some schools encourage younger students (ages 11–16) to purchase their own lab coat or wear some other old clothing over their normal wear. This helps prevent damage to normal clothes and as such can be a good idea. It is unlikely that a department could provide lab coats in sufficient quantity and range of sizes for all such students. Lab coats need regular laundering and a department must consider their safe storage when not in use.

■ Aprons

Aprons will only be required when dispensing large quantities of corrosive liquids. In such circumstances the apron should be large and made of an impervious material.

■ Protective headgear

This is unlikely to be needed except on some outside visits. Staff and students with long hair will need some arrangement to tie or clip it back well out of the way of a Bunsen burner flame or machinery.

■ Protective footwear

It is not normally necessary to provide or use protective footwear in school science. However neither staff nor students should wear open-toed sandals when there is a risk of a spill of hot water or other liquid, or where there is the chance of breaking glassware. Ordinary shoes will admit chemicals so must be removed quickly in the event of them becoming contaminated.

Along with the spill kit in the prep room, it is a good idea to keep a pair of wellingtons large enough for all staff to wear. In the very rare likelihood of a large container (e.g. 2.5 litre) of corrosive liquid being spilled, wellingtons will keep the feet well protected when dealing with the spill and cleaning up. Wellingtons should be worn when pouring large volumes of liquid air or similar substances.

■ Face masks

Face masks may sometimes be needed for such tasks as cleaning out a chemical store, or cleaning locust cages or aviaries. It is important to realise that no face mask offers complete protection and it is important to ensure a good fit. Ensure you select a type appropriate to the task in hand.

Canister-type respirators are not necessary.

LABORATORY DESIGN FOR HEALTH AND SAFETY

This is a new Topic but it incorporates elements of Chapter 10 'Chemical storage', from the previous edition. It draws on information from several publications including DfEE Building Bulletin 80[1].

1 Introduction

This Topic is not intended to provide a blueprint for laboratory design. Some sources of further detailed information on laboratory design are listed at the end of this Topic. The purpose of this Topic is to highlight some key health and safety issues facing the head of science and to provide a briefing paper that the head of science can use in discussions with senior managers when dealing with safety issues involving the design of science facilities. Few heads of science are faced with the task of designing a brand-new department from scratch but many more are charged with advising on the updating of existing facilities. This Topic aims to be helpful in both cases and also should be of use to heads of science managing existing facilities and trying to keep the health and safety provision as up-to-date as possible.

2 Strategic design for health and safety

A high proportion of accidents in school science are traffic accidents, which fall into two broad categories. The first arises from technicians transporting materials or equipment over long distances or on difficult journeys which might involve a change of level or movement from one floor to another. The second involves collision between technician and students using the same thoroughfares. The ideal solutions to these hazards involve careful initial design. The department needs to be compact, aiming for a radial rather than linear structure, and the prep room and storerooms need to be well centralised so that distances between them and the laboratories they serve are minimised. Ideally technicians and students should use separate traffic routes. One possibility is to place the prep room at the hub of radiating laboratories although this clearly causes lighting problems in most situations and may also result in problems connected with ensuring adequate escape routes for technicians.

Modern buildings will meet current fire regulations. The laboratories and prep rooms must have two exits 'if a single exit door would be in a hazardous position'. The DfEE's position is one of delicate ambiguity but many fire officers would insist on a second exit; this may be into another laboratory provided the laboratories are properly separated. Stairwells should be isolated from the corridors by fire doors. These are minimum requirements and thought should also be given to escape routes used in emergencies and factors such as the effect of door and corridor width on the speed and ease of a full evacuation. Older buildings may have laboratories which share a ceiling or roof void. Fire can spread with great speed across such voids and any upgrade should include consideration of the possibility of installing firebreaks.

There is much to be said for science departments occupying a single floor (ideally the ground floor) but this is clearly impractical for larger departments and indeed in many schools. Departments occupying two or more floors should ideally have a prep room for each floor and/or an excellent lift system designed to accommodate trolleys and technicians. In this case the head of science will need to devise methods for dealing with the loss of flexibility caused by the restrictions in movement. Where apparatus, chemicals and equipment are moved using trolleys, movement should be minimised and if possible there should be designated trolley parks. One solution involves the storage of trolleys at both ends of their journey and the provision for this should be considered at the design stage of laboratories and prep rooms. The provision for deliveries should be considered in the overall design of the department. When delivering hazardous materials or delicate equipment suppliers should be able to transfer materials as directly as possible to safe storage.

Security is an important aspect of design. The designer needs to consider the protection of the building from outside intrusion in terms both of the quality of doors, windows and locks and of eliminating blind spots where illegal entry may be unseen. Careful siting of vulnerable rooms such as stores and prep rooms may also reduce the possibility of casual theft or vandalism. Unauthorised access needs to be difficult and supervision easy. It must be borne in mind that good

---

[1] DfEE (revised 1999) *Science accommodation in secondary schools, a Design Guide,* Building Bulletin 80. Stationery Office. ISBN 0 11271039 5.

design alone will not protect a building and appropriate management of the facilities is also essential.

3 Laboratories and prep rooms

One of the main considerations in the design of laboratories and prep rooms is the extent to which they are to be specialist facilities or will cater for all sciences and all age groups. Laboratories used for chemistry experiments require the greatest additional investment for health and safety (laboratory ventilation, fume cupboards and heat-resistant benches) and services (gas and water). The counsel of perfection is to design for maximum flexibility but the decision will depend on both philosophy and finance. The size of the laboratory will depend on the numbers in the largest groups to use it. The ideal may well be practical class sizes limited to twenty students (as in Scotland) but in practice it would seem realistic to expect a maximum class size of thirty (or possibly thirty-two) in England and Wales. The DfEE recommendation is for such a laboratory to have a floor area of 79–91 m^2. If the laboratory is too small, overcrowding will result, but, if the laboratory is too large, supervision may become difficult. Floor area is only one guide; the proportions of the space are significant and a laboratory also needs to be furnished. For the most efficient general supervision of practical work the laboratory should approximate to a square (DfEE recommend a 10:8 ratio).

Laboratories and prep rooms need good ventilation and it is desirable to have 5–6 air changes an hour, but this is often difficult to achieve in a prep room. Opening windows will provide basic ventilation and, in addition, laboratories used for chemistry should be fitted with extractor fans for which air inlets will also be necessary. Air inlets need to be placed to provide a proper flow of air through the laboratory. Fume cupboards ideally need to be sited away from corners and doors where turbulence might affect their performance. If residual current devices are fitted, the fume cupboards and extractor fans should be on a separate circuit to minimise the possibility of nuisance tripping. Remember that different ventilation systems affect each other and also the response of a room to fire. Furthermore, extraction systems generate noise which affects ease of class control.

Laboratory and prep room lighting is difficult. It goes without saying that teaching areas need to be well lit and that natural lighting has obvious benefits. However, thought needs to be given to the negative effects of bright sunlight. These include rendering Bunsen burner flames invisible, dazzling students and making rooms uncomfortably hot. Fitting solar film to the glass can significantly reduce these effects but this of course reduces the light levels in the room, a particular problem if plants are grown on window sills. There is frequently a need to dim a laboratory which can be achieved using curtains, or fabric, plastic or metal blinds. Curtains are significantly less safe than the other options.

All laboratories and prep rooms need gas, water and electricity and each room should have separate isolation valves or switches for each of the services. The electricity supplies should ideally be fitted with a residual current device which can double as an isolation switch. Some consideration needs to be given to the positioning of these isolation devices. One possibility is to site them just inside the main exit door to the room but there is also much to be said for placing them by the teacher's bench. Gas regulations require a gas shut-off where the supply enters the room but this may not be ideally placed for use by the teacher in an emergency. Use of a solenoid valve allows the switch to be located anywhere convenient. Washing and eye-wash facilities are essential for all laboratories (see Topic 5).

If smoke alarms are fitted it is important that they are automatically switched off when laboratories are in use, as they will be triggered by many class activities involving heating.

The choice between fixed benching and flexible units has been extensively discussed and debated. There are two possible safety aspects. The first involves those systems which utilise service pods hanging from the ceiling. These offer great versatility but the pods themselves may interrupt the sight lines of teachers and may be easily damaged. The second arises when the flexibility is used to create a configuration which affects the emergency escape routes within a room or access to emergency equipment such as eye-wash facilities or fire extinguishers. The conventional fixed system needs, of course, to have an optimum configuration for supervision and escape which needs to be established at the design stage. Long runs of benches that split the room and awkward corners without easy local escape routes should be avoided. The position of the board is an important decision. This is frequently on a short wall although the longer wall brings the class closer on average to the teacher and should improve supervision.

The design of the laboratory or the provision of its furniture should allow for the neat storage of bags. Clearly these should not obstruct gangways or escape routes directly or, indeed, indirectly by preventing stools being stowed under benches. Possible solutions will include additional under-bench storage or shelving; an alcove is a useful design feature. Here and elsewhere good management of the laboratories is as important as good design and such storage must not become a receptacle for waste. Additional planned storage for goggles and for laboratory coats (if used) is also desirable.

There is a wide range of materials suitable for floor coverings and benches. Floors need to be hard-wearing, non-slip, chemical resistant and easily cleaned or disinfected. From the safety angle there is perhaps little to choose between the various alternative materials for floors or benches.

4 Storage

To a large extent storage will depend on the layout of the school. Modern designs have a central store and an adjacent prep room area but in existing buildings compromise is inevitable. Any store needs to be readily accessible to technicians (and possibly other staff) and inaccessible to students and unauthorised personnel. There should be additional, possibly separate, secure storage for expensive equipment. Outside stores should be avoided if possible, as such stores are susceptible to vandalism, labels rapidly become unreadable and they often lead to the creation of unofficial internal stores, to avoid journeys outside in bad weather.

Lighting should be excellent to reduce the possibility of error. Storage on deep shelves should be avoided, as should placing heavy equipment or bottles above eye level. Some stores may need provision for securing gas cylinders either on or off their trolleys.

If at all possible, there should be a separate chemical store, preferably opening off the prep room area. It needs good security and it is desirable though not essential that doors should open outwards. Ventilation can be achieved using air-bricks at a high and low level if there is an outside wall; otherwise, extractor fans on a time switch will be necessary. Ideally, the floor should slope away from the door and be made of concrete or quarry tiles. The chemical store should have a spillage kit. Running water may be helpful in emergencies unless the store is adjacent to the prep room but it should not have a gas supply.

Highly flammable liquids can be stored within the building in flammables cabinets, with a maximum of 50 litres in any one room. Other chemicals can be arranged on shelves in the locked chemical store but, if local conditions suggest that extra security is required, they can be locked in ordinary wooden cupboards.

Chemicals can be separated into:

■ corrosives chemicals;

■ oxidising agents;

■ toxic and other inorganic chemicals;

■ toxic and other organic chemicals;

■ flammable solids;

■ large bottles of made-up solutions.

Incompatible chemicals (e.g. acids and alkalis or oxidising agents and most organic chemicals) should be stored as far apart as practicable, e.g. in different cupboards, or on shelves on different walls of the store room. Large bottles should be low down but off the floor, or protected from kicking. This can be achieved by standing them in a container such as a plastic trough or on a plinth. In the latter case further protection can be achieved by using a barge board to retain an absorbent material such as sand. Chemicals that are hydrolysed by water in the atmosphere should be kept in containers with soda lime. Radioactive substances should not be kept within the chemical store, but must not be within 2–3 m of any area occupied by the same person on a regular basis.

After use, bottle necks and drips should be wiped to avoid any further evaporation within the store. Ensure caps are firmly screwed on.

Spark-proof electrical fittings (e.g. fans and lighting) are not essential unless highly flammable liquids will be dispensed there. Even then, spark-proof fittings may not be necessary if there is good ventilation and dispensing takes place some distance (e.g. 2 m) from any electrical fittings. However, with new buildings and refurbishment it is usually easy to locate switches outside the store and this is worthwhile.

Unfortunately, the design of the school may dictate that chemicals have to be stored in the prep room. In this case all but the most innocuous should be locked away to prevent the possibility of theft if students enter the room. As chemicals will be dispensed, access to a fume cupboard will be necessary, either in the prep room or in an adjacent laboratory. In addition, forced ventilation (with an extractor fan) is almost certain to be necessary.

A biology store may well need a refrigerator for micro-biological materials but higly flammable liquids must not be stored in or adjacent to it.

Effective storage requires good management of resources with equipment and materials organised in a simple but effective way that allows for rapid stock checks and easy removal of out-of-date chemicals or other materials. A possible organisation of a chemical store is illustrated in Appendix 1. Appendix 2 summarises the main options for the storage of chemicals.

Further information

ASE (1989) *Building for science, a laboratory design guide*. ISBN 0 86357 119 0.

ASE (1996) *Safeguards in the school laboratory*. ISBN 0 86357 250 2.

CLEAPSS School Science Service Guide (March 2000) L14 *Designing and planning laboratories*.

DfEE (revised 1999) *Science accommodation in secondary schools, a Design Guide,* Building Bulletin 80. Stationery Office. ISBN 0 11271039 5.

DfEE (1996) *Safety in science education*. Stationery Office. ISBN 0 11 270915 X.

Appendix 1   Possible organisation of a chemical store

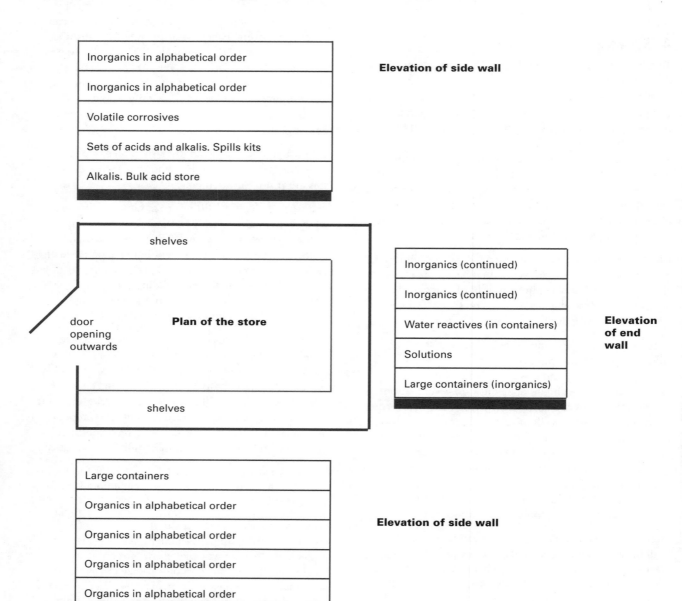

Elevation of side wall

| Inorganics in alphabetical order |
| Inorganics in alphabetical order |
| Volatile corrosives |
| Sets of acids and alkalis. Spills kits |
| Alkalis. Bulk acid store |

shelves

door
opening
outwards

Plan of the store

shelves

Elevation of end wall

| Inorganics (continued) |
| Inorganics (continued) |
| Water reactives (in containers) |
| Solutions |
| Large containers (inorganics) |

Elevation of side wall

| Large containers |
| Organics in alphabetical order |
| Organics in alphabetical order |
| Organics in alphabetical order |
| Organics in alphabetical order |

Appendix 2 Options for storing chemicals

Category	Code	Group	First option	Second option	Third option	Keep away from
Flammable substances	FL	Liquids	Fire-resistant cupboard in chemical store or prep room	External store meeting fire requirements	Strict limits on stock	GO, T
	FS	Solids	Internal chemical	Internal chemical	Locked cupboard	GO, CL, FL
	FM	Water reactives	Store in locked cupboard	Store on shelves away from GO	In prep room or store	
Toxic substances	T	Toxic chemicals	Internal chemical store always locked or in locked cupboard	Locked cupboard in prep room or store	Locked cupboard in laboratory	FL
Corrosive substances	CLa CLb	Liquids, acid Liquids, non-acid	Internal chemical store at low level in waterproof storage well	Prep room or store at low level	Laboratory in low, locked cupboard	CLb, FM, T CLa, FM, T
	CR	Volatiles	Exclusive cupboard, with ventilation to outside, located in chemical store	Dry cabinet, desiccator or plastic box with desiccant and soda lime	Internal store near ventilation	FM
	CS	Solids	Internal chemical store with general chemicals	Prep room or store in cupboard	Laboratory in locked cupboard	
General chemicals	GO	Oxidising	Internal chemical store with inorganic chemicals	Prep room or store with inorganic chemicals	Laboratory in locked cupboard	FL, FS, FM, GC, CL
	GI	Other inorganics	Internal store	Prep room or store	Laboratory in cupboard	
	GC	Other organics	Internal store	Prep room or store	Laboratory in locked cupboard	
Special cases	S	Bromine	With corrosive, volatile chemicals (anhydrous Na_2CO_3 and 1 M $Na_2S_2O_3$ to hand)			FM
		Methanal	Secure biology storage or with toxic chemicals			CL, CR
		White phosphorus	In water in locked cupboard in store or prep room, maybe with toxic chemicals			GO, FM
		Silicon tetrachloride	In dry container, cabinet or desiccator with silica gel			–
		Sulfur dioxide	These canisters are no longer available			CR, CL
		Gas cylinders	Fixed either to bench or trolley			FL
		Radioactive substances	Special cupboard (site with care) (see Topic 19)			FL, CL

FUME CUPBOARDS

This Topic replaces Chapter 15 in the second edition of Topics in Safety. *It draws on information in DfEE (1998)* Building Bulletin 88 (BB88), *Fume cupboards in schools[1], which replaces Design Note 29 (1982).*

1 Introduction

The Control of Substances Hazardous to Health (COSHH) Regulations[2] have increased the existing tendency to regard exposure to gases and vapours in school science with more concern than in the past. The COSHH Regulations sharpen the obligation of employers to provide adequate fume cupboards as they contain a requirement that employers shall provide equipment to prevent or control exposure to substances hazardous to health when, without it, exposures are assessed to be unacceptable. The COSHH Regulations also stipulate that employers must take steps to see that such control measures are used, tested and maintained.

2 When fume cupboards are needed

Fume cupboards are needed when, without them, there would be a significant exposure to dusts, vapours or gases hazardous to health. However, fume cupboards should usually be regarded as a secondary defence, and apparatus and operations should be designed to minimise release of vapours.

Appendix D2 of Building Bulletin 88 (BB88) advises on experiments and substances for which use of a fume cupboard is advisable. It dispels the false belief that fume cupboards are needed only for Advanced Level use. This information is also contained in CLEAPSS *Hazcards*[3] and SSERC *Hazardous chemicals. A manual for science education*[4].

Access to a demonstration fume cupboard is always highly desirable (see section 5). Younger classes may need access to a fume cupboard for practical work, other classes to more than one fume cupboard. Technicians frequently require access to a fume cupboard, both for preparation and disposal. In addition to their use for handling noxious fumes, fume cupboards are also valuable for handling offensive or flammable vapours.

3 In the absence of a fume cupboard

What can be done in the absence of a fume cupboard or if a fume cupboard fails a regular inspection?

The COSHH Regulations require that substances that are assigned a Maximum Exposure Limit (see Topic 10) must have their concentration reduced as far as is reasonably practicable. However, the lack of an efficient fume cupboard may not mean that experiments involving reactions for which the use of a fume cupboard is recommended cannot be carried out. There may well be alternative techniques that can be used. Clearly the 'model' risk assessments, that assume a fume cupboard will be used, cannot apply and a special risk assessment will be needed as instructed by the employer. An alternative is to seek out a model risk assessment that allows the investigation to be carried out on the open bench. Possible alternatives might include the following.

■ Carrying out experiments as teacher demonstrations with smaller quantities in a well-ventilated laboratory, e.g. the action of heat on lead nitrate can be performed safely as a demonstration or by 4 groups, if not more than 0.5 g of solid is heated at any one time.

■ Carrying out experiments on a microscale so that the quantities of gas/vapour potentially released are well below the hazard limit, e.g. the preparation of ethanal by the oxidation of ethanol.

■ Replacing the experiment with a less hazardous one, e.g. the reduction of nitrobenzene to phenylamine requires a fume cupboard because both the reactant and product are toxic. However the reduction of the methyl or ethyl ester of nitrobenzenecarboxylic (nitrobenzoic) acid presents much less risk.

CLEAPSS *Hazcards* and SSERC *Hazardous chemicals. A manual for science education* both contain a wealth of information on alternative, safer, methods for

---

[1] DfEE (1998) *Fume cupboards in schools*, Building Bulletin 88. Stationery Office. ISBN 011 271 027 1.
[2] Control of Substances Hazardous to Health (COSHH) Regulations (1999). SI No. 1999/437. Stationery Office.
[3] CLEAPSS (1995, updated 1998, 2000) *Hazcards*. CLEAPSS School Science Service.
[4] SSERC (1997) *Hazardous chemicals. A manual for science education.* (ISBN 0 95317760 2, also CD-ROM, 1998).

performing reactions that may be potentially hazardous if performed in the traditional way, without the need for a fume cupboard. Subscribers can contact the above organisations (see 'Introduction' page 2) with requests for special risk assessments.

Even if a fume cupboard fails its regular inspection, it may still be possible to use it for some experiments. This will depend on the way it fails the test and how badly. In such circumstances it should be labelled as 'ONLY TO BE USED FOR ...'

4 The standard for school fume cupboards

There is some confusion about the status of various standards for fume cupboards, and the standard for school fume cupboards. BB88 sets out the basic recommendations that apply to school fume cupboards. (This has replaced DES Design Note 29 (1982) *Fume cupboards in schools*.) The bulletin recommends standards for newly-installed school fume cupboards. It is based on experimental work carried out by the CLEAPSS School Science Service on the likely exposure to vapours produced by operations carried out in school science; 100–200 operations were considered including accidents such as spills and sulfur dioxide cylinder valves sticking open[5].

The British Standard for fume cupboards does not apply to school fume cupboards. The reason for this is summed up in Section 1 of BB88 as follows.

> *Where it is known for particular fume cupboards that the rates of release of hazardous gases and vapours are low, or where the fume cupboards are used intermittently and then only for short periods, the performance type test procedure may be too stringent. In such situations, the requirements of Part 1 of BS7258 are not applicable and reference should be made to other appropriate standards such as Design Note 29…*
> *(This bulletin [BB88] replaces Design Note 29 and is now the standard for school fume cupboards)*

It is important to be aware of this paragraph because there have been instances in the past of representatives of fume-cupboard manufacturers convincing would-be purchasers that Design Note 29 was about to be superseded by a British Standard. The Standard (BS7258) for fume cupboards is in some ways very permissive and in any case does not aply to demonstration cupboards. Unlike BS7258, BB88 makes specific recommendations, e.g. on air-flow rates. It should also be pointed out that not all HSE Inspectors and Safety Consultants are aware that BB88 has been approved by the HSE National Industry Group for Education.

Anyone concerned with the purchase or installation of a school fume cupboard should read BB88 or contact CLEAPSS or SSERC, although the information in this Topic will give some idea of the main recommendations of BB88.

4.1 Air flow

When the sash opening is 400 mm, the minimum working air velocity should be 0.3 m s^{-1} or more. Also, the difference between the greatest/least and the mean air velocities should be below 30%.

The minimum air velocity figure is a compromise. Someone walking briskly past can draw out some vapour, which would be less likely to happen if the minimum velocity were higher. On the other hand, velocities above about 0.6 m s^{-1} affect Bunsen burner flames. There is a tendency for the air velocity to go up as the sash is lowered which can increase the flow to the extent that Bunsen burner flames will lift off. This has led, on at least one occasion, to a gas tap being left running all night as nobody realised the burner had been blown out by the draught. Modern fume cupboards should have a bypass that reduces this. It comes into effect as the sash is lowered, usually by uncovering a vent at the top of the fume cupboard, and prevents the air flow under the sash from rising too much.

The 30% variation figure is important as a measure of stability of the air flow: if there is a greater variation, there is a greater tendency for eddies to occur and these bring out vapour. It is relatively easy to achieve variations of this value or less provided the duct leaves the fume cupboard more or less in the middle of the top. This recommendation effectively rules out running the duct out of one corner because it is architecturally convenient or claiming that a large glass box fitted against a window with an extraction fan in it can be considered as a fume cupboard.

The maximum sash working opening for use of a cupboard for chemical handling should be fixed by a stop; a mark on the sash is insufficient. The stop should be capable of being unlocked with a key so that the sash can be raised further for cleaning inside or for assembling tall apparatus. BB88 specifies that the maximum sash opening should be at least 400 mm. This is a compromise, which gives sufficient room for most manipulations, offers some protection to the faces of operators and makes reasonable demands on the extraction system. A stop fixing the minimum sash opening is also important. Without it, a sash can be made to close the working opening completely, thus preventing the fume cupboard from working. Its height should be fixed so that the air velocity is not so high that Bunsen burner flames are badly affected. Some believe

---

[5] Crellin, J. R. (1984) School fume cupboards. *Education in Chemistry*, **21**, 185–189

that it is important to be able to close a fume cupboard completely in case of fan failure. However, evacuation of the room is the right reaction to this event that should happen only rarely.

4.2   Materials

Fume cupboards should be glazed with toughened or laminated glass. BB88 suggests appropriate working and other surfaces; solid melamine is the favoured working surface since asbestos cement went out of fashion. Architects tend to favour light colours that soon become stained; another trap for the innocent is stainless steel, which is no match for school conditions.

4.3   Double-sashed fume cupboards

These are installations where the fume cupboard has access from two different rooms, e.g. a lab and a prep room. BB88 reinforces previous DES advice that double-sashed fume cupboards are not satisfactory. Even if properly fitted with stops to limit the minimum sash opening, there will be cross draughts, which could cause vapours to escape. If fitted between two laboratories or between a laboratory and a prep room, they also reduce security and fire containment.

4. 4   Installation

It is inappropriate to repeat most of the recommend-ations of BB88 which are concerned with installation. However, two points need to be emphasised. First, the design of extraction systems requires a ventilation specialist; architects and builders are quite capable of believing, for example, that reducing a duct diameter from 200 to 150 mm to fit it through a gap has little effect on air flow. However, they are totally mistaken. Another curious belief is that air bricks and cowls offer little impedance to air trying to travel at several metres per second. However, even ventilation specialists need educating about fume cupboards as they tend to believe the maxim 'The faster the better'. It is important to ensure that they have a copy of BB88.

Secondly, fume cupboards will work effectively only if air can freely enter a laboratory to replace that which is being extracted. Some laboratories are fitted with grills to the outside for this replacement air; otherwise a window should be opened. The best position for the air inlet is opposite the fume cupboard. The need for adequate replacement air becomes acute if several fume cupboards are operating and an extraction fan as well.

4.5   Commissioning new fume cupboards

Once a fume cupboard has been installed, it will need to be tested before it is used by staff or students. BB88

contains a schedule[6] that should be used as a part of the commissioning of a newly-installed fume cupboard. The installers are obliged, under the regulations, to test the fume cupboard. If a school wishes to have a new fume cupboard installed it should insist that the commissioning schedule contained in BB88 forms part of the contract before it is awarded. This is particularly important if the supplier is not the installer of the cupboard. The schedule makes some attempt to divide responsibilities between supplier and installer where these are not the same.

It is often difficult to site a fume cupboard well in a school laboratory but doors and windows close to it should be kept shut: replacement air should come from a distant grill or window, preferably sited opposite the cupboard so that the air flow is perpendicular to it.

5 Demonstration fume cupboards

5.1   General

These should be glazed on the back and sides. Any baffles fitted should, of course, be transparent and easily removed for cleaning. If a demonstration fume cupboard cannot be fixed permanently in the laboratory so that a class can be arranged around three sides with the operator at the sash, then it should be on castors with two locking brakes and fitted with a flexible duct attached to the fixed outlet with a swivel. Arrangements for gas and electricity supply need careful design; water and drainage are not essential but there should be some arrangement for supplying a water condenser, e.g. metal tubes with riffed nozzles passing through the glazing.

5.2   Recirculatory fume cupboards

Some schools use recirculatory fume cupboards fitted with filters. The ease with which they can be installed and wheeled round a laboratory is attractive and their cost is about half that of a ducted fume cupboard installation. BB88 suggests quite stringent conditions for these and only one or two models satisfy them. They are not suitable for use with some chemicals. The manufacturer should supply a list of chemicals safe to use with the fume cupboard. This information should be readily available to all staff who may have cause to use the cupboard and will need to be written into risk assessments for experiments.

Disadvantages and advantages of recirculatory fume cupboards

■ Their main disadvantage is their need for adequate maintenance. Air flows need to be checked frequently to ensure the pre-filter has not become blocked with dust or smoke particles. The main filters should be checked for effective absorption:

---

[6] BB88, Schedule C page 45.

this entails releasing vapours inside the fume cupboard and checking the outflow with a Draeger or similar 'sniffer'. The electronic alarms fitted to some recirculatory fume cupboards work well with fuel from the salesman's cigarette lighter but may not work with sufficient sensitivity for most toxic vapours. While replacement filters are likely to be needed only every two or three years, their cost of two or three hundred pounds will probably fall on the already stretched laboratory budget, and occasionally filters may cease to be manufactured. Recirculatory fume cupboards are not usually as robust as conventional ones. Finally, staff do not always realize that, even when working correctly, a filter must let a very small proportion of a vapour through (it is something to do with partition coefficients). They forget that the nose is a very sensitive detector and become alarmed.

■ Their main advantages are the lower cost of installation and that they are portable.

Best advice is to use a ducted fume cupboard wherever possible.

6 Existing fume cupboards

Because the replacement of a fume cupboard is expensive, it is often necessary to make do with an existing one. BB88 recommends that any fume cupboard not meeting the minimum face velocity requirement (see section 4.1) should be upgraded. It is sometimes possible to do this by making relatively small changes to the extraction system: e.g. the number of fume cupboards served by a system can be reduced, a fan or cowl can be replaced or a damper altered. Sometimes cleaning out the ducting system, maintaining the fan and fitting stops to the fume cupboard are all that are necessary.

Another relatively inexpensive improvement is to cover the glass in the fume cupboard with a safety film: CLEAPSS or SSSERC can advise where this material can be obtained. Education authorities will have policies on the replacement of asbestos products. In the past, working surfaces in fume cupboards were frequently made of asbestos-cement materials such as Sindanyo. While the dust from such a working surface is extremely unlikely to reach significant levels in normal use, policy may require it to be sealed. Dark-coloured melamine is a suitable material. It must be remembered that any employer has an obligation to protect the health of employees and others. Meeting the recommendations of BB88 is the best way of doing it. If they are not followed, the obligation on the employer to ensure that there is no serious exposure to noxious vapours becomes harder to meet.

7 The use and maintenance of fume cupboards

There is a requirement laid down by the COSHH Regulations that fume cupboards are tested at least once every 14 months. This means a visual inspection, testing of the air flow and, for recirculatory fume cupboards, testing the efficiency of the filters. A record must be kept of this regular monitoring. Such monitoring may be carried out by any person trained in the use of the monitoring equipment. This includes laboratory technicians. Methods of testing and pass/fail criteria are given in SSERC and CLEAPSS publications[8].

Fume cupboards should be kept clean and free from apparatus and bottles not immediately required. If a fume cupboard has to be used as a store for corrosive volatiles (e.g. the chlorides of phosphorus, sulfur, tin, etc.), it should be fitted with a time switch set to come on perhaps twice a day and not be used for experiments. Fume cupboards should be properly maintained: particular attention should be paid to the sash mechanism and the service controls. The air flow should be checked periodically; ducts have been known to become blocked with bird's nests, balls, etc. Between the 14 month tests a thin strip of flimsy plastic attached to the underside of the sash will at least indicate that there is air flowing and in the right direction.

When in use the fan should be left running until any reaction has ceased and the fume-cupboard duct is free of fumes. Individuals should be discouraged from passing close by the front of the fume cupboard as they are likely to cause eddies which eject vapours.

While the sash should offer some protection to the operator, eye protection should still be worn whenever there is foreseeable risk to the eyes. Fume cupboards are not replacements for safety screens, thus they are not suitable locations for experiments, such as reduction experiments, where there is risk of explosion. It is safer to use the bench with safety screens and other appropriate precautions. The exception to this is the use of carbon monoxide as a reducing agent, in which case the experiment should be carried out in a fume cupboard.

If the air speed of a fume cupboard is so high that it interferes with Bunsen burner flames, the interference can be reduced by shielding, perhaps with a cylindrical can with its bottom removed; alternatively, Meker burners, which are more draught-resistant, can be used.

There is a temptation to treat any small sink or drip pot in a fume cupboard as a disposal point for hazardous liquids. It should be resisted, although a fume cupboard may well be found to be the best place to treat and dilute these liquids before they are then disposed of in the approved manner.

---

[8] SSERC (1998) *Routine testing of fume cupboards – ducted and recirculatory.*
CLEAPSS *Laboratory handbook*, section 20.10.6, or Guide L9b (April 2000) *Monitoring fume cupboards.*

FIRE PRECAUTIONS

This Topic replaces Chapter 14 in the second edition of Topics in Safety.

1 Introduction

Major fires are not a frequent occurrence in school laboratories. Small fires resulting from laboratory accidents have been reported from time to time and a very small number of these have had serious consequences for the students or adults involved. This Topic should help preserve this generally good record by considering some of the causes of fire and the best means of avoiding them.

Whatever is recommended, staff must follow the rules or code of practice laid down by their employer.

2 Precautions

The aims of fire precautions are to:

■ minimise the risk of a fire starting;

■ avoid injury to people including fire-fighters;

■ minimise the damage to property in the event of a fire.

There may be conflicts between the requirements of security and those of fire safety. For example, if the only emergency exit from a laboratory is through a prep or store room, the Fire Prevention Officer is likely to insist that the communicating door is fitted with panic bolts or not locked at all, though the needs of security might suggest a mortise lock. Smoke alarms should not be fitted in laboratories. The best position is in the ceiling of the stairwell.

There are other matters of concern, which are equally applicable in new or old premises. Smoke check doors should be fitted with automatic closing devices and not wedged open **except** when pushing a trolley, carrying bottles in a bottle carrier or carrying a tray. Any plastic materials used in laboratories or prep rooms for con-struction, storage containers, sinks, lampshades, elect-rical conduits, etc. should not be readily flammable.

A small fire was spread dangerously by flames melting overhead plastic lampshades that then dripped over the benches.

Curtains or blinds should be of a flame-retardant material. The location of mains switches for electricity and stopcocks for gas and water should be clearly indicated and known to all teachers and technicians working in the laboratories.

In a practical class, a child lit the gas at the gas tap producing a flame 1 m in length. Acting in haste, the teacher turned on the adjacent tap, resulting in two gas flames. Thus prevented from reaching the taps again, the teacher then had to hunt for the stopcock in order to cut the supply to that bench.

Experienced teachers have a particular responsibility to give guidance in safe practice to their newly qualified or trainee teacher colleagues and to laboratory technicians. The practice of teaching across science can sometimes result in a teacher handling unfamiliar chemicals in unaccustomed ways. Here again it is the responsibility of the head of department to ensure that all concerned are adequately informed of safety hazards and safe techniques. The importance of instruction in sound handling techniques and good practice cannot be over-emphasised. Staff need to be instructed/reminded of the need to:

■ check Bunsen tubing for signs of cracking;

■ check glassware for faults;

■ make sure charcoal blocks are safe to leave after use;

■ wash down surfaces contaminated with oxidising agents;

■ ensure vapour does not build up in laboratories by checking for adequate ventilation;

■ ensure flasks and glasses of water or OHPs cannot act as lenses to focus the Sun.

Heads of science should also ensure that only minimum quantities (e.g. 100 cm^3) of flammables are available in a laboratory at any time and that teachers and students are trained to cope with small fires such as those in test tubes or beakers. Particularly useful in respect of the above is *Safe and exciting science,* the ASE pack of training activities on health and safety for science departments, which has a section designed to be used to train new teachers in science[1].

---

[1] ASE (1999) *Safe and exciting science.* ISBN 0 8635 7295 2. Unit 3D 'Fire', page c7.

Rubbish must not be allowed to accumulate particularly under benches or in stairwells. Waste bins should be of metal and be emptied daily but hazardous materials should be rendered safe before being left for disposal. Under no circumstances should oxidising agents be placed in the waste bin.

A school cleaner started a fire in a dustbin containing paper towels when she tipped in manganate(VII) (permanganate) from one waste bin followed by broken glass. This came from a flask which had been deposited in another bin in a different laboratory and which had originally contained propane-1,2,3-triol (glycerol).

3 Outbreak of fire

If a fire does start, the top priority must always be the safety of people: **everything else is secondary to this**. Smoke and toxic gases can spread very rapidly and cause panic and injury.

All establishments should have a clearly stated procedure for dealing with such emergencies and this should be known by all teachers, ancillary staff and students.

A summary should be prominently displayed in all rooms in a fire notice.

Fire exits should be clearly marked and kept free from obstruction at all times.

Regulation 7 of the Management Regulations[2] requires that a member of the school staff be nominated to implement evacuation procedures.

4 Fire-fighting equipment

Each laboratory and prep room should be provided with a fire blanket and with the means of extinguishing a small fire; a carbon dioxide fire extinguisher of 4 to 5 kg or two of 2 kg capacity being the most suitable.

However, sand is necessary for dealing with alkali metal and phosphorus fires. 'Sand buckets' tend to be used as a receptacle for all manner of things and are best avoided. Sand should be provided in a bag, or even better, a plastic bottle brought into the laboratory by the technician with the chemicals.

Any extinguisher must be used with the utmost care in the vicinity of animal enclosures and dry powder extinguishers are very messy to clean up and can ruin computers. Foam extinguishers are equally unsuitable.

The equipment should normally be situated adjacent to the teacher's area of the laboratory.

All such items should be regularly inspected and maintained in accordance with the requirements of the education authority or Fire Prevention Officer. After use, any equipment must be serviced in accordance with the supplier's recommendation.

5 Some particular hazards

5.1 Fuel gases

It is imperative that there should be no leaks in the fuel gas system; any odour of unburned gas should be investigated immediately and rectified before classes continue. Flexible pipes (e.g. Bunsen burner tubing) should be regularly checked and replaced if there is evidence of damage or poor fit. Avoid using thick-walled neoprene tubing as it is too rigid and may cause Bunsen burners to be knocked over.

Extra vigilance is required if liquefied petroleum gas (LPG) is used as the fuel source. Unlike natural gas (methane), LPG (propane or butane) is denser than air and will sink to floor level; it may then accumulate in conduits or other underfloor cavities. If LPG is used, it is preferable to have piped supplies. In that case, the cylinders will be large and the Fire Prevention Officer will insist on outside installation. All such piping will need to be inspected on a regular basis. Small cylinders may be fitted in mobile benches.

Bunsen burners fuelled by cartridges are best avoided except for occasional demonstrations or in emergencies.

Where an appliance requires an integral gas bottle or cartridge, such containers should be changed and used only in strict accordance with the supplier's instructions.

An explosion that wrecked the laboratory of a rural school, which used bottled gas, was caused by ignition of butane in an underfloor service duct. The gaseous butane had escaped from a leaking screw thread connection between a gas tap and its service pipe and collected below the floor. Students who succeeded in rotating the gas tap on the bench after removing the restraining woodscrews had caused the original leak.

Modern designs of gas tap are available with integral anti-rotation devices to obviate such problems.

Some laboratories are now equipped with lightweight island bench units with fixed, rigid service pipes.

In one incident, movement of the island unit had caused a leak in the gas pipe below the bench, allowing gas to fill the space between the drawers. Eventually a flashover occurred when a student was using a Bunsen burner and the whole unit became engulfed in flame.

Explosions involving hydrogen gas continue to occur.

---

[2] Management of Health and Safety at Work Regulations, 1999. SI No. 1999/3242. Stationery Office. Also HSE (2000) *Approved Code of Practice and Guidance L21: Management of Health and Safety at Work*. HSE. ISBN 0 7176 2488 9.

The most usual cause is failure to expel all air from the apparatus before igniting the hydrogen. Ways of avoiding this problem are given in ASE (1998) *Safety reprints*[3].

5.2 Ethanol (methylated spirits, alcohol)

A number of burns accidents involving methylated spirits have been reported. In the most serious instances, it was being used as a fuel in burners for model steam engines.

In at least three reported cases a teacher, believing the fuel to be exhausted and the flame to have gone out, was attempting to refill the trough-type burner with methylated spirits when it ignited, causing a flash fire and severe burns to students sitting about 1 m from the demonstration bench.

At least five reported accidents in a short time mean that the use of methylated spirits as a fuel for model steam engines presents an unacceptable hazard. The best solution is to use a burner specially designed for a solid fuel, such as hexamine or Meta fuel. Burners intended for solid fuels should never be used with liquid fuels.

Fires involving methylated spirits are not confined to its use as a fuel.

A technician was decanting methylated spirits after boiling with grass to extract chlorophyll; the liquid ignited causing severe burns to the person holding the vessel. In another instance, a student was badly burned when attempting to fill a 'home-made' thermometer with methylated spirits, by heating the bulb in a flame whilst the open end was dipped into the liquid.

5.3 Heating flammable liquids

Particular care must be exercised when it is necessary to heat a flammable liquid. Only the absolute minimum volume required should be used, contained in a vessel no more than one fifth full.

A bath of hot water is often a satisfactory heat source but the water should not be heated with a naked flame or hot plate on the same bench as these liquids, in order to avoid the risk of igniting the flammable vapour.

An electric kettle or thermostatically-controlled water bath is a convenient source of hot water for school laboratory purposes. For higher temperatures, a sand tray or hot plate will need to be used.

There are various definitions of highly flammable liquids, all depending on the specification of a flash point. Table 1 lists flammable and highly flammable liquids that might be used in school laboratories, with their flash points and auto-ignition temperatures. Many of the liquids in the table are capable of producing a vapour-air mixture that could be ignited by a spark even at room temperature. There have been instances reported of explosions caused by ignition of flammable vapour-air mixtures by arcing thermostat contacts.

A laboratory drying oven was completely wrecked by a solvent explosion. A spark in the thermostat ignited the vapour produced by evaporation of the final traces of solvent from crystals.

Several instances are known of similar explosions occurring when flammable solvents had been placed in refrigerators: domestic refrigerators do not usually have spark-proof thermostats. All electrical equipment, which may come into contact with flammable vapours, must be fitted with spark-proof switchgear.

5.4 Class practical work

There has always been a fire hazard associated with some clothing materials but many light-weight synthetic fabrics are particularly prone to burn if held even momentarily in a Bunsen burner flame or splashed with a burning liquid. Laboratory coats should be made of heavy-duty cotton, and not of a synthetic fabric. Substances such as Proban are available to treat lab coats to render them flame retardant.

A few years ago, there were several reported accidents in which a student's hair had caught fire. Hair normally singes when in a flame but some styling preparations can cause it to burn instead. Investigations by CLEAPSS suggest that many lacquers (holding or fixing sprays) and mousses (frothy preparations from aerosols) increase the flammability of hair. Gels (in pump-action dispensers, tubes or jars intended to make hair look wet or shiny) are relatively safe and render hair non-flammable until they have dried out. There is some evidence that styles in which hair is in tufts or separate strands increases the tendency for it to catch fire.

Students should be advised not to spray their hair at school (so that the solvent/propellant may have some chance to disperse) and also to keep hair, goggle straps, ties and scarves well away from Bunsen burners or other naked flames.

Illicit experiments can be a fire hazard. Some students have pencil sharpeners that are made of magnesium and on at least one occasion an attempt to burn one proved successful!

---

[2] ASE (updated 1998) *Safety reprints*, 'Hydrogen' page c7. This article deals with the problems associated with hydrogen in school laboratories. ISBN 0 86357 246 4.

Table 1 Flammable and highly flammable liquids

Material	Flash point[1] /°C	Auto-ignition temperature[2]/°C	Material	Flash point /°C	Auto ignition temperature/°C
Benzenecarbaldehyde[3] (benzaldehyde)	64	191	Heptane[4]	−1	233
Bromobenzene	51	566	Hexane[4]	−28	250
Bromoethane	−20	517	Hex-1-ene	<−20	−
Butanal	−7	−	Methanal solution (formalin)	50–80[5]	470
Butan-1-ol	24–29	340	Methanol	11	446
Butan-2-ol	28	406	Methylamine, 30% solution	0	430
Butanone	−6	515	Methylbenzene (toluene)	4	506
Chlorobenzene	29	638	3-Methylbutyl ethanoate (iso-amyl acetate)	20	560
1-Chlorobutane	−9	460	Methyl-2-methylpropenoate (methyl methacrylate)	10	421
Chloroethane	−50	519	2-Methylpropan-2-ol (t-butyl alcohol)	9	450
Cyclohexane	−20	260	Octane[4]	14	260
Cyclohexene	−60	−	Oct-1-ene[4]	21	−
1,2-Diaminoethane	43	−	Paraffin	47	227
1,2-Dichloroethane	17	450	Pentane[4]	−48	309
1,2-Dichlorethene	6	−	Petroleum, crude	<32	−
Diethylamine	−18	312	Petroleum spirit (petroleum ether)	−18	288
Dimethylamine 33% solution	−25	470	Phenylethene (styrene)	32	490
Dimethylbenzene (xylene)	29	~500	Propan-1-ol	15	540
Ethanal	−38	185	Propan-2-ol	12	460
Ethanoic acid (acetic acid)	43	426	Propanone (acetone)	−18	538
Ethanoic anhydride (acetic anhydride)	50	390	Pyridine	20	482
Ethanol (methylated spirits)	13	422	Triethylamine	−7	−
Ethanoyl chloride (acetyl chloride)	4	390	Trimethylamine, 30% solution	−7	190
Ethoxyethane (diethyl ether)	−45	180	Turpentine	35	293
Ethylamine, 70% solution	−18	384	White spirit	40	−
Ethyl ethanoate (acetate)	−5	427			

Notes

[1] The flash point of a liquid is the temperature at which the vapour above it is capable of being ignited.

[2] At the auto-ignition temperature a liquid or its vapour will ignite without the aid of an external source of ignition.

[3] Benzenecarbaldehyde has been included because, although its flash point is above 60 °C, its auto-ignition temperature is low.

[4] Branched isomers have lower flash points.

[5] Varies according to methanol content.

5.5 Demonstrations

It is very important that the teacher should at all times demonstrate safe techniques and never be seen to take chances. Eye protection should be used by both teacher and students, together with suitably positioned safety screens, whenever an experiment, which might result in an explosion, is to be performed. Nearly all the serious accidents occur during demonstrations. Therefore, students should not be seated too close to the demonstration bench: 2–3 m is usually a suitable minimum gap.

5.6 Clearing away

Problems can also arise in clearing away after an experiment.

A fire started in one laboratory, when small pieces of phosphorus ignited in a plastic sink, thereby causing the plastic to burn as well.

Another accident arose when a bottle containing an aged sample of sodium was rinsed with water, the metal exploding and starting a fire that rapidly spread.

Blocks of charcoal can smoulder unseen for a long time after use even after dousing with water. A number of fires have been caused by ignition of charcoal blocks returned to a store cupboard before being completely cold. Such materials are best stored in a metal container with a well-fitting lid and not returned to the store for at least 24 hours after use.

5.7 Newly published texts and courses

Many newly published courses are now published with health and safety advice. It is the duty of the head of science to ensure that, notwithstanding the advice given, the activities suggested in the text do not present an unacceptable fire risk.

6 Fighting small fires

Teachers using school laboratories need to know how to tackle small fires. Training of staff and students in dealing with small fires should form a natural part of teaching and departmental meetings. Fire brigades and equipment suppliers run courses and it is suggested that at least some science teaching and support staff at a school be encouraged to attend one of these. The advice in the following paragraphs could form the basis of local rules.

Burning furnishings

Tackle only in the initial stages. If gaining a hold, the priority is evacuation of students and staff.

Flammable liquid fires

■ If the flammable liquid is **burning in a container such as a beaker**, the preferred first treatment is to cover with a bench mat or damp cloth (or smother with a fire blanket). If the volume of flammable liquid involved is small, it is probably safer to leave it to burn out by itself. The use of a fire blanket can, in inexperienced hands, create problems, as they tend to be awkward to handle and may spread a small fire by knocking over the apparatus containing the burning liquid. If smothering does not extinguish the fire, a carbon dioxide extinguisher may then be necessary to complete extinction. If a blanket *is* used, it should be left in place while the area cools.

■ If **spilt liquid is on fire**, it may be possible to allow it to burn out. Alternatively, smothering is possible. If a fire extinguisher is used, direct it towards the edge of the fire and sweep towards the centre. Two persons can better tackle large fires, each with an extinguisher from different angles but not opposite each other. However, unskilled use of fire extinguishers can lead to the fire spreading.

■ If **burning liquid is spilt on a person's clothes**, they should be made to lie down with the flames on top in order to burn away from the body and be wrapped tightly in a fire blanket.

Gas fires

A fire extinguisher should not be used on the gas jet. Use the extinguisher only on residual fires that may be burning after the gas has ceased to flow.

■ **Hydrogen cylinders**: if safe to approach, shut off the gas supply at the main cylinder valve. The key should be on the valve at all times for this purpose. If for any reason this is not possible, evacuate.

■ **Natural gas:** if safe to approach, shut off the supply. The main gas cock may have to be used and it is better if it is close by.

Metal fires

Small fires involving **sodium, potassium, calcium, lithium** or **aluminium.** (**Note**: eye protection should already be in use.) Smother with a large excess of dry sand, **not** a carbon dioxide extinguisher. Leave to cool. Sodium residues should be disposed of in propan-2-ol, potassium residues in 2-methyl propan-2-ol and, in all cases, the sand should be cautiously added to a bucket of water in a fume cupboard afterwards to decompose silicides formed. Spontaneously flammable gases may form at this stage but are not a hazard in an efficient fume cupboard.

Phosphorus fires

Water is a suitable extinguishing medium. It is most convenient, usually, to cover the burning phosphorus with wet sand.

SIGNS AND LABELS

This Topic replaces Chapter 12 in the first and second editions of Topics in Safety *and Appendix 1 of Chapter 5b in the second edition. Some material from Chapter 12 is now in Topic 8.*

1 Safety signs on walls, cupboards, etc.

A range of safety signs may be used in and around buildings to give safety information. The Safety Signs Regulations[1] implement a European Council Directive aimed at standardising safety signs in workplaces across Europe. Signs fall into five categories.

Prohibition signs are circular with a black pictogram on a white background, red edging and a red diagonal line.

DO NOT DRINK THE WATER

NO SMOKING

Warning signs are triangular, with a black pictogram on a yellow background and black edging.

DANGER OF ELECTRIC SHOCK

TOXIC MATERIAL

Mandatory signs are circular with a white pictogram on a blue background.

EYE PROTECTION MUST BE WORN

GLOVES MUST BE WORN

Emergency signs are rectangular or square, with a white pictogram on a green background.

FIRE ESCAPE ROUTE

EYEWASH

Fire-fighting signs are rectangular or square with a white pictogram on a red background.

FIRE EXTINGUISHER

FIRE HOSE

---

[1] The Health and Safety (Safety Signs and Signals) Regulations 1996 or, in Northern Ireland, the Health and Safety (Safety Signs and Signals) Regulations (NI) 1996.

More extensive examples can be found in several publications[2]. The pictogram alone may be sufficient, but it is permitted to add text. For example, a chemical store may contain substances with a range of hazards. Rather than confuse the situation with a proliferation of signs, it would be more appropriate to use the general DANGER sign, as below, with a caption as shown.

HAZARDOUS CHEMICALS

Despite a widely-held belief to the contrary, it is **not** compulsory to display safety signs in most situations, although if safety signs are used, they must conform to the standard specification. However, they are only required where the risk cannot be controlled by other methods. Putting signs, for example, on the doors of chemical stores may simply increase the risk of vandalism, although it is usual to put the HIGHLY FLAMMABLE sign on the doors of the highly flammable cabinets **inside** the store or preparation room. The main risk from chemical stores would be to fire-fighters, and the local Fire Officer may be prepared to agree that if the information about the location of chemical stores is made available by other means (e.g. by the caretaker or site manager in an emergency) then no sign is needed. AM1/92[3] and (in Scotland) SED Circular 1166[4] require the RADIOACTIVE sign to be on the door of the cupboard in which sources are kept and require the Fire Officer to be informed.

HIGHLY FLAMMABLE

RADIOACTIVE

Similarly, there is no need to put up a sign saying EYE PROTECTION MUST BE WORN in every laboratory. If there were such a sign, it would mean that every person entering the laboratory – students, science staff, the headteacher with a group of visitors – would have to put on eye protection, whether or not practical work was under way. The risks from practical activities with chemicals, etc., are better controlled by verbal instructions from the teacher, notes on worksheets, etc. However, there may be advantages for teaching

purposes in having a **removable** EYE PROTECTION MUST BE WORN sign, as long as it really is removed when there is no risk.

The Regulations define certain standard signs, although minor variations in the pictogram are permitted. Where no suitable standard sign exists, the user can define one, provided that it is simple and conforms to the general principles. For example, a gas isolation valve might be identified by using a rectangular green sign, with a white pictogram of a spanner and an arrow to indicate the off direction and the caption GAS ISOLATION VALVE.

Changes to fire extinguisher code

As a result of a new European Standard[5], the colour code for fire extinguishers has recently changed. All new fire extinguishers must now be coloured red, although existing extinguishers do not need to be changed. The Standard does permit a zone of a different colour, provided that it does not exceed 5% of the total area. Different countries are likely to use different colours in these zones, but in the UK the colours will be the familiar ones.

- ■ Black   carbon dioxide
- ■ Blue   dry powder
- ■ Green   vaporising liquid, e.g. halogenated hydrocarbons
- ■ Cream   foam
- ■ Red   water

2 Labels on bottles

The labelling on bottles is governed by different regulations[6] to those dealing with signs around a building, although some of the same pictograms are used[2]. Symbols should be square with a black pictogram on an orange background, for example, CORROSIVE. These regulations only apply to suppliers. There is no requirement for schools, as users, to put any labels on their chemicals. However, it is good practice to do so and goes some way to meeting the requirements of the COSHH Regulations by informing users (i.e. teachers, technicians and students) of the main hazards of a particular chemical. It also contributes to the health and safety education of students, as required by the National Curricula in England and Wales and Northern Ireland[7].

---

[2] See, e.g. ASE (1996) *Safeguards in the school laboratory* (10th edn., ISBN 0 86357 250 2); CLEAPSS (1997) *Student safety sheets*; SSERC (1997) *Hazardous chemicals. A manual for science education* (ISBN 0 95317760 2, or CD-ROM version, 1998).

[3] Administrative Memorandum 1/92 *The Use of Ionising Radiations in Education Establishments in England and Wales*.

[4] SED (1987) Circular 1166 *Procedures for the use of ionising radiations in educational establishments*.

[5] BS EN 3 and BS 7863: 1996.

[6] The Chemicals (Hazard Information and Packaging for Supply) Regulations 1994 (CHIP2) as later amended in 1996, 1997, 1998, 1999 or, in Northern Ireland, the CHIP Regulations (NI) 1995 as amended.

[7] See, for example, the preamble to the Programme of Study at all key stages in *Science in the National Curriculum, England and Wales*, DfE, 1995; or the *Health and Safety* statement, common to all practical subjects, in the *National Curriculum for England*, DfEE/QCA, 1999.

Where labels are used, they should be accurate. Concentrated sulfuric acid is CORROSIVE, as are solutions which are 1.5 M or more. Solutions equal to or more than 0.5 M are IRRITANT. Below 0.5 M they are LOW HAZARD (for more information, see Topic 10). It would be educationally unsound and would promote an unreasonable fear of chemicals if the solutions were wrongly labelled. Suppliers of chemicals are obliged to show one or two hazard symbols, together with various risk phrases (see Topic 10) and safety phrases. The symbol alone should be sufficient for labels used in schools.

Pictograms are available from several commercial suppliers on rolls or sheets of sticky tape. They can also be reproduced by printing from some software packages, e.g. the CD-ROM version of the *Hazardous Chemicals Manual* (SSERC, 1997). The labels look better if printed on a colour printer.

3 Signs and labels as control measures

When a risk assessment is carried out, one of the control measures to reduce the risk from a particular hazard might be the use of a sign or label. This is particularly true of risks in and around the prep room. Examples of signs and labels which might be useful include the following.

THIS BOX HAS A MASS OF 20 KG. ONLY TO BE LIFTED BY 2 PEOPLE.

THIS APPARATUS ONLY TO BE USED BY THOSE WHO HAVE BEEN TRAINED.

DO NOT ISSUE THIS CHEMICAL WITHOUT CHECKING WITH HoD.

USE A STEP-LADDER TO REACH THIS APPARATUS.

CHECK THAT THE STEAM VALVE IS OPERATING BEFORE USE.

CHECK THAT AIR IS FLOWING BEFORE USING THIS FUME CUPBOARD.

DO NOT STORE CHEMICALS IN THIS FUME CUPBOARD.

DO NOT PUT SOLID WASTE DOWN THIS SINK.

STUDENTS ARE NOT ALLOWED TO ENTER.

STAFF: LOCK THIS DOOR WHEN THE ROOM IS NOT IN USE.

NO FOOD / NO FLAMMABLE LIQUIDS IN THIS 'FRIG.

WARNING: THIS HOT PLATE IS HOT.

CHARCOAL BLOCKS COOLING – DO NOT OPEN LID.

However, be warned against a proliferation of signs – they will be ignored.

If an experiment has to be left running outside lesson times, or a piece of equipment (other than that obviously designed for continuous operation, such as a refrigerator) left switched on, there should be a suitable label. An example is given as Appendix 1 to this Topic – it may be freely copied.

Appendix 1   Unattended running of apparatus outside normal working hours

.... School/College   Room ....

Apparatus/Investigation ....

....

....

Date/Time started ....   To run until ....

PLEASE LEAVE ON

Services switched on (tick as appropriate):

Electricity ....   Computer ....

Water ....   Gas ....

Other (specify) ....

IN AN EMERGENCY ....

....

....

Emergency contact(s):

	Name	*Position*	*Phone*	*Address*
1				
2				

Signature of person in charge ....   Date ....

Place this sheet adjacent to/fastened to the apparatus/investigation.

Published by the ASE (adapted from an HSE ESAC publication). May be photocopied for use in schools.

10 USING CHEMICALS

This Topic replaces Chapter 7, 'Chemistry experiments' and Chapter 8, 'Restricted chemicals', in the first and second editions of Topics in safety.

1 Introduction

This Topic is written for anyone who uses chemicals, not just chemists. The first and second editions of *Topics in safety* had extensive tables giving guidance on the suitability of various chemicals for school use. Since the second edition was published, other publications have become available with more extensive information, e.g. CLEAPSS *Hazcards*[1] and SSERC *Hazardous chemicals. A manual for science education*[2]. The DfEE (1996) *Safety in science education*[3] has a table clearly derived from those in *Topics in safety*. At the time of writing, the ASE has DfEE approval to update the table and publish it on the ASE website.

The lists that appeared in the first two editions of *Topics in safety*, therefore, have now served their purpose. There is a broad consensus about the chemicals that can be used in school science and under what circumstances. However, problems do arise when the hazards of a particular chemical are re-classified by the regulatory authorities or when a previously uncommon chemical finds a new use in school science. This new Topic is intended to address those issues.

2 Assessing the suitability of chemicals for school science use

The systematic classification of hazards in recent years has led to a greater awareness of the hazards of substances that have been used routinely in school science for many years. Merely because the hazards are better known does not necessarily mean that the risks are greater or unacceptable. The general public, and sometimes scientists as well, tend to use the word '*safe*' as meaning '*completely safe*' or '*free from risk*'. This is unrealistic and unscientific. Nothing is completely safe[4]. Science teachers should promote the word to mean '*safe enough*' or '*safer than it was*'. There is an

important place in chemistry teaching for the spectacular demonstration, which conveys an important chemical message and which students will remember for many years to come, provided that it can be made '*sufficiently safe*'.

One justification for teaching science is to teach youngsters about the hazards and risks of the world in which they will live and work. This can only be achieved by allowing students to have hands-on experience, in a controlled environment, of substances and activities that present some hazard. Wrapping students in cotton wool would not be a good preparation for life. The difficulty lies in deciding what is sufficiently safe. Does the educational advantage outweigh the risks? In general, the risk from category 1 carcinogens, etc., is likely to be so great that their use is rarely justifiable in schools. Category 3 carcinogens, however, and in some circumstances category 2 carcinogens, may be justified if conditions are suitable. Similarly, it might be inappropriate to give younger students solid barium chloride (TOXIC) but such students could be given 0.1 M[5] barium chloride solution (HARMFUL) because they would need to consume implausibly large amounts to do themselves harm. Sixth-formers would probably be deemed to be sufficiently trustworthy to handle the solid.

In assessing the suitability of some chemicals for school use, it is important to consider the role of technicians. Whereas students will often use relatively dilute, low-hazard solutions, the technician may have had to handle the much more hazardous solute. Because the technician is handling much larger quantities, face shields and pvc aprons may be necessary. Ventilation is often poor in prep rooms and the technician may well need to use a fume cupboard. Dust masks complying with a suitable standard may be necessary sometimes, e.g. when weighing out chemicals classed as SENSITISERS.

Increasingly, open-ended project or investigative work is finding a place in school science at all levels. With younger students and/or larger classes, it is best to permit investigations only in relatively safe contexts,

---

[1] CLEAPSS (1995 or 1998/2000 update) *Hazcards*.

[2] SSERC (1997) *Hazardous chemicals. A manual for science education* (ISBN 0 95317760 2, also as CD-ROM, 1998).

[3] DfEE (1996) *Safety in science education*. Stationery Office. ISBN 0 11270915 X.

[4] See, for example, D. R. Williams (1998) *What is safe? The risks of living in a nuclear age*. Cambridge: RSC.

[5] In this topic, M is used as a convenient abbreviation for mol dm^{-3}.

e.g. using acids and alkalis, sufficiently dilute as not to be classified as CORROSIVE. With different groups working on different activities, even the best teacher's supervisory skills are fully tested, without adding health and safety to the problems. The more hazardous chemicals should be used only where students can be given clear instructions and supervision is relatively straightforward. In sixth-form project work, it is inevitable that some students will want to use chemicals not normally found in schools. Even where students are expected to consider health and safety issues as part of the project, the teacher/lecturer must still check their risk assessments. This is not a job for technicians – the supervising teacher or lecturer has a duty to carry out such a check. With novel chemicals and/or procedures in use, staff may well need to have a special risk assessment carried out, for example, for members, by CLEAPSS or SSERC. There could be factors that teachers may not have considered, for example, the inability of most school fume cupboards to withstand fumes from hydrofluoric acid.

3 General principles of risk assessment when using chemicals

We feel that a pragmatic approach is best. Over many years ASE, CLEAPSS, SSERC and the HSE have collected information about accidents in schools. Indeed, much of the advice given in model (general) risk assessments such as *Hazcards* or *Hazardous chemicals. A manual for science education* is based on information about accidents and near-misses collected over many years. Where the use of a novel substance or activity is proposed we believe it is normally quite straightforward to extrapolate the risks from the known into the unknown, provided that the hazards of the unknown can be identified. The SSERC book[6] *Preparing COSHH risk assessments for project work in schools* gives useful guidance.

Factors to take into account include the following:

■ whether the chemicals will be handled by technicians, teachers or students;

■ the nature of the hazards of the chemicals used or made;

■ the amount of chemicals to be used or made;

■ the route by which chemicals might be taken into the body;

■ if handled by students, their age, ability and degree of responsibility;

■ the presence of students with special educational needs, where relevant;

■ whether students handle the pure substance or only a dilute solution;

■ the ability of the teacher to supervise the class adequately (class size, experience and other issues);

■ the facilities, e.g. access to a suitable fume cupboard or facilities for heating flammable liquids without using Bunsen burners;

■ the availability of gloves (if necessary) and goggles giving chemical splash protection as opposed to safety spectacles;

■ training for staff and/or students, e.g. how to heat a chemical or sniff a vapour safely.

If your employer has provided you with model risk assessments for using chemicals, e.g. *Hazcards*, *Hazardous chemicals. A manual for science education*, etc., the risk assessment process becomes much simpler. All you have to do is to check that the model applies to your situation and consider whether any modification is necessary to deal with the particular situation of your school, laboratory or class. Then a simple record is made to show that the thinking has taken place and to convey the significant findings of risk assessment to others, for example, by annotating teachers' guides, schemes of work, etc.

4 'Banned' chemicals

There is a common misconception that a variety of chemicals and procedures are banned. This is untrue; under national legislation, almost nothing is banned even for educational use. In fact, only the following are banned under the COSHH Regulations[7] for educational purposes:

■ benzene;

■ anything containing more than 0.1% benzene (e.g. most samples of petrol);

■ benzidine (and its salts);

■ 2-naphthylamine (or napthalen-2-amine) (and its salts);

■ 4-aminodiphenyl (and its salts);

■ 4-nitrodiphenyl.

In 1970, the then-DES issued an Administrative Memorandum[8] on carcinogens, stating that a range of amines, including *o*-tolidine, β-naphthylamine and those

---

6 SSERC (1991) *Preparing COSHH risk assessments for project work in schools.*
7 The Control of Substances Hazardous to Health (COSHH) Regulations 1999, or, in Northern Ireland, the COSHH Regulations (NI) 1995.
8 Administrative Memorandum 3/70, *The Avoidance of Carcinogenic Aromatic Amines in Schools and Other Educational Establishments*, DES, 1970.

listed above should not be kept or used in school laboratories (see Topic 12). There has been similar guidance in Scotland[9]. This was purely advisory, but virtually all education authorities acted upon the advice and instituted local bans. It is therefore simplest to consider all of these amines as effectively banned.

There is a range of chlorinated hydrocarbons that are damaging to the ozone layer. Under European Regulations[10] it is now illegal to supply these for educational or most other uses. However, schools that hold stocks can continue to use them quite legally, although they will be unable to obtain further supplies. Chemicals in this category include:

- tetrachloromethane (carbon tetrachloride);

- 1,1,1-trichloroethane.

Sometimes, education employers (especially education authorities) have produced local codes of practice, which have included lists of banned chemicals. As employees have a duty to cooperate with their employers on health and safety matters, teachers and technicians must respect any such ban. However, it is worth checking the status of any alleged ban: when it was last reviewed, whether it is mandatory or advisory, if there are exceptions for use in the sixth form, etc.

The lists in the first and second editions of *Topics in safety*, in *Safety in science education* and elsewhere include a category of NOT RECOMMENDED. This means exactly what it says: the substance or procedure is not, in general, recommended for use in schools. There is no national ban but there may be a local ban. Even if not banned locally a special risk assessment would be needed before using it:

- to evaluate the educational justification for doing something which is generally not recommended

- to ensure staff are fully aware of the particular health and safety precautions needed to control the risk from this rather special hazard.

In many cases, members could obtain such special risk assessments by applying to CLEAPSS or SSERC, but might well face some interrogation about why the activity was considered necessary, the facilities available and the skills and experience of the staff involved.

Table 1 Hazards of chemicals.

Hazard group	Hazard
Physico-chemical properties	Explosive Oxidising Extremely flammable Highly flammable Flammable
Health effects	Very toxic Toxic Harmful Corrosive Irritant Sensitising by inhalation Sensitising by skin contact Carcinogenic (categories 1, 2, 3) Mutagenic (categories 1, 2, 3) Toxic for reproduction (categories 1, 2, 3)
Environmental effects	Dangerous for the environment

5 Hazard and risk when using chemicals

The Health and Safety Executive (HSE) defines a hazard as anything with the potential to cause harm. This is inherent in the nature of many chemicals. Concentrated sulfuric acid is corrosive. This is an unalterable property of the acid, just like its density.

Risk, on the other hand, is the probability of harm actually being caused by the hazard. Risk depends upon:

- how likely it is that something will go wrong;

- how serious the consequences of something going wrong would be.

Under the CHIP Regulations[11] the hazards of chemicals are classified under three headings (see Table 1).

Some substances may be listed not because they present a hazard themselves, but because they form a hazardous substance when in contact with water, acid, etc. About 60 *risk phrases* are defined in legislation[12] (although more logically they should be called hazard phrases). For many industrially important chemicals, the associated risk phrases have been approved by the Health and Safety Commission and are published as the

---

[9] SED Circular 759, *The use of Carcinogenic Substances in Educational Establishments*, SED, 1970; most recently, SED Circular 8/95, *Guidance on the Use of Carcinogenic Substances in Work in Schools*, SED, 1995.

[10] EC Regulation 3093/94, Council Regulation on Substances that Deplete the Ozone Layer (this makes the use of these substances illegal throughout the EC) and SI 1996 No. 506 The Environmental Protection (Controls on Substances that Deplete the Ozone Layer) Regulations 1996 (this provides penalties and enforcement mechanisms in the UK).

[11] Chemicals (Hazard Information and Packaging for Supply) Regulations 1994 (CHIP2 Regulations) (as later amended in 1996, 1997, 1998 and 1999) or, in Northern Ireland, the CHIP Regulations (NI) 1995 as amended.

[12] Chemicals (Hazard Information and Packaging for Supply) (Amendment) Regulations 1997 (CHIP97): *Approved Guide to the Classification and Labelling of Substances and Preparations Dangerous for Supply*, 3rd edn., 1997, or, in Northern Ireland, the CHIP (Amendment) Regulations (NI), 1998.

Table 2 Risk phrases.

Risk phrase (i.e. hazard)	LD_{50}*	Example
LOW HAZARD	> 2000	Sodium carbonate (4090 mg/kg)
R22 HARMFUL IF SWALLOWED	≤ 2000	Copper sulfate (300 mg/kg)
R25 TOXIC IF SWALLOWED	≤ 200	Barium chloride (118 mg/kg)
R28 VERY TOXIC IF SWALLOWED	≤ 25	Potassium cyanide (5 mg/kg)

• in mg/kg oral, rat.

Approved Supply List[13]. Examples include R8 CONTACT WITH COMBUSTIBLE MATERIAL MAY CAUSE FIRE (e.g. potassium nitrate), R14/15 REACTS VIOLENTLY WITH WATER, LIBERATING EXTREMELY FLAMMABLE GAS (e.g. sodium) and R40 POSSIBLE RISK OF IRREVERSIBLE EFFECTS (e.g. thiourea). Detailed criteria for assigning these risk phrases are given in the guidance. For example, substances labelled HARMFUL may cause death or damage when administered (orally, to the skin, or inhaled) in moderate amounts, whereas those labelled TOXIC do so in small amounts and those labelled VERY TOXIC do so in very small amounts. The LD_{50} (lethal dose) is the amount of substance required to kill 50% of the animals in a sample (commonly rats.) The figures are scaled as if the animals weighed 1 kg.

The risk phrases in Table 2 apply to the solid. If a solution is used then the concentration is important as this will affect the volume needed in order to consume the lethal dose. Thus copper sulphate solution needs to be labelled HARMFUL only if the concentration is 1 M or above. Similarly, barium chloride solution is TOXIC if the concentration is 0.2 M or above, HARMFUL if it is 0.02 M or above (but less than 0.2 M) and LOW HAZARD below that. It is important to emphasise that in sufficient quantity almost any chemical can be lethal – consuming a large excess of sodium chloride or of water has killed in the past! Guidance on how solutions of varying concentrations should be labelled can be found in various publications, e.g. the *Laboratory Handbook* (CLEAPSS), *Hazardous chemicals. A manual for science education* (SSERC).

CARCINOGENIC substances (and those classed as MUTAGENIC or TOXIC FOR REPRODUCTION) are particularly emotive. There are three classes of carcinogens, but it is important to recognise that these do NOT represent a hierarchy of potency. See Topic 12.

6 Occupational Exposure Limits

For a limited range of substances, the COSHH Regulations specify Occupational Exposure Limits[14] (OELs). Mostly, these relate to gases or volatile liquids, as inhalation is the most likely route of intake in most workplaces. However, if skin absorption could contribute significantly, this is also indicated.

Two types of OEL are defined. Occupational Exposure Standards (OESs) are concentrations (e.g. of chlorine) which should not be exceeded, but to which it is believed workers can be exposed day after day, without risk of damage to their health. On the other hand, Maximum Exposure Limits (MELs) are set for the most hazardous substances (e.g. benzene, wood dusts) where 'safe' levels of exposure cannot be defined. Not only must the MEL never be exceeded but also every effort must be made to keep exposure as far below these levels as is reasonably practicable.

For both types of OEL, the limit is defined as the concentration (in $mg\ m^{-3}$ or ppm) averaged over a specified time period. Two time periods are used: 8 hours (long-term exposure limits, LTELs) and 15 minutes (short-term exposure limits, STELs). Higher doses can often be tolerated if exposure is for a shorter period of time. 15-minute exposure is typical of the way in which chemicals are often used in school science and so STELs are often the appropriate figures to use for classroom work, but this might not be true of technicians working in ill-ventilated prep rooms.

The model risk assessments commonly used in school science, e.g. *Hazcards* or *Hazardous chemicals. A manual for science education,* will have taken account of OELs when suggesting control measures such as suitable quantities for particular practical activities. Examples of how to use OELs in exposure calculations can be found in several publications[15]. It is important to put OELs in perspective. Sucrose (sugar) has an OEL (STEL) of $20\ mg\ m^{-3}$. This may be relevant in a sugar-bagging plant, but is no reason to avoid putting sugar into a cup of tea!

7 Interpreting Safety Data Sheets

Under the CHIP Regulations a supplier is obliged to provide Safety Data Sheets when hazardous substances are supplied. The exception to this is when substances are sold to the general public and sufficient information is provided by other means. Schedule 5 of the Regulations specifies the information that must be given on Safety Data Sheets.

---

[13] Chemicals (Hazard Information and Packaging for Supply) (Amendment) (No. 2) Regulations 1999: *Approved Supply List*, 5th edn., 1999, based on 67/548/EEC the Dangerous Substances Directive.

[14] *EH40/** Occupational Exposure Limits*, HSE (updated annually, the ** being the last two digits of the year).

[15] See CLEAPSS (1997) *Laboratory Handbook*, section 7.9; or SSERC (1991) *Preparing COSHH risk assessments for project work in schools*, Appendix 6 .

It is important to stress that Safety Data Sheets are *not* risk assessments. Risk assessment requires knowledge about the quantities of a chemical to be used, how it is to be used, the skills, experience and training of the user and other factors that the supplier could not possibly know about. The sheets provide information about hazards. The user then takes this information and carries out a risk assessment.

Many teachers and technicians find Safety Data Sheets very alarming. The information can run to several pages. The toxicological information can be frightening. Would the average science teacher or technician think a substance with an LD_{50} of 261 mg/kg (oral, rat) and described as '*Should be treated as a suspected carcinogen. Evidence of reproductive effects.*' was suitable for use in schools? Yet this is caffeine, something we nearly all consume in small quantities in coffee, tea or cola drinks. Caffeine certainly presents a hazard. Whether there is a significant risk depends on the amount and how it is used.

Suppliers, and especially those from the USA with its greater tendency for litigation, tend to go overboard in warning about hazards from which there could be little risk in the context in which the substances are used in school science. Despite the guidance available, where risk phrases are not given in the *Approved Supply List,* there are frequently inconsistencies between suppliers about the hazards of, and hence the risk phrases to be used for, a particular chemical (see section 8).

Hazards may be different depending upon the route by which a chemical is taken into the body: by inhalation, by skin contact or by swallowing. In assessing the risk, the likelihood of exposure must be taken into account. For example, a fine powder might well be inhaled, but the same substance in the form of large crystals would not. Gases and vapours are readily inhaled, of course.

8 Some illustrative examples

In this section we give examples of activities where there are hazards, but where the risk can be reduced to acceptable levels by suitable control measures. The intention is that these examples might act as models to show how risk assessment could be carried out in more unusual situations.

1 Occasionally there are reports of hydrogen exploding, e.g. when being passed over hot copper oxide. Usually, the problem is that excess hydrogen is being ignited at a jet before all the air has been flushed out. There are safe ways of ensuring all the air is flushed out but, even if it is not, an explosion is not disastrous if the students and staff are well protected by safety screens, eye protection and distance. The key here, as in many similar cases, is (in-house) training for those staff who need to know and a sufficiently robust management procedure to ensure that untrained staff cannot, and do

not, carry out this activity. Methane (natural gas) is sometimes suggested as a safer alternative to hydrogen. Whether it is suitable depends on what the educational objectives are; in some contexts, use of methane would be confusing. Hydrogen from cylinders is arguably safer than generating the gas chemically because the large volume of hydrogen which is readily available flushes the air out very quickly.

2 Reactions of sodium and the other alkali metals with water are one of the more memorable demonstrations carried out in many schools. Even when the school has adopted apparently suitable precautions, there are occasional reports of incidents, e.g. pieces of sodium reacting with unexpected violence and being projected over the safety screen. The problem is sometimes caused by using too large a piece of sodium or, occasionally, potassium (perhaps as a result of over-zealous encouragement by the class). Sometimes, against advice, teachers attempt to constrain the sodium in order to collect a sample of gas. Whatever the cause, injury can be avoided by having the safety screens very close to the reaction vessel and students and staff some distance away (2–3 m). A piece of sodium would then need to be travelling almost vertically to project over the screen, and would thus come down almost vertically into the safe, unoccupied space. Even better would be to have three safety screens arranged in a triangle, totally surrounding the reaction vessel, with a fourth placed on top as a lid. Cooling the water with ice will also help.

3 Both potassium (di)chromate(VI) and ammonium dichromate(VI) are VERY TOXIC BY INHALATION, and CATEGORY 2 CARCINOGENS. They MAY CAUSE CANCER BY INHALATION. They are also TOXIC IF SWALLOWED and HARMFUL IN CONTACT WITH SKIN. They MAY CAUSE SENSITISATION BY SKIN CONTACT. Normally, it is only technicians and sixth-formers who handle the potassium dichromate(VI) solid and, because the crystals are usually relatively large, inhalation is implausible in this context. Gloves should be worn to protect from possible skin contact. On the other hand, electrolysis of dichromate(VI) solutions could produce an aerosol of dichromate(VI) mist and so steps would need to be taken to control exposure to this. The sort of work that younger students are likely to do with potassium dichromate(VI) involves relatively dilute solutions (0.1 M or less), which would be TOXIC IF SWALLOWED, but present much less risk of causing problems by skin contact and could not be inhaled. A school would need to decide whether the class could reasonably be trusted not to swallow the solution. On the other hand, ammonium dichromate(VI) is used almost entirely because of its interesting and highly memorable exothermic decomposition once ignited. Handling the ammonium dichromate(VI) solid should present no greater risk than potassium dichromate(VI). However, as the particles decompose, small specks of chromium(III) oxide are carried into the air. Although LOW HAZARD, it is conceivable that they could carry tiny amounts of undecomposed ammonium dichromate(VI) which therefore might be inhaled. Consequently, this decomposition should be carried out in a way which prevents inhalation of the particles, e.g. by use of a fume cupboard (although this would contaminate the inside) or in a conical flask fitted with a mineral wool plug to act as a filter.

4 Concerns have been expressed about the use in school science of thermometers containing mercury. Mercury is TOXIC BY INHALATION. There is a DANGER OF CUMULATIVE EFFECTS. There are alternative ways of measuring temperature, such as liquid crystal strips, digital thermometers and temperature probes connected to computers. However none of these is appropriate in all circumstances, if only because of the cost. On some occasions, at least, liquid-in-glass thermometers are needed. There are various alternative liquids to mercury. In primary schools and in much work in lower second-ary it makes sense to use such alternatives (although the thread breaks more easily and is harder to re-join). Where accuracy is important mercury offers a number of advantages, e.g. it responds more quickly (and is thus less confusing in inexperienced hands). It is also less susceptible to errors due to immersion to the incorrect depth (and correct immersion is not always possible because of the nature of the apparatus.) Provided schools are aware of the hazards of mercury and are vigilant at clearing up any breakages there is little risk.

5 Sometimes, the risk can be reduced with no educational disadvantage. For example, sulfuric acid is classed as CORROSIVE at concentrations of 1.5 M or more, and IRRITANT at concentrations of 0.5 M or more (but below 1.5 M). Traditionally, 'bench strength' sulfuric acid has been 1 M or 2 M, but for most purposes 0.4 M works perfectly well. Not only is it safer, but it is more economic as well. Where a safer alternative exists that works just as well, the COSHH Regulations require that it be used. Hence, for example, for routine tests of the action of acids on indicators, metals, oxides and carbonates, 0.4 M sulfuric acid should be used. If the intention is to prepare crystals of a salt, for example by evaporating the water after titrating sulfuric acid with sodium hydroxide, then use of 0.4 M solutions would result in a need to evaporate a large amount of water. It is more practical to use more concentrated solutions in this case, but that does not invalidate the general point that most work can be done with quite dilute solutions and, where they are satisfactory, they should be used. ***Bench solutions should normally be below 0.5 M.*** Similarly, when testing for reducing sugars in food, it is far safer for children to heat Benedict's solution (LOW HAZARD, although the reaction product, copper(I) oxide, is HARMFUL) than Fehling's solution (CORROSIVE). As Benedict's solution works just as well it should be used.

At A-level, however, Benedict's is not satisfactory in testing for alkanals (aldehydes) and therefore Fehling's solution should be used there. Alternatively Sandell's reagent could be used[16] although there is the possibility that examiners might not recognise this as a valid test.

6 There is an increasing tendency to use microscale techniques for practical chemistry. Microscale[17] chemistry offers many advantages – it is cheaper, since smaller amounts are used, it is quicker and it may be safer. Smaller volumes of gas are produced and so open laboratory working may be possible, avoiding the need for fume cupboards. On the other hand, more concentrated solutions are often necessary. Dispensing small volumes requires teat pipettes with the possible risk of accidents arising through misbehaviour or carelessness, especially where more concentrated solutions are used.

7 In biology teaching, methanal solution (formalin) has been used in the past for fixing and preserving biological specimens and in microbiology for killing microorganisms before examination. Methanal is TOXIC BY INHALATION, IN CONTACT WITH SKIN AND IF SWALLOWED; it CAUSES BURNS; there is a POSSIBLE RISK OF IRREVERSIBLE EFFECTS and MAY CAUSE SENSITISATION BY SKIN CONTACT. Clearly, its use should be avoided where possible but it has been used in small amounts for very many years in biology without any evidence of problems. For fixing specimens there is no alternative – nothing else works, therefore its continued use is justified. Similarly, soaked onto a piece of filter paper, it is placed into an inverted agar plate to kill off the microorganisms prior to examination. Clearly, there are other disinfectants which would kill the microorganisms but a liquid sloshing around on the agar gel would destroy, or at least damage, what was to be observed. The advantage of formalin is that the methanal vaporises from the filter paper so that no liquid comes into contact with the gel. Given the tiny quantities involved, the continued use of formalin is justified in this context, as long as steps are taken to avoid skin contact. Traditionally, the main use of formalin has been for preserving biological specimens. Nowadays, there are safer alternatives, e.g. propylene phenoxetol, and these should be used for new specimens. However, we would not recommend the automatic replacement of formalin in existing specimens. This may be necessary after a leak, for instance, but routinely replacing all formalin could expose technicians to much higher levels of methanal than would otherwise be the case.

8 Where a chemical is not listed in the *Approved Supply List,* there are frequently inconsistencies between suppliers about the hazards of, and hence the risk phrases to be used for, that chemical. Table 3 shows

---

[16] SSERC (1997) *Hazardous chemicals. A manual for science education* (or CD-ROM, 1998).
[17] See, for example, J. Skinner (1997) *Microscale Chemistry.* RSC.

Table 3 Risk phrases given in catalogues for copper(II) chloride.

Supplier	Copper(II) chloride-2-water
Aldrich	HARMFUL BY INHALATION, IN CONTACT WITH SKIN, AND IF SWALLOWED; IRRITATING TO EYES, RESPIRATORY SYSTEM AND SKIN.
Beecroft	TOXIC IF SWALLOWED; IRRITATING TO EYES, RESPIRATORY SYSTEM AND SKIN.
Merck (BDH)	HARMFUL IF SWALLOWED; IRRITATING TO EYES, RESPIRATORY SYSTEM AND SKIN.
Fluka	TOXIC IF SWALLOWED; IRRITATING TO EYES, RESPIRATORY SYSTEM AND SKIN.
Griffin Education	TOXIC IN CONTACT WITH SKIN AND IF SWALLOWED.
Philip Harris	TOXIC (does not give risk phrases in catalogue).
Scientific and Chemical (Hogg)	TOXIC IF SWALLOWED; IRRITATING TO EYES, RESPIRATORY SYSTEM AND SKIN.
Sigma	HARMFUL BY INHALATION AND IF SWALLOWED; IRRITATING TO EYES, RESPIRATORY SYSTEM AND SKIN; RISK OF SERIOUS DAMAGE TO EYES.
Timstar	TOXIC IN CONTACT WITH SKIN AND IF SWALLOWED.

the risk phrases given in catalogues by a number of suppliers, for a chemical which schools commonly use. In the *Hazard Data Sheets* supplied by Merck Eurolab (BDH) it is interesting to note that the LD_{50} for copper(II) chloride-2-water is given as as 584 mg/kg (oral, rat).

It should also be noted that the risk phrases for the anhydrous compounds are generally different from those shown above (more hazardous). The complete lack of consistency between suppliers emphasises that assignment of risk phrases is not a precise science. Therefore, it is entirely reasonable for health and safety experts involved in science education to use their judgement in balancing the apparent hazards against the educational advantages. Copper chloride is often used in solution when teaching electrolysis because of the nature of the products at each electrode. It has been used for many years with no evidence of any problems and there is no valid reason to stop using it.

11 DISPOSAL OF WASTE AND UNWANTED MATERIALS

This Topic replaces Chapter 13 'Disposal' in the first and second editions of Topics in Safety.

1 Legislation to protect the environment

In recent years, concern over the environment has led to ever-tightening regulations and significant changes to the law, so this Topic has been completely rewritten as compared with the equivalent chapter in the earlier editions. Many of the changes have resulted from the implementation of European Directives, mostly implemented in the UK through the Environmental Protection Act 1990 and its various regulations. Since 1996, enforcement of environmental protection legislation has been the primary responsibility of the Environment Agency (in England and Wales), the Scottish Environment Protection Agency (SEPA) and the Environment and Heritage Service (in Northern Ireland). In this Topic, we refer to these bodies collectively as environmental agencies. Two years or so before publication of this edition, we tried to initiate a discussion with the Environment Agency and with the Department of the Environment, Transport and the Regions. Unfortunately, progress was very slow and at the time this edition went to press there was no consensus on how various regulations would be interpreted in a variety of scenarios relevant to science teaching. Therefore, this Topic gives much less detailed guidance than expected. However, it is hoped that full guidance on waste disposal by science departments will be issued in the future.

2 Waste from science departments

Science departments often want to dispose of unwanted materials. Options for dealing with these may include:

■ re-using (e.g. sending unwanted textbooks to third world countries or pre-war apparatus to antique dealers);

■ recycling (e.g. distilling a solvent for re-use);

■ discharge to the atmosphere (e.g. gases from fume cupboards, see Topic 7);

■ discharge to the sewage system (i.e. as effluent);

■ depositing in the solid waste collection (i.e. as refuse);

■ disposal via the services of an authorised waste contractor;

■ turning the waste into a different, less hazardous, form before disposal by one of the above methods (e.g. neutralising acidic waste before discharging as low hazard effluent).

Strictly speaking, in law, waste is anything that the owner or producer does not want and which has reached the end of its normal commercial cycle or chain of utility. However, legislation on waste is very complex and it would be for a court to decide what constituted waste and therefore whether an item was covered by the waste legislation. Disposing of labelled bottles of uncontaminated chemicals that a science department no longer requires might not be disposing of waste if the chemical can be used without any specialist recovery operation[1,2] and if the department is quite sure that the person taking it will not dump it. On the other hand, putting the same bottles in the general refuse collection, or paying an authorised waste contractor to take them away, certainly is waste disposal.

Very different regulations apply to the disposal of waste (mainly solids, but in general anything which will be removed from the premises by road), effluent which is poured into the sewage system and fumes discharged directly to the atmosphere. However these are all covered by the Environmental Protection Act.

3 Waste removed by road (controlled waste)

Waste which is taken away by road, either by the local authority refuse collection or by a waste contractor, is known as **controlled waste**. Under the Environmental Protection Act 1990, there are three types of controlled waste, depending on who produces it, i.e.

■ waste from households,

■ waste from commercial premises, and

---

[1] See *Circular 11/94* (Department of the Environment), *Circular 10/94* (Scottish Office), *Circular 26/94* (Welsh Office).
[2] *Environmental Protection Act* 1990. *Section 34. Waste Management. The Duty of Care. A Code of Practice,* Department of the Environment / Scottish Office / Welsh Office, HMSO, 1996. ISBN 0 11 753210 X.

■ waste from industrial premises.

Subject to certain exceptions, waste from schools and other educational establishments is to be regarded as household waste. If the waste is hazardous in some way then disposal is further controlled by the Special Waste Regulations 1996 (as amended). In particular an effect of the Special Waste (Amendment) Regulations is that controlled waste from school *laboratories* has to be treated differently from other waste classed as household waste.

Any waste which is to be disposed of must be taken by an authorised transporter to an authorised facility. Authorised transporters must be either registered or exempt from registration. Those which are exempt include local authorities, charities (e.g. Labaid, collecting surplus equipment to ship to third-world schools), voluntary organisations (e.g. a PTA collecting for a jumble sale) and the producer of the waste transporting his/her own waste. Thus a science department could transport its own waste quite legally. Any establishment using a waste contractor should always look at the registration certificate or an authorised copy (not a photocopy). Exempted bodies will obviously not have a certificate, but should be able to demonstrate that they are exempt, e.g. by showing stationery with their Registered Charity Number on it.

In practice, as far as chemicals are concerned, small quantities of some substances can be dealt with by do-it-yourself (DIY) methods which render the waste low hazard. However, larger amounts will require an authorised waste contractor. There are, in any case, some chemicals, e.g. mercury and its compounds or chlorinated hydrocarbons, for which there is no DIY disposal option available (although recycling may be possible). Governing bodies and head teachers should be made aware that science department budgets will need to reflect the cost of occasional visits by an authorised waste contractor.

Even where the Special Waste Regulations do not apply, a duty of care implies that, when disposing of unwanted materials, science departments have to consider who might be affected by their action or inaction and adopt suitable control measures to reduce the risk of injury. For example, technicians clearing apparatus away or cleaners emptying rubbish bins might be injured by broken glass. Therefore, uncontaminated broken glass should be collected separately and placed in a recycling bin. Contaminated glass and other sharps should be placed in tough containers (e.g. recycled coffee tins or thick cardboard boxes), sealed and labelled before disposal via the refuse collection service. Large

quantities of gases released into the atmosphere may adversely affect the health of neighbours. Therefore, even where a fume cupboard is used, only small-scale operations should be considered.

4 Avoiding the need to dispose of waste

It may well be possible to avoid disposing of chemicals, if they can be recycled. For example, at GCE A-level, methyl benzoate may be synthesised (esterification) as a first step, nitrated and then the nitro-derivative used for the next stage, i.e. reduction to 3-aminobenzoic acid. Or lead(II) iodide, precipitated in a class experiment on stoichiometry, can be collected, washed and used for electrolysis. These serve as good examples of conservation to pupils. A local fire station may be willing to accept some flammable chemicals, for burning during training in the use of fire extinguishers.

Often problems of waste disposal could be avoided by better planning and stock control. The increasing use of microscale techniques[3] in chemistry will inevitably reduce the amount of waste for disposal. Although it is tempting to buy large quantities because that is cheaper, it becomes extremely expensive if half of it is eventually surplus and has to be disposed of. Disposal problems begin when a purchase order is signed.

5 Disposal of waste materials as effluent

Waste disposed of as effluent (i.e. down the drains) is *not* considered as 'controlled waste'.

It is often possible to treat water-soluble waste so that it does not present a hazard to employees or to the system itself[4]. For example, water should be discharged at a pH between 5.5 and 9.0. Thus acids and alkalis should be roughly neutralised, oxidisers should be 'neutralised' with reducing agents, etc. Clearly, substances which are classed as DANGEROUS FOR THE ENVIRONMENT (or carrying relevant risk phrases, see Topic 10) should not be poured down drains. Table 11.1 shows the concentration at which solutions of various types of hazardous material would not be considered hazardous. The position is quite complicated, because the critical concentration depends on the precise risk phrase (see Topic 10.) Table 11.1 is a simplified version, but it takes a worst case scenario, i.e. some solutions could be more concentrated than those shown here and still not be considered hazardous. The concentrations are given as percentages, i.e. grams of solute per 100 cm[3] of solution (or solvent).

---

[3] For example, see J. Skinner (1997) *Microscale chemistry*. RSC.
[4] For example, correspondence between SSERC and East of Scotland Water and SSERC and the Water and Drainage Department of the former Lothian Regional Council.

Table 11.1 Concentration below which different types of waste would not be considered hazardous.

Classification of hazardous substance	Concentration below which waste is not considered hazardous
VERY TOXIC	Less than 0.1%
TOXIC (category 1 or 2 carcinogen or category 1 or 2 mutagen or category 1 or 2 toxic for reproduction)	Less than 0.1%
TOXIC	Less than 1%
HARMFUL (sensitising, category 3 carcinogen, category 3 mutagen or category 3 toxic for reproduction)	Less than 1%
HARMFUL	Less than 10%
CORROSIVE	Less than 1%
IRRITANT (sensitising)	Less than 1%
IRRITANT	Less than 10%
LOW HAZARD	Not specified

Mercury and cadmium compounds should not be disposed of down the drain. Liquids which do not mix with water should also not be disposed of in this way. Petroleum spirit, other highly flammable liquids which do not mix with water and chlorinated hydrocarbons should never be poured down the drain. Science departments therefore need to have an organic waste solvent bottle, which will have to be collected from time to time by an authorised waste contractor. In fact, it would be better to have more than one bottle, so that incompatibles are kept apart. Also, it will probably be cheaper to dispose of chlorinated hydrocarbons if they are kept separate from other solvents.

6 Disposal of waste which is insoluble in water

Disposal of insoluble solid waste materials and liquids which are immiscible with water present a considerable problem to science departments. If classed as hazardous, waste from school **laboratories** (but not waste from other parts of the school, including workshops, or waste from primary science activities) should be considered as **special waste**. Hence the law requires that it is disposed of via an authorised waste contractor. Table 11.2 shows the concentrations at which waste containing various types of hazard would not be considered as special waste[5].

Table 11.2 Concentration below which solid waste is not classed as special.

Classification of hazardous substance	Concentration below which it is not special waste
VERY TOXIC	Less than 0.1%
TOXIC (CATEGORY 1 OR 2 CARCINOGEN)	Less than 0.1%
TOXIC	Less than 3%
HARMFUL	Less than 25%
CORROSIVE	Less than 1%
IRRITANT	Less than 10%
LOW HAZARD	Not specified

[5] Environment Agency (1997) *Classification of Special Waste. Special Waste Regulations 1996. Information sheet 1.*

Note that, like Table 11.1, Table 11.2 has been slightly simplified in that some substances would in fact not be classed as special waste at concentrations higher than shown here.

Note also that whilst there is a concentration threshold, there is no quantity threshold which can lead to some absurd anomalies.

Advice in previous editions of *Topics in Safety* was that solid waste, including chemicals which are insoluble in water, could be diluted with a cheap, inert material, such as sand, to concentrations below those shown in Table 11.2, well mixed, wrapped securely and then placed in the solid refuse collection. Under recent and impending legislation, especially the EU Landfill and Hazardous Waste Directives, that is probably no longer legal in most cases. In general, we can no longer recommend the sand dilution method, except in special cases (e.g. as part of a spill clear-up procedure). Although at present much special (i.e. hazardous) waste ends up in general landfill, it will be increasingly necessary to separate them. Article 3(4) of the Landfill Directive reads:

The dilution or mixture of waste solely in order to meet the waste acceptance criteria (e.g. for non-hazardous landfill sites) is prohibited.

7 Use of authorised waste contractors

Science departments will need to use authorised waste contractors from time to time. There are some waste and unwanted materials which cannot be rendered low hazard by DIY methods, and others where the quantity is such that it would be impractical to do so. Buying in a contractor is expensive, although because charges are calculated in various ways, it is always a good idea to obtain at least three quotations. Some charge quite a lot simply to visit the premises, but then only a relatively small additional amount per bottle disposed. Thus disposing of a lot of chemicals may not cost very much more than disposing of a few.

Substances for which you must use authorised waste contractors include:

■ mercury and its compounds;

■ cadmium and its compounds;

■ chlorinated hydrocarbons;

■ asbestos.

When chemicals are collected by an authorised waste contractor, the educational establishment will be given a transfer note, which must be kept in a safe place for at least 2 years (in some cases 3 years). We suggest you copy it, giving one copy to the main office and keeping the other in the science department, and retain both for at least 3 years. Any chemicals for disposal must be

properly packaged and contained, for example, incompatibles must be kept apart. A responsible contractor will be able to give guidance on what is required and will probably supply suitable packaging. Note that most contractors will not be able to handle asbestos. The local waste-collection authority may well be in a position to help with asbestos. In general anyone using a waste contractor who claims to be authorised (whether for asbestos or more generally) is under a duty to check that s/he does in fact have a licence or is exempt.

8 Summary of recommendations

The legislation governing disposal of waste is very complex. Waste disposed of via the drains as effluent is covered by different legislation to that for waste taken off the site by road. This list summarises the options for waste disposal, in order of priority.

■ Can the waste be re-cycled or re-used in some way?

■ Is the waste hazardous in some way? If not, dispose as effluent (down the drains) or in the refuse collection, depending on solubility, etc.

■ If it is hazardous, but cannot be re-cycled, can it be treated chemically (e.g. neutralised, hydrolysed, reduced or precipitated) so that it becomes low hazard? If so it may then be possible to dispose of it as above. Treatment to reduce the hazard may also be worthwhile if the waste is being stored pending collection.

■ If it is hazardous (even after treatment), it will usually be necessary to store it in a safe place for eventual collection by an authorised contractor. This is likely to be especially the case when managing chemical storage (i.e. prep room clearouts!)

For further guidance, members may contact ASE, CLEAPSS or SSERC.

12 ASSESSING CARCINOGENIC HAZARDS

This Topic replaces Chapter 9 in the second edition of Topics in Safety. *The Appendix[1] is available only on the ASE website because of the need for regular updating.*

1 Introduction

Many chemicals are known to be carcinogenic, including some that are found in schools. It has been estimated that up to 6% of all cancers are caused by occupational exposure[2] and that the majority of cancers are caused by diet and life style. Many carcinogens are encountered in everyday life, examples being components of paints, adhesives, epoxy resins, cigarette smoke, some foodstuffs and traffic fumes, all of which are used or encountered in a relatively uncontrolled way. On the other hand, in the school laboratory, substances of lower carcinogenic potency will be handled with care and on a much smaller scale.

There is a danger that the emotive nature of cancer will cause the relatively remote risk of a chemical's low carcinogenic potential to be exaggerated, compared to its more immediate hazards such as flammability and toxicity. The purpose of this article is to present the known facts about those chemicals with carcinogenic potential which are likely to be found in schools and to suggest precautions in their use. The awareness raised of the hazards of carcinogens in the laboratory can obviously transfer with benefit to life outside. In Section 2 carcinogenic agents are discussed under a number of groupings. Section 3 contains recommendations for particular applications in schools. The website Appendix[1] extends the range of chemicals, listed under the same headings used in Section 2. It includes:

■ the Category of Carcinogen and the Risk Phrases of substances as stated in the Approved Supply List[3];

■ those which are banned;

■ estimates of the relative potencies of the carcinogens where the information is available[4].

1.1 Toxicity[5] and carcinogenicity

Acute toxic effects are manifested immediately and are thus readily understood. On the other hand, dangerous carcinogenic effects are usually seen only many years after the exposure and some carcinogens may be effective at levels that do not produce obvious toxic effects. The same, of course, applies to other chemicals which exert chronic toxic effects, which may at first go unnoticed. It is important to realise that some carcinogenic chemicals may be treated with insufficient care because they are not unduly toxic in the short term.

Those substances which may cause cancer in lengthy and high levels of exposure in industry are most unlikely to cause a threat to a careful laboratory worker using sensible laboratory techniques to avoid the risk from toxic as well as from any possible carcinogenic effects. In schools, many chemicals are used only a few times in a year and usually in low concentrations and quantities. Even so certain potent carcinogens are rightly excluded from school use.

Some substances lead to cancer only if taken into the body by a particular route and it is often simple to ensure that such an entry route is blocked. For example, potassium bromate(v) is a carcinogen by ingestion, but it is hard to see how a titration with standard bromate(v) solution can lead to an exposure. Pipette fillers are used and in any case the bromate(v) solution is in the burette. It is interesting to note that until a few years ago potassium bromate(v) was added to flour for baking as an improver. Other examples where knowledge of the route of entry plays a part are given in sections on particular chemicals.

1.2 Recognising carcinogens

Teachers, and others in schools, wishing to find out information on carcinogens, can consult a range of publications. Apart from this Topic and its website Appendix, the sources of help most readily available to

---

[1] See ASE website: www.ase.org.uk.

[2] Doll, R. (October 1992) *Carcinogenic risk: getting it in proportion*, a paper given at the conference, Cancer in the Workplace. HSE and Society of Chemical Industry.

[3] Chemicals (Hazard Information and Packaging for Supply) Regulations 1994 (5th edn. 1999) (as amended). These are commonly called the CHIP Regulations.

[4] Searle, C. E. (1990) *Chemical carcinogens model rules and notes for guidance.* Universities Safety Association. ISBN 0 85958 580 8.

[5] The word *toxic* is used here to refer to substances which, if inhaled or taken internally, or absorbed through the skin, may involve serious, acute or chronic health risks or even death.

schools are suppliers' catalogues (see (c) below) and the *Hazardous chemicals. A manual for science education* (SSERC) or *Hazcards* (CLEAPSS). The primary source and classification of substances legally defined in the UK as carcinogens is given in the COSHH Approved Code of Practice (ACOP) and the associated Approved List ((a) and (b) below). However, many other substances which are considered to be carcinogens are missing from these Lists and some of these are discussed here. It is also valuable to have a feel for the type of chemical structure or groupings likely to confer carcinogenicity on a molecule (see (d) below).

(a) *Consulting the regulatory lists of the UK, i.e. the COSHH Regulations[6] and the associated Carcinogens ACOP, the current HSE Guidance Note EH40[7] and the current Approved Supply List*

Category 1 and 2 carcinogens should have the relevant Risk Phrases on their labels – either R45 (may cause cancer) or R49 (may cause cancer by inhalation) as well as the Toxic pictogram:

Category 3 carcinogens carry the Harmful pictogram,

unless they are also toxic in other ways, and the Risk Phrase R40 (may cause irreversible changes). The bottle or container bears the Risk Phrase and the Hazard pictogram, but not usually the Category. Catalogue entries sometimes list the Category. The information is given in the *Hazardous chemicals. A manual for science education* (SSERC) or in *Hazcards* (CLEAPSS).

Category 1 carcinogens are those recognised as being carcinogenic to humans, usually on the basis of studies of lengthy industrial exposure. Examples which might be used in schools are zinc chromate(VI), chromium(VI) oxide, and sulfides and oxides of nickel. Note the last three are carcinogens only by the inhalation route and the oxides and sulfide of nickel are only likely to be found as fume and dust, i.e. states likely to be inhaled, in the extraction and industrial refining of the metal.

Category 2 carcinogens are recognised on good evidence as animal carcinogens and are regarded as potentially carcinogenic to humans. Examples used in

schools might include chromium(VI) compounds in general, cadmium chloride, cobalt salts or epichlorohydrin (hardener for epoxy resins).

Category 3 carcinogens are also 'experimental animal carcinogens', but are not placed in Category 2 because (i) either they have been insufficiently investigated but raise concern for humans, or (ii) they are of low potency, tumours only appearing after feeding very high doses. Examples are tetrachloromethane, phenylamine, ethanal or nickel salts.

(b) *Consulting Schedule 1 of COSHH Regulations*

Those referred to which might be relevant to schools are aflatoxins, arsenic (and presumably its compounds), hardwood dusts, used engine oils, coal soots, coal tar, pitch and coal tar fumes. Several processes are also listed, e.g. the manufacture of magenta and auramine dyes and the fume or dust from rubber manufacture.

(c) *Consulting a supplier's catalogue or manufacturers' safety data sheets (MSDS)*

Beware – some suppliers, especially US-based companies, seem to be more motivated by the fears of possible litigation than that of providing sensible and helpful advice. An unfortunate result of this crying wolf is that customers might begin to ignore all such advice, possibly with serious consequences. Suppliers will sometimes advise in their catalogues that a substance is an experimental carcinogen and append one of the Risk Phrases R45, R49 or R40 even when it is not listed in the CHIP Approved List. It is likely that many of these substances are very weak carcinogens, causing tumours in experimental animals at very high dose rates, often over extended periods, by which time the animal may have become terminally ill from other toxic effects.

(d) *Making predictions by examining the structure*

A glance at the type of functional groups can provide a useful pointer to the likelihood of a substance being a carcinogen. Figure 1 shows the main groups which may confer carcinogenicity on a molecule. In a few instances closely related isomers show quite different carcinogenicities.

In the preparation of the list of carcinogens in the Appendix and in the discussion in Sections 2 and 3, the reports of other agencies, e.g. the International Agency for Research on Cancer (IARC), and the regulatory lists of other countries, e.g. MAK and BAT Values[8], have been consulted.

---

[6] Control of Substances Hazardous to Health (COSHH) Regulations (1999). SI No. 1999/437. Stationery Office.

[7] HSE *EH40/2000 Occupational Exposure Limits*. This is updated annually.

[8] *List of MAK and BAT Values 1999, Maximum Concentrations and Biological Tolerance Values at the Workplace, Report No 35*. Deutsche Forschungsgemeinschaft (Wiley VCH Verlag GmbH).

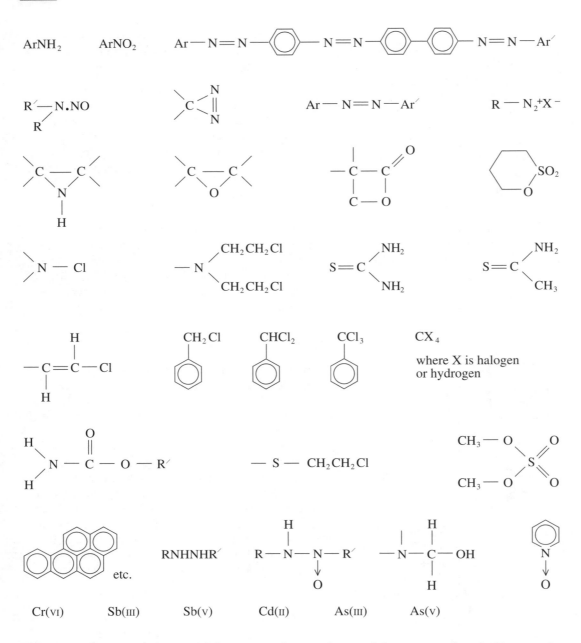

Figure 1 Main groupings which may confer carcinogenicity on a molecule (Ar = aryl = aromatic ring).

1.3 Potency

The three CHIP categories do not represent a rank order of potency. Most substances currently identified as Category 1 (human carcinogens) were those used in industry in the nineteenth and first half of the twentieth century when industrial hygiene was poor. This resulted in people receiving high exposure for long periods of time. Category 2 contains more of the relatively modern chemicals for which there has been little or no human exposure thanks to improved industrial practices. This Category will almost certainly contain carcinogens more potent to humans than those in Category 1. It is unfortunate that Category 3 covers two types of possible carcinogen and would have been more useful if it had

been sub-divided, thus allowing clear identification of those with low potency.

Ideally, for the purposes of setting up regulatory standards, and for making risk assessments, quantitative information on the carcinogenic potency of a range of chemicals on humans would be highly desirable. Unfortunately such a list does not exist, and the information that does exist is patchy. There is an extremely wide difference in the magnitude of the exposure to or of the dose of different chemicals needed to give rise to tumours. This can range from a short exposure lasting minutes to repeated contact or quite high doses over a period of many years.

There is, however, a wealth of information on the carcinogenic potency of many chemicals in animals. One of the main parameters used is the TD_{50}. This is the dose rate, generally expressed as the mass (g, mg, µg or ng) per kg bodyweight per day, required to produce well-defined tumours in 50% of a population of test animals compared with the controls. A small selection from a database is shown in Table 1. The potencies are seen to range over 6 or 7 orders of magnitude from 1 µg for aflatoxin to just under 1 g for 8-hydroxyquinoline and there seems to be, strictly speaking, no clear boundary between a weak carcinogen and a 'non-carcinogen'. The majority of carcinogens of most interest fall in the middle range.

Extrapolating from these data to make predictions for humans is beset with several difficulties. As well as the TD_{50}, other factors such as the variations in response by different species of animals (including humans) have to be considered, namely differences in metabolic pathways and detoxification mechanisms, normal life spans, etc. This having been pointed out, it can nevertheless be seen that the order on the table reflects fairly well most of the generally held opinions on the magnitudes of potency to humans. Where available such a potency grading has been marked against certain chemicals in the website Appendix.

Certain types of carcinogen react directly with some of the nucleotide bases in DNA. These **genotoxic carcinogens** are generally electrophiles, or are metabolised to electrophiles which then form adducts on the nucleotide bases. The resulting corrupted coding in the DNA may be propagated when further cell division occurs. **Epigenetic**, or **non-genotoxic,** carcinogens do not react directly with DNA. They may act as promoters or co-carcinogens, which means that, although they may not themselves initiate tumours by attacking DNA, they can accelerate the carcinogeneses which had been initiated by other agents. Other epigenetic carcinogens act by suppressing the immune system or by inducing peroxisome formation leading to the production of free radicals.

The existence of these two types of carcinogens has implications for human health. Because of the mode of action of a genotoxic carcinogen, a single molecule of it could in theory lead to cancer and hence it is generally believed that there is no safe threshold for such a chemical. In practice this is unlikely to be the case as the chemical will have to reach the target organ. For this to happen the chemical has to pass many barriers, namely being absorbed and the many digestive and detoxifying processes. For an agent or its active metabolite to be present at the site of its target organ it would need to be reaching the site faster than it is being

TD_{50}	
100 ng	TCCD (a dioxin)
1 µg	aflatoxin
10 µg	*bis*-chloromethylether (*bis*-CME)
100 µg	
1 mg	Direct Black 6 cadmium sulfate hydrazine 1,2-dibromoethane
10 mg	2-naphthylamine 1,1,2,2-tetrachloroethane, Cupferron potassium bromate(v)
100 mg	phenylamine, caffeine, thiocarbamide
1 g	8-hydroxyquinoline trichloroethene, 1,4-dioxane sodium sulfate ethanamide
10 g	hydrogen peroxide carageen
100 g	FD&C Green No1 (food dye)

Table 1 Scale of carcinogenic potencies based on animal tests (Gold *et al.*)[9].

removed by the other processes. This might happen only after a sustained exposure. With powerful carcinogens zero exposure must be the goal. On the other hand, some epigenetic carcinogens lead to tumours often only after lengthy and repeated high levels of exposure cause physiological abnormalities and prolonged tissue damage. Thus 'safe' thresholds almost certainly exist for many epigenetic carcinogens, although it may be many years before these levels can be quantified.

[9] Gold, L. *et al.* (1984) A carcinogenic potency database of the standardized results of animal bioassays. *Environmental Health Perspectives*, **58**, pp. 9–319.

1.4 Legal requirements

Regulation 4 of the COSHH Regulations prohibits in the UK the manufacture or use of 2-naphthylamine, benzidine, 4-aminobiphenyl, 4-nitrobiphenyl and their salts. The COSHH (Amendment) Regulations 1991 prohibited benzene and preparations containing more than 0.1% of benzene apart from applications in research and development, and in industry. The DfEE, SOEID, DENI and the Welsh Office have recommended a ban on the use of several chemicals [10].

Prevention of exposure to carcinogens is the main objective of the Carcinogens ACOP asssociated with the COSHH Regulations. The most certain way of eliminating the risk of cancer is by substituting the carcinogen with a non-carcinogen, whilst ensuring that the replacement is not highly hazardous in terms of toxicity, flammability or instability, etc. If a sufficiently large educational benefit does not accrue then the use of a carcinogenic substance cannot be justified.

Where substitution is not possible, the risk must be reduced to very low levels by using control measures which are appropriate to the nature of the risk. This ideally means enclosing the substance so that exposure by inhalation or via skin absorption is extremely unlikely, e.g. by using a fume cupboard for substances which are volatile and using glassware and apparatus which will contain it well. A flask and reflux condenser provides better containment than an open beaker. Solids should preferably be used in crystalline form rather than as fine powders. Where a substance, or its carrier solvent if it is in solution, is known to enter the body easily by the dermal route, then gloves made of *suitable materials* should be worn.

2 Carcinogenic agents

2.1 Aromatic amines and nitro compounds

Certain aromatic amines are the only chemicals widely believed to have caused cancer in laboratory workers, but these chemicals are all banned for use in schools, either by the COSHH Regulations or by individual employers' health and safety policies.

Generally, single-ring aromatic amines have low carcinogenic potential. Phenylamine (aniline), over which suspicion had hung for a long time, has recently been assigned the status of a Category 3 carcinogen. In animal experiments high doses of this substance fed over a long period of time resulted in a low yield of tumours. Any carcinogenic risks from this substance are

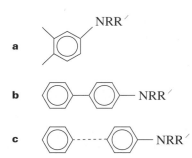

Figure 2 Some carcinogenic structural types.

greatly overshadowed by its high toxicity and capacity for being rapidly absorbed by the skin. It should be handled with care. Tests on the *N*-acetylated derivative, *N*-phenylethanamide (acetanilide), have failed to show evidence of tumours. Other derivatives such as the 2-methylphenylamine (*o*-toluidine) are carcinogenic, but the methyl or ethyl esters of 4-aminobenzoic acid have not been shown to be carcinogenic.

Carcinogenic compounds identified so far in this group almost all have an amino group at a position on an aromatic ring equivalent to the 2-position in naphthalene (Figure 2a) or *para* to a biphenyl link (Figure 2b). The biphenyl link may also be extended by inclusion of other structures (Figure 2c). Compounds corresponding to these structural types should not be prepared in schools.

Substituting certain *electron-donating substituents,* such as methyl, methoxy or halogeno in a 2- or *ortho* position to the amino group in any of the amines mentioned above greatly increases the potency. A recent HSE Alert Notice describes 2-methoxyphenylamine (*o*-anisidine) as a potent bladder carcinogen in animals and though the results for the 4-isomer were less clear, there was concern that it might be capable of inducing tumours. One might therefore expect the corollary to be true, that the substitution of *electron-withdrawing groups* would reduce the potency. Good examples of this effect are the esters of 4-aminobenzoic acid referred to above.

The presence of one or more solubilising sulfonate groups in the nucleus of an aromatic amine ensures that the amine is rapidly excreted, thereby reducing the carcinogenic potential, usually to negligible proportions. A good example of this effect is the fact that 2-naphthylamine sulfonic acids fail to produce tumours in mice, even after very heavy doses [11].

Nitro compounds corresponding to carcinogenic aromatic amines should be assumed also to be carcinogenic. In general nitroarenes are biologically

---

[10] DfEE (1996) *Safety in science education* (Stationery Office, ISBN 0 11 270915 X); SOEID (1995) *Circular No 8/95 Guidance on the Use of Carcinogenic Substances in Work in Schools and in Non-advanced Work in Further Education Colleges*; DENI (1972–97) *Circular 1972/97: The Uses of Carcinogenic Substances in Educational Establishments.*

[11] Anliker, R. in M. Richardson (ed) (1986) *Toxic assessment of chemicals*, Chapter 14 'Organic Colourants'. RSC. ISBN 0 85186 897 5.

transformed in the body to the corresponding arylamines. Nitro derivatives of unsaturated hydrocarbons formed in the combustion of diesel oil are potent carcinogens.

2.2 Dyes, benzidines and azo compounds

Some azo dyes are carcinogenic but the generalisation that all are is unfounded. The human gut flora breaks down azo compounds by reductively cleaving the azo bond to form two aromatic amines. Hence, if either product is a carcinogenic amine then the parent azo dye will also be carcinogenic.

Substitution with a sulfonic acid group often renders an azo dye non-carcinogenic. This generalisation is true for azo dyes, especially where both moeities astride the azo link contain a sulfonic acid, e.g. Sunset Yellow. The molecule as a whole is water soluble, but so are the two amines formed when the azo link splits (Figure 3).

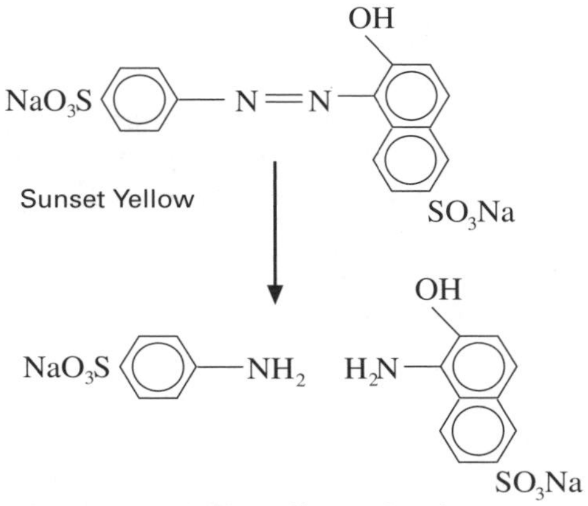

Figure 3 Sunset Yellow.

However this generalisation is not true for *diphenylazo dyes or benzidine dyes,* e.g. Direct Blue 6. Here, although the parent dye molecule is soluble, the biotransformation in the gut will yield the recognised human bladder carcinogen, benzidine, in addition to the two sulfonated amines (see Figure 4).

Direct Black 38, Direct Brown 95, Trypan Blue, Direct Red 6, Congo Red and other 4,4′-diarylazobiphenyl dyes have a similar skeletal structure and will almost certainly be carcinogenic regardless of the substituents on the outer aryl or naphthyl nuclei. As for amines, the presence of methyl and other electron-donating groups in a position *ortho* to the azo nitrogen and hence in the 2-position to the amino group will increase the potency of the parent dye.

It is suggested that year 12 (England, Wales and N. Ireland) and sixth year (Scotland) preparations of azo dyes be restricted by:

- avoiding the preparation of dyes which conform to the structural types given for carcinogenic aromatic amines or contain such components;

- purchasing commercial dyes in as pure a state as possible because of the risk that commercial samples of many dyes may contain carcinogenic intermediates or by-products as impurities. Many dyes are now manufactured overseas and quality control during manufacture may be poor;

- avoiding the possibility of a diazonium salt coupling with undiazotised amine to form azoaminoarenes. This can be achieved by ensuring that diazotisation is complete before proceeding to the next stage. Use excess of nitric(III) acid (nitrous acid) and check for its presence with starch/iodide paper (Figure 5).

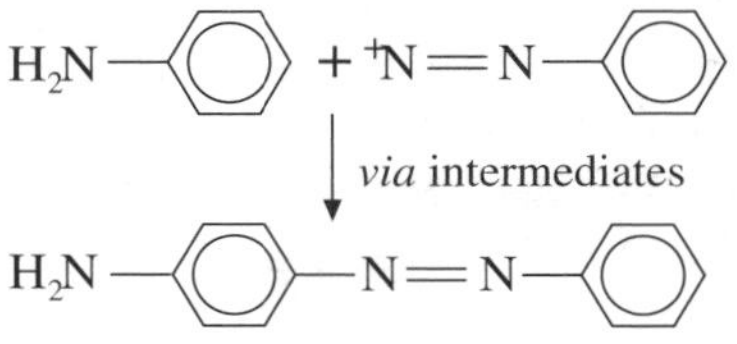

Figure 5 Ensuring diazotisation is complete.

- preparing water-soluble azo dyes where possible, e.g. Methyl Orange. A better choice is to diazotise sulfanilic acid, $NH_2.C_6H_4.SO_3H$, and couple it to a heavily sulfonated naphthol.

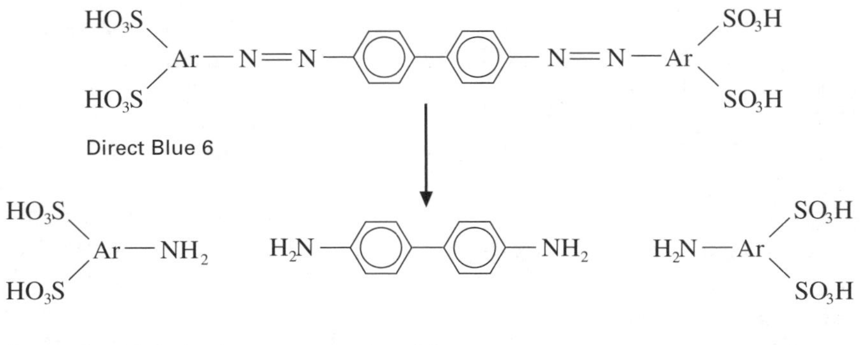

Figure 4 Direct Blue 6, a diphenylazo or benzidine-based dye (Ar = aryl = aromatic ring).

In the recent past some school courses have used various dyes including Disperse Yellow 3, Direct Red 23 and Acid Blue 40.

Sudan I, II, III and IV are probably weak carcinogens, with the evidence against Sudan IV seeming to be more reliable.

There is no evidence of either Magneson I or Magneson II being carcinogenic, although, as is the case with the Sudan dyes, the structures hint that the possibility exists.

The metallochromic indicators used in complexometric titrations, e.g. of metals with EDTA, are mostly naphthyl azo dyes, all of which are water soluble. Solochrome Black T (also called Eriochrome Black T), Solochrome Black 6B, Patton and Reeder's indicator, Calcon and Calmagite all have one sulfonic acid grouping. Beryllon II contains four sulfonic acid groupings, two on each naphthalene nucleus and would therefore be expected to be non-carcinogenic. Unfortunately its colour change at the end point is not easy to see! Ponceau 3R is a suspected carcinogen.

There is no evidence that, in general, the reactive dyes which have been used in schools are carcinogenic. The great care which must be taken on account of their sensitising potential means the risk of any possible tumour formation should be virtually non-existent.

Some anthraquinone and triphenylmethane dyes may be carcinogenic depending on the presence of particular substituents. It is relevant to emphasize here that **all** dyes should be handled with care as some may contain carcinogenic impurities. Dyes that are known to carry this risk, although thought to be safe themselves, and that are used in schools, are Magenta (basic fuchsin or rosaniline) and Disperse Yellow 3. The quoted purity for the latter is often as low as 30%. However Disperse Yellow is widely used in textile dyeing without discernible adverse effects and it is unlikely that it could be hazardous in small-scale experiments in school science.

2.3 Nitroso compounds

Many of these compounds are potent carcinogens and they should not be used in schools. *N*-nitroso-compounds could accidentally be made if nitric(III) acid (nitrous acid) was generated in the presence of secondary or tertiary amines. Even nitrogen dioxide gas in the laboratory atmosphere can react with amines in this way.

1-nitroso-2-naphthol, a commonly used reagent for several metals, is only weakly carcinogenic. There is some evidence that Cupferron (*N*-nitroso-*N*-phenylhydroxyamine, ammonium salt), a reagent for several metals, is moderately carcinogenic.

2.4 Hydrazines

Large doses of hydrazine itself have produced a low incidence of tumours in mice. Both 1,1- and 1,2-dimethylhydrazine are quite potent. Hydrazine has been used for making small fuel cells, but its use should be discontinued. Phenylhydrazine seems to be of a low potency, but the commonly used 2,4-dinitrophenyl-hydrazine is not thought to be carcinogenic.

2.5 Aromatic hydrocarbons

The only pure chemicals of this group likely to be found in schools are methyl- and some other substituted benzenes, naphthalene and possibly anthracene. Benzene, which was widely used as a chemical to study aromatic properties and as a solvent, is now banned in educational establishments. This also means that unleaded petrol and crude oil, which often contain 1% or more of benzene, cannot be held or used in schools, other than as a fuel in vehicles, lawnmowers, etc.

For showing aromatic substitution reactions, methyl benzoate or methylbenzene are alternatives for benzene. For solvent purposes a variety of other alternatives can be used, e.g. cyclohexane with a short term occupational exposure limit (OES) of 300 ppm, methyl and dimethyl-benzenes (with short term OES values of 150 ppm). Because of their volatility and flammability, an efficient fume cupboard should normally be used together with all the usual precautions taken to prevent fire.

Anthracene and naphthalene are both quite toxic. There is evidence that naphthalene is weakly carcinogenic and it is absorbed by inhalation and via the skin. There is no evidence that simple derivatives of any of these hydrocarbons (including those of benzene), with the exception of amino, nitro and azo compounds, are carcinogenic but they may be toxic.

Carcinogenic polycyclic aromatic hydrocarbons are present in most samples of genuine crude oil and in the tarry messes left after some distillations of organic materials or compounds, including wood or coal. Tars are readily absorbed through the skin and hence the main danger of significant exposure arises when apparatus is being washed up. The wearing of suitable gloves for this operation is strongly recommended. In practice, real crude oil is now difficult to obtain and in any case would be banned on account of its benzene content which is well above concentrations of 0.1%. Using artificially made crude oil [12], whether DIY or obtained from a supplier, does not completely solve the problem. Although made from ingredients of low hazard, the resulting tarry pyrolysis products are almost certainly potent carcinogens. Tars collected in demonstration 'smoking machines' should also be disposed of carefully.

---

[12] Relevant entries in SSERC (1997) *Hazardous chemicals manual. A manual for science education* and CLEAPSS *Hazcards*.

2.6 Halogeno compounds

Many of these are severely toxic to the liver and, in addition, some are carcinogenic. The simple halogenated compounds vary greatly in their physiological activities. While 1,2-dibromoethane, 1,2-dichloroethane and iodomethane do appear to have significant carcinogenic activity, others such as trichloromethane (chloroform), triiodomethane (iodoform), tetrachloromethane (carbon tetrachloride) and trichloroethene (trichloroethylene) are of lower activity. A recent HSE Alert Notice has described bromoethane as an experimental animal carcinogen and a possible human carcinogen.

The use of these substances as solvents should be restricted to those instances (rare in schools) where no satisfactory substitute is known. Unfortunately there is no universal substitute for the relatively safe 1,1,1-trichloroethane which had been an alternative for the toxic tetrachloromethane and trichloromethane for several years. It is a case of horses for courses and each application which formerly used the chlorinated hydrocarbon solvent may use a different solvent. In view of current concern about its toxicity and possible carcinogenicity, trichloroethene is not a favoured substitute solvent. Generally these compounds should not be first choice for use as solvents.

As a solvent for extraction purposes, dichloromethane has long been used on account of the combination of its solvent properties and high volatility. It is a weak carcinogen and is assigned Category 3 status, but the HSE has been considering removing even this status. It can be used with care for extraction purposes, e.g. of caffeine.

Many of the recognised analytical methods in the standard texts (such as Vogel[13]) for determining several metal ions often recommend tetrachloromethane or trichloromethane for extracting the organometallic complexes from aqueous solutions and for spectrophotometric methods. It is usually possible to find alternatives, e.g. in the case of the lead dithizone complex, butyl ethanoate is found to be a good alternative of much lower toxicity, though flammable.

The HSE[14] has recommended that no exposure or contact by any route – respiratory, skin or oral, as detected by the most sensitive methods – shall be permitted to 1,2-dibromoethane. This compound should neither be used nor prepared in schools. However, the use of bromine water (not bromine in other solvents) as a test for ethene is safe as only a trace of dibromoethane

is formed, the main product being hydroxybromoethane. In this application, the quantities of the products are minute and the contents of the tube can be disposed of immediately without isolating the products.

2.7 Direct alkylating agents

Again, these compounds, some of which are very potent carcinogens, should not be used in schools. However one potent carcinogen of this type may be met in schools as a product of a chance reaction. Methanal (formaldehyde) and hydrochloric acid vapours react to give trace amounts of chloromethoxy-chloromethane (*bis*-chloromethylether or BCME) which is highly carcinogenic (concentrations of greater than 1 part per thousand million in air are forbidden in industry).

It has been stated that, depending on the humidity and temperature, as little as 10 ppm each of methanal and hydrogen chloride could give rise to this order of concentration of BCME. Other investigations have failed to confirm this. Because of the uncertainty[15] it is best that methanal vapour should not be allowed to interact with hydrogen chloride from hydrochloric acid or from volatile, easily hydrolysed chlorides.

Dimethyl and diethyl sulfate are reasonably potent carcinogens, both readily absorbed by the skin.

2.8 Miscellaneous organic compounds

Various other organic compounds have been reported to be carcinogenic and are discussed below.

Thio compounds

Thiourea has produced thyroid cancer in rats; it is classed by IARC as a Group 2B carcinogen[16] and by the CHIP Approved List as Category 3, i.e. it is possibly carcinogenic to humans. The Department of Cancer Studies at Birmingham University has carried out a literature search on phenylthiourea (PTU, phenylthiocarbamide, PTC) and concluded that it should be acceptable for limited taste-testing experiments with necessary precautions to limit possible intake. Use only one paper strip containing no more than 0.1 mg of PTC per student. Purine and pyrimidine analogues, e.g. thiouracil, should be handled extremely carefully, if at all.

8-hydroxyquinoline

This substance is of low carcinogenic potency. Where necessary it may be handled with care.

---

[13] Vogel, A. I. (1979) *Handbook of quantitative inorganic analysis,* 4th edn. Longman. ISBN 0 582 46321 1.

[14] Health and Safety Executive, *EH15/79, Threshold Values.*

[15] Kallos, G. J. H. and Solomon, R. A. (1973) *American Industrial Hygiene Association Journal,* 34, 469; Tou, J. C. and Kallos,G. J. (1974) *American Industrial Hygiene Association Journal,* 35, 419; Travenius, S. Z. M. (1982) Formation and occurrence of bis(chloromethyl)ether and its prevention in the chemical industry. *Scand. J. Work Environ. Health,* 8, Supplement 3.

[16] Commission of the European Communities (1989) *The toxicology of chemicals: Carcinogenicity Vol 1.* ISBN 92825 9381 9.

Ninhydrin

There have been rumours that this substance is carcinogenic, but there is no reliable evidence that this is so. Nevertheless it is a biologically active compound and the spraying of chromatograms should only be carried out in a small disposable spray booth[17] in a fume cupboard.

Cotton Blue stain

This contains phenylamine and will therefore be a weak carcinogen.

Janus Green

There seems to be no evidence against Janus Green. It is available in highly pure form.

1,4-dioxane

This substance, sometimes used as a solvent, is weakly carcinogenic. In addition it is highly flammable and like ether readily forms peroxides which can be explosive.

Methanal (formaldehyde)

This is a very toxic chemical with an MEL of 2 ppm. It is relatively easy to comply with this limit in schools if sensible precautions are taken in handling preserved specimens, etc. (such as rinsing before examination). Epidemiological tests do not show any cancer risk to humans.

Monomers and polymers

In general monomers are by definition reactive species and several of them are carcinogenic; there are even reports of ethene being carcinogenic. Usually the polymers are safe, but there is probably no guarantee that polymerisation is complete. Burning or destructively heating polymers may release monomers.

In the past some schools made their own polyacrylamide gels for electrophoresis by purchasing the monomer and carrying out the polymerisation. Apart from its medium carcinogenicity, acrylamide is a powerful neurotoxin and great care is needed in preparing a solution of the monomer (which is a light powder). Fortunately the alternative of agarose gel works satisfactorily for many applications. If acrylamide gel is necessary it can be purchased as a pre-polymerised sheet.

2.9 Inorganic compounds and minerals

Chromium, cobalt and nickel compounds are now commonly reported to be carcinogenic. Much of the evidence of carcinogenicity for these compounds comes from industry, particularly mining, where workers are exposed to high levels of dust or fumes for lengthy periods. In pottery many of these may be used as fine powders.

Chromium compounds

Chromium compounds in mining operations have been reliably associated with nasal and lung cancers; and the use of chromate baths in the plating industry has given rise to non-malignant skin ulcers. Most experimental evidence points to the Cr(VI) oxidation state alone being carcinogenic; and then the highest potency is shown in the less soluble compounds such as the chromates(VI) of lead, zinc or calcium, but not barium.

Hexavalent chromium compounds can cause ulcers on the skin, but are carcinogenic by inhalation of dust or aerosol. Inhalation of dust is highly unlikely if the usual crystalline salts are used to prepare solutions. Avoid electrolysis of the solutions or any process where a gas is released in solution, or carry out such procedures in a fume cupboard. The only slight possibility of raising some dust of a dichromate(VI) would appear to arise from the 'volcano' experiment. This should be done preferably using a containment method[18] or in a fume cupboard. It is found, of course, outside the laboratory, in the form of fireworks.

Nickel compounds

Industrial exposure to insoluble, dusty nickel compounds such as nickel(II) oxide and the sulfides has been shown to be a source of industrial cancer. The soluble salts used occasionally in school science are of low potency. The chloride, nitrate and sulfate, generally used in hydrated form, are crystalline and would not form a dusty aerosol. However the oxide, hydroxide and carbonate are usually in the form of powders and could form a dust if not handled carefully. If solutions of the salts are electrolysed, this should be done in a fume cupboard. In nickel plating no gases should be evolved when a nickel anode is used and the current density kept to the recommended value. Nickel salts are appreciably toxic if ingested and are well known skin and respiratory sensitisers. Following the good laboratory practice needed to avoid possible sensitisation or toxicity should ensure the carcinogenic risk is minimal.

Cobalt metal and compounds

These are generally considered to be of low potency by inhalation (R49). No reliable epidemiological data is available as those industrially exposed to cobalt and its compounds were simultaneously exposed to nickel, chromium and arsenic. Crystalline soluble salts can be handled safely. Care is needed with the powdery forms.

---

[17] SSERC (1997) *Hazardous chemicals manual. A manual for science education*, entry on ninhydrin; or SSERC Bulletin 124.
[18] See relevant entry in either SSERC (1997) *Hazardous chemicals manual. A manual for science education,* or CLEAPSS *Hazcards*.

Minerals

Many ores are a mixture of minerals and should be handled carefully. Depending on the mineral, e.g. sulfides which may be mixed with arsenides, it may be prudent to take extra precautions if these are to be roasted/digested, etc., prior to analysis. Other minerals may be radioactive. Careful choice of sites for collection of minerals or ore samples should be made.

2.10 Carcinogens of biological origin

Aflatoxins and other mycotoxins, metabolites of fungi such as *Aspergillus* and *Fusarium* spp and other fungi, are usually absorbed through the gut and the mould is easily dispersed. The spores of bracken fern are quite potent and field trips should avoid walking through bracken-covered areas during late summer when the fronds are bearing spores.

2.11 Physical agents

(a) *Ionising radiations*

Work with ionising radiations and the sources producing them is controlled by the Ionising Radiation Regulations 1999. The *sealed* radioactive sources, when used in accordance with the Administrative Memoranda (from DfEE, Welsh Office, DENI) or Circular 1166 and Explanatory Notes (from SOEID and SSERC respectively) on the use of ionising radiations in schools, do not present a significant risk of producing even a skin cancer. Open sources are a greater risk. Fine powders which are very easily spread and inhaled present greater risk than crystalline, non-dusty, salts (see Topic 19).

Another significant source of radiation, which in some areas of the country is rather high, comes from radon gas seeping from the ground underneath the building. Ensuring minimisation of this risk is rightly the responsibility of the employer.

(b) *Fibres*

The main hazard is via the inhalation route. Asbestiform minerals have long been banned from schools, though they can occasionally still be found in odd places. Where the asbestos is broken and fibrous, e.g. oven door seals, it should be replaced, but hard unbroken cement panels are often best sealed and left. Care is needed in collecting and handling certain minerals on field trips. Of the man-made mineral fibres (MMMF), the wools (Rocksil, slag wool, and glass wool) are of low potency, and the glass wools made of drawn filaments rather than by spinning are of very low potency. Glass wools are unpleasant to use but are less potent than ceramic fibres (Category 2 carcinogens and R49)[19]. After prolonged heating the ceramic fibres change to cristobalite or mullite which are even more toxic than the original ceramic fibre. Dust from Kevlar (1,4-aramid) fibres is carcinogenic, but that from Nomex, the 1,3-isomer, is not. There is weak evidence linking graphite fibres with tumour formation.

For the Arculus 'wet asbestos' method the mineral wool can be replaced by glass fibre, though scrunched-up filter paper serves as a liquid reservoir superior to that made of any of the wools. Vermiculite is another alternative.

Platinised ceramic wool can still be used, but handling should be reduced to a minimum. Place it in the 'catalytic chamber' (usually a combustion tube or side-arm test-tube) in a fume cupboard with a small loose pad of glass wool at the ends to help retain it. After use stopper the ends and store for next time.

(c) *Ultraviolet radiation (UVR)*

In the laboratory, UVR is used for locating purposes in chromatography or for demonstrating fluorescence and the photoelectric effect. In general, avoid lamps emitting radiation with wavelengths under 300 nm. However, lamps designed for viewing specimens or chromatograms commonly use 265 nm, but are safe in that they are arranged to shine on artefacts or chromatograms without being viewed directly. More likely to cause skin cancer is the UVR received from sunlight (see Topic 18).

3 Summary of guidelines

3.1 Strategy for limiting exposure

The main approach is that of carrying out a risk assessment and setting up adequate control measures as for any hazardous substance, but with carcinogens the emphasis on using an alternative is greater than is the case for other chemicals. Situations which can lead to releases and significant exposures are as follows.

■ Handling volatile carcinogens or using processes which might result in a release of vapour, e.g. distillation. Ensure stores are well ventilated.

■ Weighing out powders to made up solutions (often once this stage is complete the chance of an exposure is minimal).

■ During solvent extraction, especially if using a separating funnel.

■ Absorption through the skin. Many chemicals, including solvents, are rapidly absorbed through the skin and through gloves of materials unsuited for that chemical. Chapter 11 of the *Hazardous Chemicals Manual*[20] includes a discussion and guidance on choice of glove types.

[19] Rossiter, C. E. (1994) Mineral fibres – what research is still needed? *Ann. Occup. Hyg.*, Supplement, 1. pp. 603–608.
[20] SSERC (1997) *Hazardous chemicals manual. A manual for science education.*

Some compounds, particularly aromatic amines and several dyestuffs, although themselves relatively safe, may contain carcinogenic impurities. An example is diphenylamine which is not thought to be carcinogenic, but some commercial samples of it may contain the potent carcinogen 4-biphenylamine. In general, any compound that is likely to contain as an impurity any of the substances listed in Section 3.2 should be avoided or at least obtained in as pure a form as possible and handled carefully.

3.2 Compounds that should definitely NOT be kept or used in schools

(a) Benzene, petrol and crude oil.

(b) Naphthalen-1-amine or naphthalen-2-amine (α- or β-naphthylamine).

(c) Biphenyl substituted by
(i) at least one nitro or primary amino group, or by at least one nitro and primary amino group;
(ii) further substitution by halogeno, methyl or methoxy groups, but not by other groups in addition to substitution as in (i) above. 3,3'-dimethyl-biphenyl-4,4'-diamine (*o*-tolidine) and 3,3'-dimethoxybiphenyl-4,4'-diamine (*o*-dianisidine) were used as reagents for detecting sugars or determining chlorine. These uses should be discontinued. The active end of a Clinistix strip contains *o*-tolidine and should not be touched. Diabur test strips are a safer alternative.

(d) Naphthylbiphenylazo dyes in general. Some may be safe.

(e) The nitrosamines. (*N*-nitroso compounds should not be prepared. Avoid accidental preparation.) (Cupferron reagent contains a similar structure; where possible use an alternative, but normal good laboratory practice should ensure nil risk.)

(f) The nitrosophenols. (4-nitrosophenol is thought not to be carcinogenic and may be used in schools.)

(g) The nitronaphthalenes.

(h) Chloroethene (vinyl chloride monomer).

(i) 1,2-dibromoethane, 1,2-dichloroethane.

3.3 Highly toxic compounds which may also be carcinogenic

Hydrazine, iodomethane (methyl iodide), methanal (formaldehyde, formalin), phenylamine, tetrachloromethane (carbon tetrachloride), trichloroethene (trichloroethylene)

Use substitutes wherever possible. If the chemicals are used avoid breathing their vapours or splashing them on the skin. Wear suitable gloves and eye protection. 1,1,1-trichloroethane, which had been used as a safer

substitute for tetrachloromethane and trichloromethane in some solvent applications, is no longer manufactured. Possible alternatives are cyclohexane, butyl ethanoate, Lotoxane, Volasils. In the case of the nylon rope trick, it is better to use a solution of the dioyl chloride in cyclohexane which will then form the upper layer over the aqueous diamine solution. To show the typical reactions of phenylamine, substitute esters of 4-aminobenzoic acid.

3.4 Less toxic compounds of possible carcinogenic potential

Bromoethane, dioxane, ethanal, ethanamide, 8-hydroxyquinoline, naphthalene, thiocarbamide (thiourea), thioethanamide (thioacetamide), α-mono-, α,α-di- and α,α,α-trichloromethylbenzenes

Ethanal is very volatile (boiling point 21 °C) and to show the properties of alkanals it is preferable to use the less volatile propanal, which has not been demonstrated to be a carcinogen. Naphthalene is quite volatile and is readily absorbed by inhalation or through the skin; for cooling curves to show liquid/solid transition naphthalene should be substituted by octadecanoic acid or by the alkanols, hexadecanol and octadecanol. Side-chain chlorinated methylbenzenes should be used with care. They are in any case extremely irritating. As with other toxic substances, wear gloves and eye protection when handling these compounds and take care to avoid contact with the skin.

3.5 Azo dyes

Use water-soluble indicators where possible. Avoid staining the skin with indicator solutions. In preparation of azo dyes check that diazotisation is complete in the first stage by testing for excess nitric(III) acid (nitrous acid). (Starch/iodide paper goes blue.)

Prepare water-soluble azo dye in which both 'halves' contain many sulfonic acid groupings by diazotising sulfanilic acid and coupling it to a disulfonated naphthol. 2-naphthol-3-6-disulfonic acid, 1-naphthol-3-6-disulfonic acid and 4,5-dihydroxy-2,7-disulfonic acid (chromotropic acid, sodium salt) are available and work well. Methyl Orange is another suitable example.

Avoid using diphenylazo or benzidine-based dyes. Where a microscope stain is of this type and no alternative is available, take precautions to avoid skin contact.

3.6 Methanal (formaldehyde) together with hydrogen chloride

To avoid possible formation of BCME, store methanal separately from concentrated hydrochloric acid or volatile, easily hydrolysed chlorides such as phosphorus(III) chloride, aluminium chloride and ethanoyl chloride. Where concentrated hydrochloric acid is specified in a chemical reaction also involving methanal, e.g. preparations of condensation polymers involving methanal, use 50% sulfuric acid instead. Glassware that has contained methanal (or formalin) should not be cleaned with hydrochloric acid.

3.7 Thorium and uranium compounds

Check the condition of the plastic tubing and bottle of radon generators regularly in case they become cracked or split. Take care to avoid spillages and keep a paper-lined tray underneath when handling. Store and use protactinium generators in a small beaker.

3.8 Chromates

Chromates, Category 2 and R49 (by inhalation only), should always be handled wearing gloves and eye protection. The generation of dust or spray (as in electrolysis) should be avoided. The preparation of a solution is unlikely to lead to an aerosol as the crystalline salts are used. Although dichromate(VI) is a primary volumetric standard, it can be substituted with potassium manganate(VII) for titration of iron(II). Tests for reducing agents, e.g. sulfur dioxide, and tests on alkanals, alkanones and alkanols can be carried out on a small-drop scale, using 0.1 M or less. The ionic migration experiment can be demonstrated, but copper sulfate and potassium manganate(VII) can be used instead. Organic preparative oxidations, e.g. of alkanols, should be carried out on a small scale only. The 'volcano' demonstration can be carried out on a small scale using enclosed techniques. Anyway, the scale of use of chromium(VI) compounds will, on environmental grounds, have to be limited.

3.9 Nickel and cobalt and their compounds

Handle the powdery forms of the metals or their compounds with care and avoid generating aerosols. When nickel catalysts are used for hydrogenating oils, they should not be recovered as a metal, but left embedded in a block of the solidified fat. Finely divided nickel catalysts are pyrophoric. The demonstration of water loss through the skin has often been done by holding cobalt chloride paper against the skin. As cobalt salts are carcinogenic only by the inhalation route, there should be virtually no risk of inducing cancer. However, cobalt salts are also skin sensitisers and it is therefore essential to wash hands after handling cobalt chloride paper.

Sources

Consulted in the preparation of this Topic were the *IARC monographs*, Sax's *Dangerous Properties of Industrial Materials*, Casarett and Doull's *Toxicology*, the relevant HSE *Toxicity Reviews* and *Guidance Notes*, and the *8th Report on Carcinogens of the National Toxicology Report*. We are grateful to the University Safety Association for permission to reproduce the potency ratings of several carcinogens; these are reproduced in the Appendix on the ASE website.

13 ALLERGIES AND ASTHMA

This is a new Topic, which was not included in the first or second editions of Topics in Safety.

1 Allergy

Allergy is increasingly common. Some research suggests this is because we live in increasingly clean environments and so children do not build up immunity at a young age. This is not the whole story however. Peanut allergy is now common (although still rare compared with some other allergies) and is believed to be the result of peanut-derived products present in nipple creams. These products are no longer used and so peanut allergy may disappear again within a few years. Many other domestic products, including cosmetics, carry warnings that they may produce an allergic reaction. If we attempted to remove from everyday use every substance which might cause allergy in somebody, it is likely there would be very little left.

Allergy results initially from exposure to a sensitiser. Respiratory sensitisers cause asthma (see section 4). Once sensitisation has occurred individuals will respond to much lower exposures in the future, although there is no way of determining the threshold concentration for sensitisation or for subsequent triggering of an allergic reaction in sensitised individuals. Sensitisation usually takes months, or even years, of exposure to the sensitiser. Symptoms may occur immediately after exposure, or may be delayed for several hours. There is some evidence to suggest that individuals with one significant allergic reaction may be more likely to develop allergy to other substances.

Some substances can produce pseudo-allergic (anaphylactoid) reactions, with symptoms similar to allergy, but by different mechanisms. These reactions can appear on first exposure and are induced, for example, by sulfate(IV) ions (sulphites), benzene-carboxylic acid (benzoic acid), acetylsalicylic acid (aspirin) and derivatives and dyes such as tartrazine.

There are a number of symptoms which may result from an allergic reaction, including:

- wheezing or difficulty in breathing;
- swelling of the face, lips, tongue or throat (which may result in difficulty in swallowing);
- a metallic taste in the mouth;
- runny nose or prickling eyes;
- a reddening of the skin;
- itchy spots on the skin;
- an increase in the rate of heart beat;
- abdominal cramps or nausea;
- collapse or unconsciousness.

In severe cases the victim may suffer anaphylactic shock. This is a rapid allergic reaction, with circulatory collapse and low blood pressure and can be life-threatening. Urgent medical treatment is essential in such cases. If students are very sensitive to a common allergen (e.g. peanuts, fish or dairy products) they are very unlikely to reach secondary school age without being aware of this and trained how to deal with it. Usually, they will carry an EpiPen (a device which does not have an exposed needle and which is used to self-inject a measured dose of adrenaline). Staff in the school should be made aware of who such individuals are and how to deal with an emergency[1]. Some individuals may suffer anaphylaxis as a result of bee or wasp stings, which has implications for fieldwork. For example, such individuals might need to apply an insect repellent containing diethyl-*m*-toluamide (such as *Repel* or *Jungle Juice*) before going into the field.

Problems of allergy are not confined to science lessons. There needs to be a whole school policy on how to deal with it. Staff may need training[2]. However, because of the materials used in practical science, there may be unexpected problems. For example, lycopodium powder is sometimes used in physics to dust onto the surface of water in the oil-drop experiment or to demonstrate dust explosions. Lycopodium powder is in fact the spores of *Lycopodium* (club moss), hence a protein and a potential sensitiser. We have never heard of any problem resulting from its use in schools but teachers should certainly

---

[1] See *Supporting pupils with medical needs. A good practice guide*, DfEE/Department of Health, 1996.
[2] Training on dealing with an asthma attack and identifying science activities likely to trigger an attack is given in Unit 3C of *Safe and exciting science*. ASE, 1999. ISBN 0 86357 295 2.

control its use very carefully and be alert to the possibility of an allergic reaction.

2 Allergy to chemicals

Ultimately, all allergic reactions are the result of exposure to chemical substances. However, it is convenient to separate out those found in biological materials (see section 3) and those causing asthma (see section 4) from chemicals in general (this section).

These days, chemicals which may cause sensitisation will be identified by a risk phrase (see Topic 10 'Using chemicals'). Relevant phrases are:

■ R42 MAY CAUSE SENSITISATION BY INHALATION;

■ R43 MAY CAUSE SENSITISATION BY SKIN CONTACT.

It is important to put these into perspective. In the *Approved Supply List*[3] nickel metal is listed as R43. However, nickel metal is often used in cheap jewellery, which will certainly be in close skin contact over long periods of time. Indeed, 'nickel rash' is quite well known but this does not stop people using it in jewellery, nor indeed, alloyed with other metals, in UK coins.

In a similar way, cobalt chloride is listed as R42/43. Students often handle paper impregnated with cobalt chloride as a test for water. Sometimes, they put a small strip of paper onto their skin to show the formation of sweat. This has been done over many years and there is no evidence that it has ever caused a problem. Quantities are tiny, duration of exposure is very limited. Even so, sensitisation is possible so care should be taken to minimise handling by using small pieces, washing hands after handling, etc. Technicians, handling larger quantities when preparing the papers, might wear protective gloves, especially as they will be exposed repeatedly, year after year.

Gloves should not be seen as the ideal way of dealing with the risk of skin sensitisation. Rubber gloves are commonly used, although pvc and nitrile alternatives are available and satisfactory. Latex (rubber) allergy is not uncommon and in fact is a serious problem in the health service. It is normally associated with the use of surgical gloves, especially powdered gloves. During manufacture of the gloves corn starch is added in order to make them easier to remove from the mould and easier to put on the hand. The powder absorbs latex protein which may then be dispersed when the gloves are removed. The problem is particularly severe with gloves because of the large area of contact and the added effects of the powder. A technician might well develop an allergy to latex and should be alert for any signs of a reaction. In the late 1990s we heard of two

cases of latex allergy amongst students. One school reported that it was not difficult to reduce exposure, e.g. by using neoprene Bunsen-burner tubing, cork stoppers in test-tubes, etc.

Some chemicals occasionally used in schools which may cause sensitisation are shown in the following table. Note, however, that some of these present other hazards, which may be more immediately serious than the risk of allergy. The fact that they are sensitisers is not a reason to avoid their use – it is a reason to ensure they are used carefully. This may include allowing students to handle only dilute solutions, using solutions as dilute as possible, working on as small a scale as practicable, wiping up spills, washing hands, etc. Technicians, whose exposure may be greater, may need to wear protective gloves, dust masks (if the sensitiser is supplied as a fine powder), and/or use fume cupboards, etc. Other substances, not listed below because they do not have the relevant risk phrase, are also known sensitisers. These include glycidyl resins (used in several glues).

Substance	Risk phrase
Ammonium dichromate(VI)	R43
Benzene-1,4-diamine (*m*-phenylene diamine)	R43
Chromium(VI) oxide	R43
Cobalt metal	R42/43
Cobalt chloride (and sulfate)	R42/43
Copper(II) chromate	R43
1,2-diaminoethane (ethylene diamine)	R42/43
Di(benzenecarbonyl) peroxide (benzoyl peroxide)	R43
Dyes (powders) (especially reactive dyes as they bond to protein)	Some may be R43
Enzymes (powders)	Some may be R43
Hydroxylammonium chloride (and other salts)	R43
Indicators (powders)	Some may be R43
Methanal (formaldehyde) gas and solutions > 0.2% (0.07 M)	R43
Methyl 2-methylpropenoate (methyl methacrylate) liquid and solutions > 1% (0.1 M)	R43
Nickel metal	R43
Nickel carbonate	R43
Nickel chloride	R43
Nickel sulfate	R42/43
Potassium dichromate(VI) or chromate(VI) (or sodium salts)	R43
Sodium (or ammonium) peroxodisulfate	R42/43

[3] *Approved Supply List* (5th edition, 1999) approved under the CHIP (Amendment) (No. 2) Regulations 1999.

3 Allergy to biological materials

Allergic reactions may develop (sensitisation), or be triggered, in response to exposure to a wide range of biological materials[4]. These include the following.

- Small mammals.

- Insects (notably locusts and the brown tail moth).

- Plant material such as hyacinth bulbs, primulas, pollen, some natural oils, peanuts and giant hogweed (which promotes skin disorders, with photo-sensitisation developing after exposure to sunlight).

- Fungal cultures (especially those such as *Penicillium* or *Aspergillus* species) which produce abundant airborne spores.

- Powders and dusts such as enzymes, antibiotics and agar.

Avoiding all exposure to any allergens in the first place, so that no sensitisation can develop, is one solution that has commonly been adopted, with the offending animals, plants, fungi, etc., banished from the laboratory. This is, however, usually an over-reaction.

Allergies may develop only after prolonged exposure to significant amounts of the allergen. Thus, keeping a small number of, say, gerbils in a laboratory may never cause students to develop allergies since they do not come into contact with sufficient amounts of the allergens for long enough. Teachers and technicians may, however, be at greater risk because they handle the organisms or materials more often or are in a laboratory or prep room, where the organisms, etc., are located, for much longer periods. Control measures involve reducing exposure to the fine hairs and faeces from animals, spores from fungi, powders from enzymes, etc. When cleaning out animal cages, as far as possible staff should avoid generating dust which could then be inhaled. (Note that the bags in most vacuum cleaners are permeable to fine particles, permitting the spread of these into the air.) Weighing out enzyme and agar powders requires particular care to avoid raising dust. Fungal cultures are best investigated or transferred before they have sporulated. Disposable gloves should be worn to avoid direct skin contact when handling, e.g. hyacinth bulbs or other organisms which have a history of provoking allergic reactions. Ensure a room is well ventilated to help prevent the build up of airborne particles. If it is impossible to avoid generating dusts, it would be sensible to wear a face mask able to filter out small particles[5].

Locusts are best *not* kept in *continuous* culture. Although breeding the animals will ensure there is a constant supply, they are often required only at certain times. Maintaining a cage of locusts throughout the year adds to the exposure of staff to their allergens and there has been a sufficient number of cases of locust allergy in science department staff to indicate that this is an unwise practice. When required, locusts can be purchased most cheaply from pet shops or by post from specialist companies which breed them to provide food supplies for reptiles and amphibians.

Burning-peanut investigations are some of the more popular science activities but in recent years have become contentious. The concern here is not so much that students will build up an allergy but that students who have already become sensitised will suffer a severe response to even the smallest exposure. A secondary school will know if any of its students have a severe allergy to peanuts. Therefore, if there are no allergic children in the school or none likely to be anywhere near the laboratory when the investigation is performed, abandoning the activity is unnecessary. Nevertheless, in the presence of students allergic to peanuts, action is obviously needed and alternatives to peanuts should then be used. Switching to other types of nut is not an answer since students may have allergies to more than just peanuts. Teachers report, however, success in the use of a variety of snack foods or pasta as substitutes for peanuts. For more guidance on safe procedures and alternatives to peanuts, refer to CLEAPSS leaflet PS10[6].

4 Asthma

Asthma is a condition in which the airways narrow, leading to breathing difficulties, as a result of exposure to various triggers. It is therefore a type of allergy. Common triggers include grass pollen (leading to hay fever), cold air, exercise, cigarette smoke, animal fur and house dust mites. Occupational asthma, i.e. asthma resulting from exposure to respiratory sensitisers (triggers) at work, is a major cause of absence from work. In 1996 about 1100 new cases of occupational asthma were diagnosed, with the most common triggers being:

isocyanates	15%
flour, grain, hay	9%
wood dust	6%
solder fume	5%
laboratory animals	5%
glutaraldehyde	5%

However, many other sensitisers have been identified[7].

---

[4] See *What you should know about allergy to laboratory animals*. Education Services Advisory Committee, HSC, HMSO, 1990. ISBN 0 11 885527 1.

[5] Purchase dust masks which meet the requirements of the European standard EN149 which are marked FFP3S or FFP3SL. These will filter out airborne spores, bacteria, enzymes and other fine dusts.

[6] PS10 (October 1998) *The burning peanut investigation and allergies to nuts*. CLEAPSS.

[7] See, for example, Annexes 1, 2 and 3 in Rory O'Neill (1995) *Asthma at work*, , TUC/Sheffield Occupational Health Project (ISBN 1 874751 02 1); or HSE (1994) *Preventing asthma at work. How to control respiratory sensitisers*. ISBN 07176 0061 9.

About 15% of children are diagnosed with asthma at some point and about 5% have asthma to a degree which requires regular medical supervision. With suitable medication, asthma is a controllable disease and students of secondary school age should know how to control their asthma. Treatment involves the use of relievers (if an attack takes place) and preventers (to reduce the likelihood of an attack). The usual view is that asthmatics should follow a normal school curriculum[8]. However, some special measures may be necessary. For example, before physical activity (such as taking exercise prior to investigating its effect on the heart rate) asthmatics may need to use their inhalers. Similarly, before using known triggers in the laboratory, science teachers should check that they know who the asthmatics in the class are and that they have their inhalers with them. Beware of triggers that are prevalent outside the laboratory, e.g. pollen or dust from furry or feathery animals – it is easy to remember chemicals, but easy to forget everyday triggers.

In the laboratory, chlorine, nitrogen dioxide, amines and sulfur dioxide have been known to trigger an asthma attack. Ammonia and hydrogen chloride gases also might well do so. Again this is no reason to avoid use of these chemicals. They are in any case hazardous for other reasons and if used in any quantity should be used only in a fume cupboard. Very small quantities might be used outside the fume cupboard in a well-ventilated room, with asthmatics warned to sit as far away as is reasonably practicable and to avoid inhaling the fumes. When a risk assessment for a proposed activity is carried out, control measures are likely to include the need to identify asthmatics and consideration of the facilities available in the room to be used – is a fume cupboard available, can the windows be opened?

A popular rate of reaction investigation involves the effect of acid on sodium thiosulfate solution. Sulfur dioxide is produced as a by-product. Mostly, the sulfur dioxide remains in solution so if the solution is poured away quickly (preferably into a fume cupboard sink but, if not available, into a large volume of cold water) little problem will arise. Students therefore must be encouraged to pour it away, rather than leaving it to stand until the end. If the solution is heated, to investigate the effect of changed temperatures, sulfur dioxide becomes much less soluble and there is a risk of unacceptable levels building up. Asthmatics at least might need to work in a fume cupboard, although this may be of only limited use if others are working in the open laboratory. Alternatively, use of hot solutions can be reduced if, for some of the samples, the solution is cooled (using ice or cold water) to show a decrease in the rate.

Similarly, small amounts of chlorine are generated by the electrolysis of dilute solutions of sodium (or other) chloride(s). If the electrolysis was allowed to proceed for 10 or 15 minutes, unacceptable levels of chlorine might result even in a well-ventilated room. However, if the current is switched off as soon as a trace of chlorine has been detected by its effect on moist indicator paper, and if asthmatics are warned not to inhale, few problems should arise.

The fumes from rosin-based solder, sometimes called colophony, are well-established as a cause of industrial asthma. Recently, a maximum exposure limit (see Topic 10) has been assigned to the fumes. This means that rosin-based solders should not be used except with local exhaust ventilation (i.e. fume extraction). Because of the possibility of becoming sensitised (which could seriously limit future careers) it is best to avoid rosin-based solders altogether, whether used by students or staff.

5 Advice for science departments

In order to minimise the risk that allergy will cause problems in science, departments need to ensure that they:

- have a mechanism for collecting information about those individuals (students, teachers, technicians) who are allergic to particular substances;

- handle such information sensitively;

- draw to the attention of those who may need to know (including new or temporary staff) information about individuals' allergies;

- have a policy that risk assessments should highlight the possibility of an allergic reaction, where there is a significant, known risk for a particular practical activity;

- monitor that the above policy is being implemented, including the adoption of suitable control measures;

- report to ASE, CLEAPSS or SSERC any unexpected cases of alleged allergy.

---

[8] National Asthma Campaign, Providence House, Providence Place, London N1 0NT. Tel: 020 7226 2260; Helpline: 0845 701 0203; Website: www.asthma.org.uk.

14 LIVING ORGANISMS

This is a new Topic.

1 Introduction

Ask science teachers or students what is meant by the term 'biology' and it would be surprising if they did not respond 'the study of living things', or something similar. And yet, in many schools, investigations involving *living* organisms, especially animals and microorganisms, are relatively rarely encountered. Practical biology may often be limited to the use of stereotyped enzyme studies or activities with seeds, seedlings or adult flowering plants. Students rarely have the opportunity to experience at first hand the behaviour, growth and physiology of an extensive range of organisms. Even practical activities involving the students themselves as the subjects of investigation are often restricted or absent. Good biology teaching should encourage the study of a wide variety of living organisms and this should occupy a central role in the science curriculum. An appropriate balance should be achieved between activities with living organisms (both inside and outside the laboratory) and those which just involve the study of biological processes such as enzyme action, osmosis, etc.

Several reasons are often cited for the absence of living organisms in biology teaching. These include, with varying degrees of justification:

■ limited finances and reduced amounts of technician support, especially during holiday periods;

■ moral objections to keeping animals in captivity;

■ difficulties in ensuring the welfare and humane treatment of animals in the laboratory;

■ legal restrictions on experiments involving animals, as stipulated by the Animals (Scientific Procedures) Act (but note that this defines 'animals' only as *vertebrates*);

■ prohibitions on the collection of animals and plants from the wild, as controlled by the Wildlife and Countryside Act (but note, it is only endangered species, not common organisms, that are fully protected);

■ restrictions caused by health and safety considerations.

This Topic is not the vehicle for a discussion of the first five issues listed above. However, teachers and technicians often report that, on grounds of health or safety, activities involving the keeping or using of living organisms have been abandoned. There is often little real justification for such curtailments. Many of the widely-held beliefs of health and safety restrictions are complete myths. Even when there is legitimate concern for health or safety, the adoption of simple precautions can often permit an activity to take place. Nevertheless, some of the restrictions in biology teaching may have been elevated to the status of a ban by an employer, most often an Education Authority but sometimes a governing body of, for example, an independent school or FE college. Such official instructions not to keep a particular organism or carry out a specified procedure must be obeyed, though they *should* be challenged if they are thought to be unreasonable.

So, what are the health and safety fears that have contributed to an impoverishment of biology teaching in many schools and how many of such fears are justified?

2 Hazards: real or imagined?

How serious are the hazards in the use of living organisms and materials of living origin? Listed below are the main concerns for health and safety in biology teaching.

■ Infectious diseases from humans, animals, animal organs and microbiological cultures.

■ Infestation by parasites.

■ Allergies caused by animals, plants, spores or chemicals.

■ Physiological or mental stress from investigations on students.

■ Hazardous substances in plants, seeds or biological reagents.

■ Animal bites, scratches, stings, etc.

3 Risk assessment

Faced with such a catalogue of possible hazards, as outlined above, the response of some teachers is to abandon a planned activity or observation in order to ensure the health and safety of students and/or staff.

Employers, mindful of their statutory duties to ensure a healthy and safe working environment, may go further and issue instructions restricting the keeping of certain organisms or the performance of specified activities. However, the observation that an organism may cause harm in some way should not in itself be sufficient reason to 'ban' it or restrict an activity involving it. What is required is a systematic assessment of the risk that harm will occur, together with a consideration of the seriousness of the consequences. Such an approach may identify situations in which it would be unwise to proceed with the intended activity or the need to restrict it in some way. However, in the majority of cases, the risk assessment will reveal that, by adopting simple precautions, if any are needed at all, the risk of harm occurring can be reduced to zero or an acceptably low level. Elimination of risks by banning an organism or activity is very often unnecessary and unrealistic; no aspect of life can be completely free of risk and a balanced approach to risks in biology teaching should be the only sensible strategy to consider.

The following section provides guidance on the hazards of using organisms and biological materials to help in risk assessment. Guidance on the hazards of microbiology and working with DNA can be found in Topics 15 and 16.

4 Guidance to assist in assessing risks for biological hazards

4.1 Infectious diseases

Zoonoses

These are infections transmitted from animals to humans[1]. In most schools and colleges, the risk of disease transmission from the animals likely to be studied will be very low or negligible. In the majority of cases, simple hygiene after direct handling of the animals will be an effective control measure. Captive-bred, laboratory small mammals which have not come into contact with wild mammals are most unlikely to carry any zoonoses. In the past, it was strongly recommended that small mammals should only be obtained from accredited breeders subscribing to schemes organised by the Medical Research Council Laboratory Animals Centre and, later, the Laboratory Animals Breeders Association, to ensure a disease-free status. However, it is now very difficult for schools to obtain animals from organisations on the current register of breeders, set up to supply healthy stock for medical research. Small mammals (and other animals too) should therefore be obtained from as reputable a source

as possible. If a local pet shop is used, choose one that maintains its animals in excellent conditions.

Because of the obvious risk of transmission of unknown diseases or parasites from *wild* mammals and birds, it is not recommended that native species of these vertebrates, found dead or alive, should be brought into schools to be studied. Injured animals, found and brought in by students, should be handled with care and kept isolated from other animals already in the school before being humanely destroyed or taken to a local vet or animal treatment centre.

Specific zoonoses have been associated with certain animals encountered in schools or during school-based activities. **Salmonellosis** has been linked particularly with terrapins and tortoises. *Salmonella* bacteria in fact may be carried by a range of animals, both invertebrate and vertebrate (including fish, amphibians and reptiles in general, chickens, ducks and other wild or domesticated birds). The 'bad press' that terrapins have received, leading to several supposed or actual bans, should be seen now as historical and an unwarranted over-reaction. Animals that are healthy and well-maintained are less likely to be infected anyway and, if hands are always washed after handling animals or cleaning out animal enclosures, risks of transmission are extremely low. However, animal material, such as hearts and lungs, that is obtained from a butcher or abattoir for dissection, may be contaminated with food-poisoning bacteria including *Salmonella*. Good hygiene is therefore required during and after the handling of such items.

Psittacosis (ornithosis) is a disease caused by the microorganism *Chlamydia*, particularly associated with birds of the parrot family, including budgerigars. Again, fears of transmission to humans have generated a variety of mythological or actual bans. In fact, the disease can be found in *all* birds, exotic, caged or wild. Transmission is usually through dust from faeces and feathers. It is highly unlikely that students and staff are endangered by, for example, a pair of zebra finches, particularly if the birds are healthy and have been resident for some time. Those who will be more at risk in schools are the staff who are responsible for the upkeep and cleaning out of a large collection of birds, particularly in an outdoor aviary where contact is possible with reservoirs of the disease in wild birds. Control measures involve excellent hygiene and avoiding the creation of airborne dust when cleaning out the cages or aviary. If this is unavoidable, it would be prudent to wear a dust mask able to filter out the finest particles[2].

---

[1] For details, refer to HSE (1993) *The Occupational Zoonoses*. Stationery Office. ISBN 0 11886397 5.
[2] Purchase dust marks which meet the requirements of the European standard EN149 which are marked FFP3S or FFP3SL. These will filter out airborne spores, bacteria, enzymes and other fine dusts, provided they fit well against the face.

Leptospirosis (Weil's disease) is another bacterial infection, transmitted typically by rats in their urine. This disease is potentially life-threatening, though it can be treated successfully with antibiotics, particularly when diagnosed early. However, the chance that captive-bred, laboratory rats would be carriers of the disease is extremely small. Animals obtained from a reputable source in healthy condition should not be considered hazardous in this respect. Staff and students involved in pond-dipping activities, mammal-trapping investigations and other aspects of fieldwork near streams and ponds may be at risk from water contaminated by rat urine carrying the bacteria. However, people in schools who are most at risk are those involved in canoeing and other water sports. Control measures are simple. For wild animals caught in live traps or brought into school by students, ensure that gloves are worn when handling them (which also provides rather good protection against bites and scratches!) and wash hands thoroughly after any activities near or on natural waters. Avoid touching the face, particularly the lips, with hands that are wet (as the *Leptospira* bacterium can enter the bloodstream through mucous membranes). Open wounds should be protected with water-proof dressings. For further guidance, see CLEAPSS leaflet PS1[3].

Cryptosporidiosis is caused by a protozoan which can be found in the faeces of many animal species, particularly those of cattle and sheep. It usually causes little more than diarrhoea and flu-like symptoms in healthy individuals but can be much more serious in those with compromised immune systems. It is most commonly transmitted by drinking contaminated water supplies but, as with Weil's disease, those coming into contact with natural waters, particularly in recreational water sports, may also be at risk. Control measures are as for Weil's disease. There have been reported transmissions to children following farm visits, emphasising again the need for good hygiene after handling animals such as lambs and calves and ensuring that no food is consumed during that part of the visit. Agricultural colleges plus the few schools that still maintain a rural studies department and keep sheep and cattle will already be aware of the need for such hygiene.

Spongiform encephalopathy in its most notorious bovine form, or BSE, is thought to be transmitted by the consumption of an infectious protein, or prion, from cattle. This may have originated from a similar spongiform encephalopathy in sheep, causing a condition called scrapie that has been known about for several hundred years. In humans, the most well-known symptoms of spongiform encephalopathy are found in

Creutzfeld-Jakob disease (CJD). The risk of transmission of BSE and similar diseases in science activities is virtually non-existent but this has not prevented a great deal of speculation and concern about the use, for dissection or other purposes, of any tissues from cattle or sheep (sometimes extended to *all* food products obtained from abattoirs and butchers). If there is a risk, it is in handling organs mainly of the central nervous system of infected animals: the brain, spinal cord and eyes. Of these tissues, only the eyes are regularly used for dissection purposes. Even government education departments admitted that the risk of transmission by handling such materials was *'remote and theoretical'*[4] but nevertheless recommended that the dissection of eyes from cattle should cease. Since then, legislation to prevent the possibility of infectious prions (or other agent) entering the human food chain has controlled the supply from abattoirs of nervous tissues from cattle, sheep and goats, so that it is now very difficult, if not impossible, for schools to obtain eyes from these animals for dissection. However, there are no such legislative restrictions on the supply of eyes from pigs or other animals slaughtered for food or other materials such as deer or llamas. Supplies can, however, sometimes be difficult to obtain because pig's eyes may not be easy to remove or few animals of other types are slaughtered. If eyes (of any animal) are dissected, the normal control measures of good hygiene must always be observed.

Lyme disease is a bacterial infection, transmitted to humans by ticks which are located on ground vegetation. The reservoir of the bacteria is likely to be deer and wild rodents. In the context of science education, the disease is only likely to be of significance for those involved in field work in areas of woodland, bracken and long grass. Control measures primarily involve avoidance of exposure to ticks by ensuring that the skin is covered. Long sleeves and long trousers should always be worn when working in potentially hazardous areas. Clothing and the body should be inspected for ticks afterwards. (Schools on trips to Germany or other European destinations should note that ticks carrying a virus causing a serious form of encephalitis might be encountered in forested areas. Control measures as for Lyme disease are required. Advice can be sought from foreign authorities before trips commence.)

Other zoonoses, which are only likely to be of relevance for agricultural colleges, schools with rural studies departments and those visiting farms, include **ovine chlamydiosis, ringworm** and **Escherichia coli** (strain 0157). The first is a disease of sheep causing abortions. There has been concern that pregnant women coming

---

[3] PS1, *Pond dipping and Weil's disease*, CLEAPSS, March 1996.
[4] As discussed in PS2, *The dissection of eyes*, CLEAPSS, May 1997 and *Science and Technology Bulletin,* 186, Autumn 1995, page 20, *Bovine eyeball dissection,* SSERC.

into close contact with sheep at lambing time may be considered at risk. This risk of abortion would make it prudent before a farm visit to warn teachers and students, who are or may be pregnant, to avoid contact with ewes and lambs. Ringworm is a non life threatening fungal skin infection which may be transmitted from infected farm animals such as cattle, sheep and pigs. Spores enter the skin through cuts and abrasions. Covering scratches and wounds with suitable dressings and practising good hygiene after contacting farm animals are obvious control measures. The 0157 strain of *E. coli* is particularly hazardous and may be passed to humans following contact with infected farm animals and their faeces. However, as with ringworm, good hygiene is an effective control measure.

Parasites

Small mammals and birds, taken from the wild, might be infested with fleas and mites which could transfer to humans or other animals in the school. It is not therefore recommended that they should be studied in schools. Care should be taken if these vertebrates are examined during field work. Items such as old bird's nests may be similarly infested. When these are brought into school (if it is known that they have not been used for some time), if autoclaving is not possible or appropriate, they should be sealed inside a plastic bag to prevent the escape of parasites. It would also be prudent to autoclave owl pellets before they are examined, in case they contain intestinal parasites or other sources of infection.

Giant African snails have been the source of some controversy in that, several years ago, government education departments warned that these animals might be carrying a parasite that could transfer to humans, causing symptoms of meningitis. It is true that, in some Asian countries to which the animal has spread, snails may be the intermediate host of a parasitic worm that infests the lungs of rats. If the snails are then used as food by humans and inadequately cooked, the parasite may survive to infest its human host. However, it seems rather unlikely that this mode of transfer will be involved with giant African snails kept and studied in schools. Furthermore, snails bred in this country (and they are prolific) cannot be infested with the parasite as its life cycle will have been disrupted. Only animals recently imported from areas where the parasitic infestation is common could be at risk of carrying the parasite. With so many snails reproducing in this country, there must now be little, if any, demand for further specimens to be imported.

Worms that infest domesticated animals such as dogs may transfer to humans in the faeces of infected animals. Illnesses produced include hydatid disease (caused by the canine tapeworm) and toxocariasis. Risks are, however, low since the host animals are unlikely to be encountered in schools, except perhaps on playing fields or when studying in local parks, and the spread of the parasite can easily be controlled by good hygiene.

Human diseases

For a full discussion, refer to section 4.3.

4.2 Allergies

For a detailed discussion of allergic reactions caused by biological materials, refer to Topic 13.

4.3 Investigations using students

Several activities which use students as the subject of the investigation are often thought to be banned, and indeed they may have been by some employers. Other activities are sometimes tackled in the laboratory without careful thought about the precautions that are advisable. Investigations involving students are invariably motivating and therefore very useful educational 'tools' and so it would be a pity if teachers were to reject them out of hand as being too hazardous to contemplate. A major concern revolves around the use of **human body fluids and cells**, typically those taken from the inside of the mouth. The fear is that if these fluids and cells are studied, diseases such as HIV or hepatitis might be transmitted from carriers to other students or to staff. In 1987, government education departments advised employers against the practise of taking '(human) blood and cell samples' in schools. This resulted in most education authorities instructing teachers not to take **blood samples or cheek cells**. However, after 1992, with the implementation of the Management of Health and Safety at Work Regulations which require risk assessments for all hazardous activities in the workplace not already covered by the COSHH Regulations, the practice of analysing activities for their inherent hazards, and adopting suitable control measures to ensure that investigations can be conducted safely, has become widespread. The Institute of Biology, with the support of other agencies, has also campaigned that cheek cells can be sampled safely.

As a result, increasing numbers of teachers and others began to question whether a widespread ban on studies of blood and cheek cells was warranted. In 1996, the DfEE changed its earlier guidance[5] for England and Wales, indicating that cheek cells *could* be sampled if the lining of the mouth is wiped with a cotton bud, rather than scraped, and if contaminated items are disposed of safely. Following this amendment of earlier recommendations, many employers have now altered their instructions to schools, permitting cheek-cell

---

[5] In Table 17.14 of DfEE *(1996) Safety in science education*. HMSO.

sampling using a safe procedure[6]. Indeed, it would not be logical for employers to maintain a prohibition on cheek-cell sampling, given that the advice on which the original restrictions were made has been reversed.

Although not recommending that restrictions on blood sampling should also be similarly lifted, the DfEE has relaxed somewhat its earlier advice[7], indicating that blood samples may be taken, if permitted by the employer. Several such employers now allow the taking of blood samples from students (usually restricted to sixth formers), if they are sure that a thorough assessment of risks has been made and that the use of a safe, sterile procedure, both for staff and for students, can be guaranteed. Appendix 1 provides further guidance on taking blood samples safely, including a suitable sterile procedure, which teachers might find useful in supporting a case they wish to make to their employers, requesting approval to take blood samples from students.

Activities involving the study of **saliva** (typically for its amylase content) and of **urine** (e.g. to analyse chloride ion concentrations) are also often not attempted. Sometimes this is because of the mistaken belief that there have been recommendations or instructions not to study these body fluids. Apart from in Northern Ireland, there has never been any national advice that work with these fluids should be restricted. Indeed, even the DfEE indicates that they can be investigated safely[8], if suitable precautions are taken to ensure that infections cannot be transmitted from one person to another. Nevertheless, some employers have issued instructions that these body fluids should not be investigated and these must be obeyed until the employer can be persuaded to alter its ban. It should be noted that there have been a number of reports of staff developing allergies to commercial amylase preparations which have been used instead of saliva. Such preparations may also behave unpredictably. Further guidance on the safe study of human body fluids is available in CLEAPSS and SSERC publications[9].

Activities involving studies of students' **ventilation** and **heart rates** and the influence of exercise are relatively frequently carried out. Perhaps because such investigations are so commonplace, they are sometimes tackled without sufficient thought about the possible adverse effects on a minority of students who, through peer pressures, may not readily identify themselves. What is a normal level of exercise for most people may be inappropriate for an overweight student or one with a

medical condition. Even mild exercise might provoke an attack in those suffering from asthma. Teachers should therefore ensure that they know who all the asthmatics are in each class and should also identify any student who has been excused from taking part in PE or sports activities for medical reasons. Before any activities involving exercise are commenced, asthmatics should be privately warned to use their inhalers and students, for whom exercise would be unwise, allowed not to take part. Teachers should, however, be sensitive in their management of these investigations. By, for example, pairing up students so that one performs exercise while his or her partner takes readings, it is easy to protect those for whom exercise might be unsafe, without drawing the attention of a class to students' disabilities. It is also important to ensure that exercise does not become competitive, with some students over-exerting themselves. This aspect of class control is also relevant if students are asked to blow into a manometer to raise the height of water in a tube.

The use of **spirometers** and **sphygmomanometers** raises special requirements. The Management of Health and Safety at Work Regulations demand that staff are trained in the use of any pieces of hazardous equipment which include these items. Such training is best arranged in-house, for example, at a regular science department staff meeting. Full guidance on the safe use of spirometers and sphygmomanometers can be found in CLEAPSS publications[10], but the main issues to be considered are discussed below.

Spirometers

■ *Avoiding infection from mouthpieces, nose clips and corrugated tubing.* This will involve adequate disinfection, allowing sufficient time. 'Milton' is very effective and recommended but takes 30 minutes; ethanol is quicker (5 minutes) but leaves an unpleasant taste, so rinsing with water is essential. The internal surfaces of tubing should be disinfected with ethanol before the spirometer is stored after use.

■ *Ensuring that there is an adequate supply of oxygen to maintain normal body functions.* Oxygen will be quickly exhausted if the spirometer is filled only with air, so it is customary to fill the spirometer with pure oxygen if more than a few breaths are to be taken when connected to the equipment. If exhaled carbon dioxide is removed with sodalime or 'Carbosorb', the normal ventilation stimulation mechanisms which typically accompany a decrease

---

[6] Guidance on a safe procedure is given by the Institute of Biology (1996) *Living biology in schools*, ISBN 0 90049032 2; by the CLEAPSS School Science Service in the *Laboratory Handbook*, 1992, section 14.4.2 and PS6, *Cheek cell sampling*, May 1996; and by SSERC in *Science and Technology Bulletin*, 178, September 1993.

[7] See the information in footnote reference 5.

[8] See the information in footnote reference 5.

[9] PS27, *Human body fluids*, CLEAPSS, June 1997; *Science and Technology Bulletin*, 178, September 1993, SSERC.

[10] Refer to the *CLEAPSS Laboratory Handbook*, 1992, sections 14.3, 15.11 and 15.12.

in oxygen will not operate. Monitoring a subject's mental alertness by asking him or her to perform simple spelling or arithmetic exercises will identify if the reduction of oxygen in the spirometer is approaching a dangerous level.

- *Controlling the time spent breathing on the spirometer.* See above.

- *Avoiding the inhalation of corrosive dust from the sodalime canister.* Much dust can be removed by repeatedly pouring the absorbent from one container to another. This should be done outdoors, while facing away from the prevailing wind. At the very least, ensure that the valve is fitted correctly so that air is not breathed in through the carbon dioxide absorbent.

- *Avoiding respiratory distress induced by excessive exercise while breathing on the spirometer.* Older designs of spirometer have smaller-diameter tubing than is now used. This offers greater resistance to air breathed in and out. With such models, levels of exercise may need to be restricted to prevent 'fighting for breath'.

- *Choosing a healthy volunteer to breathe on the spirometer.* Someone who plays in a school sports team is unlikely to have any medical problems which might be exacerbated by using the spirometer.

Sphygmomanometers

- *Controlling the time when blood does not flow to the tissues.* When the sphygmomanometer cuff is inflated around the upper arm, blood flow to the extremities of the arm must not be cut off for longer than is needed to record the blood pressure.

- *Avoiding making medical diagnoses.* It is all too easy to make a pronouncement on a seemingly abnormal blood pressure reading. However, the sphygmomanometer may not have been operated correctly and there are several factors that can elevate or otherwise influence the blood pressure measurements. These include previously smoking a cigarette, having recently taken exercise, the position of the arm relative to the heart during a measurement and constriction around the upper arm caused by sleeves rolled up. A sphygmomanometer must therefore only be used to teach about the *principles* of blood pressure regulation.

Science departments invariably have a 'no-eating and drinking' policy for students working in all laboratories. However, it is not uncommon for teachers to conduct taste-testing investigations, for example to map the 'taste-sensitive' areas of the tongue, in a laboratory without thinking about the risks or how this undermines the normal laboratory rules. Such work is best done in a food technology room, canteen or equivalent area where

hygiene can be assured. If a laboratory *really* has to be used, it should be clear to the students how exceptional the circumstances are. The very strict hygiene precautions that must be taken should be *seen* to be taken, i.e. washing down/ disinfecting benches to remove any discarded or spilt chemicals or micro-organisms and the use of disposable paper or plastic utensils (*not* laboratory glassware), straws, swabs etc.

4.4 Use of hazardous chemicals

These are encountered in a variety of ways in biological investigations. When the use of harmful or irritant chemicals in an investigation is contemplated, they are rarely considered sufficiently hazardous to warrant restricting the activity. Corrosive chemicals are treated with greater caution but **toxic chemicals** often provoke an extreme response, perhaps with a decision taken to abandon the activity involving them. This may, of course, be a legitimate action following a full risk assessment. However, adopting suitable control measures, such as modifying the procedure or wearing eye protection and gloves, could often allow the activity to continue. In many cases, worries about the effects of toxic chemicals on *students* are an over-reaction since the chemical will be diluted so that its hazard classification is only harmful or it is not even classified as hazardous. Examples include the use of plant growth substances in tissue culture or the application of animal hormones such as adrenaline in animal physiology studies. However, a technician who prepares the dilution will be more at risk and control measures must be applied. Harmful or toxic fungicides may have been used to treat seeds but these can nevertheless be handled safely wearing disposable gloves or by ensuring that hands are washed immediately afterwards.

Breeding investigations with *Drosophila* fruit flies are sometimes restricted because of the use of **ethoxy-ethane** (diethyl ether) as an anaesthetic. This has a narcotic action and is extremely flammable but, with good ventilation and the strict avoidance of working near naked flames, it will often be acceptable to use the chemical rather than seek out alternatives which may be less effective. Another genetics investigation involves the tasting of the chemical **phenylthiocarbamide** (PTC) [also known as phenylthiourea (PTU)]. An ability to taste this substance is genetically controlled and there is a fixed proportion of the population that inherits the allele for tasting PTC. However, the chemical is toxic, generating the widespread belief that its use is not allowed. It may seem bizarre to suggest that tasting a toxic chemical is quite permissible, but we do this all the time with, for example, caffeine. Provided the amount tasted is very low, there will be no toxic effects. With PTC-impregnated papers, purchased from educational suppliers, the dose is strictly limited to a safe level. If PTC papers are to be prepared in schools by soaking filter paper in PTC solution, each strip should contain no more than 0.1 mg of PTC[11].

When the hazardous chemicals are part of the armoury of plants and animals, however, it is not uncommon for concerns to escalate often to unwarranted, extreme heights. It is recognised that there are many species of **poisonous plants**[12] commonly found in gardens, school grounds, etc., but it is often only certain parts that accumulate toxins and simply *handling* the materials carries no risk. Some plants, and especially some fungi, are highly toxic and it would be prudent to avoid them. However, even if poisonous parts of a plant are eaten, for many species, significant quantities need to be ingested before ill effects are experienced. As an example, for the castor oil plant, the seeds contain quantities of ricin. This is one of the more potent plant toxins. Case histories have shown that, on different occasions, young children have consumed between three and twelve seeds and suffered fatal effects. Doses would probably need to be higher for older students to consume lethal amounts. In assessing the risks of using castor oil seeds in school, teachers need to consider the likelihood that their students would have the inclination and the opportunity of eating a sufficient quantity of seeds during practical work. Similarly, the fears expressed by teachers about the poisonous wild plants that often grow in a natural wildlife garden can often be allayed after a careful analysis of the actual risks of plants being eaten.

Some species of animals also use toxins for attack and defence. Those which produce particularly potent **venoms** such as many species of poisonous snake are subject to the requirements of the Dangerous Wild Animals Act and cannot be kept and handled without a licence. Such animals will not be encountered in schools and it is very unlikely that students could bring them in to school from home. Other animals, including various species of insect and arachnid, produce venoms and consequently are regarded with deep suspicion. **Tarantula spiders** kill their prey by injecting poisons and many teachers question their suitability for studies in schools. However, many species are unlikely to bite humans and, even if they did, the effects of injected venom are not usually extreme. There is therefore no reason, on the grounds of their dangerous behaviour, why suitable species should not be kept in schools. It is, however, recommended that they are not regularly handled as their sharp body hairs may produce an allergic reaction or enter the eye, and the welfare of the animals is improved if they are left undisturbed. A hive of **honey bees** would make a valuable addition to many school grounds but teachers regularly express concerns about the dangers of students being stung. In fact,

students are less likely than adults to suffer any distress if they were to be stung, which is not likely to occur unless a colony is vandalised. An extremely large number of stings would need to be made to induce a serious toxic effect. A very small minority of students, however, are hypersensitive to bee stings and suffer an allergic reaction but their presence in a class would normally be known. Common-sense respect for a colony of bees is more appropriate than an inordinate fear of its dangers. One final example is the **Florida stick insect,** or two-striped walking stick, which may spray an irritant chemical when handled. The eyes are most at risk but sensible precautions will protect the handler from harm.

[11] See CLEAPSS (1992) *Laboratory Handbook*, section 15.13 'Tasting Investigations'.
[12] For details of which plants are poisonous, refer to M. R. Cooper and A. W. Johnson (1998) *Poisonous Plants and Fungi in Britain: Animal and Human Poisoning* (2nd edn). Stationery Office. ISBN 0112429815.

Appendix 1 Human blood sampling: recommended procedures

Warning: Government education departments recommend that blood samples should not normally be taken. Only proceed if: (i) your employer (education authority, governing body, etc.) has authorised the procedure and (ii) you can guarantee that all students and staff will follow the required precautions.

A Introduction

A.1 Why study blood ?

In the study of human blood, a part of many biology courses, it is important that the blood is shown to be a composite liquid containing several different components, including red cells. Aspects of physiology, including the determination of blood groups, clotting time and measurements of blood sugar levels, are also very valuable and suitable topics for practical studies. Most students are fascinated by such work and eager to look at blood smears under the microscope, determine their blood groups and so on. However, there are difficulties in obtaining blood samples, even the drop or two required for such activities.

Some establishments have found it possible to obtain time-expired blood from a local hospital or blood bank of the National Transfusion Service. (The latter is more likely to be willing to supply red cells from time-expired blood suspended in saline, which will not be suitable for all investigations.) However, it is more exciting and in some cases more appropriate for students to study their own blood; hence the need for this guidance. (Precautions 2, 3, 4, 10, 11, 12, 13 and 14 of the Suggested Sterile Procedure (Appendix 2) apply if time-expired blood or red cells are used.)

A.2 The risks involved

Wherever blood samples are taken, whether in a hospital clinic or in an educational establishment, there is a slight possibility of transmitting blood-borne viruses, the most significant being human immunodeficiency virus, HIV (the cause of AIDS) and hepatitis viruses B and C. However, blood-borne viruses are only transmitted if blood from a carrier or infected person infects another person via, say, a scratch in the skin. **There is no significant risk if the correct sterile procedure is fully carried out**.

In 1987, **government education departments recommended strongly that the taking of blood samples in schools and colleges should cease. Most education authorities adopted this recommendation and issued guidance restricting the practice in maintained educational establishments**. (In Scotland, it was recognised that the practice should continue for certain post-16 vocational courses.)

With the implementation of the Management of Health and Safety at Work Regulations in 1992, the principle was established of assessing risks before any hazardous operation is begun. In schools that had become grant-maintained and in colleges that had become incorporated, and therefore no longer under local authority control, several teachers argued that they should be able to take blood samples *if their assessment of risk indicated that suitable precautions could be taken to ensure that there could be no possibility of disease transmission.*

The advice now given by the DfEE (*Safety in Science Education*, 1996) is no longer as rigid as that in 1987: '*Blood samples must not be taken from staff or students unless permitted by the employer's guidelines. Unless specifically required, for example in some post-16 vocational courses, most education employers do not permit blood samples to be taken. If, exceptionally, it is permitted by the employers' guidelines, sterile conditions must be strictly enforced and all materials contaminated with blood should be autoclaved before disposal or treatment. If samples from a blood bank are investigated, autoclaving before disposal is again recommended.*' It is therefore now possible that education employers may be prepared to allow the taking of blood samples, if they are satisfied that strict precautions can and will be taken. The guidance given in these notes can form the basis of the required sterile procedures that will be used.

B Procedure

B.1 Approval required

After an assessment of risk has indicated that blood sampling can be performed safely, the approval of the education employer must be obtained before work involving blood sampling starts. This will require submission of the documentation of the assessment. The risk assessment must take into account the maturity and behaviour of the students involved and an appraisal of the ability to ensure safe working. The documentation should include a description of the activities to be attempted, the circumstances in which they will be carried out, details of the sterile procedure to be adopted (e.g. Appendix 2) and all other precautions that will be taken.

B.2 Precautions to be taken

Teachers must ensure that students fully understand the precautions that must be taken and the possible consequences of not taking them. This is valuable as a contribution to general education as well as essential for blood sampling to be safe.

Any students or staff who know that they are HIV-positive or have tested positive for hepatitis B and/or C viruses must not give blood samples. Procedures must be such that affected students can be excluded from, or allowed to opt out of, the sampling activity without having to admit publicly that they have tested positive for HIV or hepatitis. Confidentiality must be preserved at all times. Teachers and lecturers need considerable skills in managing such situations. As many as 2–3% of students in some areas may be hepatitis B and/or C positive but their identity in a group will often not be known to teaching staff. It should be made clear to students that they must not take part if they have good reason to believe that they may pose a particular risk to others. At the same time, however, the teacher or lecturer must allow students to decline to take part without in any way drawing attention to any possibility of infection; see B.3 below.

B.3 Student participation

There must be no pressure on a student to give a blood sample. Teachers should make it clear by their attitude that it is perfectly normal for some students not to want to have a sample taken and not to want to take any part in the work involved. If this is done well, it is likely that such students will gradually become involved in the work. Students should be allowed to change their minds either way.

B.4 Parental permission

For students below the age of 16, the permission of parents or guardians must be obtained, well in advance. This may also be considered advisable for post-16 students. A suitable form is given in Appendix 3.

B.5 Who takes the blood samples ?

It is recommended that the teacher should supervise the activity closely but that students take their own samples of blood. However, students who are quite willing and eager for a sample to be taken may find it impossible to do it themselves and in such circumstances, the teacher should take the blood sample. In this case, it is recommended that teachers ask students to sign the relevant part of the form in Appendix 3, or some similar statement.

The use of an automatic finger-pricking device (see Appendix 4) is strongly recommended. The teacher can be responsible for assembling the instrument with a fresh lancet and then handing it to the student who simply presses the device onto the skin and triggers the lancet. The instrument is handed back to the teacher who then disposes of the lancet safely (see Appendix 2).

B.6 Suitable sites for taking blood samples

Blood should be taken with a sterile lancet from the side of a student's finger, near the nail, using a new lancet for each person. It is not recommended that blood is taken from a finger tip because of the greater thickness of the skin at this point and the risk of subsequent infection. The ear lobe is sometimes suggested as an alternative site but this is also not recommended because of danger if a student jerks his or her head as the sample is taken and the difficulty of transferring drops of blood for investigation.

The best position is 5–10 mm from the lower corner of the nail (see diagram). It is easier to insert the lancet if the finger has been crooked at the top joint.

To help ensure a sufficient flow of blood from the punctured skin, the hand should be warm (so encouraging blood flow to the skin). It is sometimes helpful to force blood to the extremities by vigorously shaking the hand or rapidly moving the arm in a circle around the shoulder joint (take care to ensure that the arm cannot hit anything!).

B.7 Care with lancets

Teachers must supervise the issue, use and subsequent disposal of the lancets (using a 'sharps' container: see Appendix 4) extremely carefully.

B.8 Sterile procedure

A sterile procedure, approved by a Community Health Physician (e.g. as in Appendix 2), must be adhered to.

Appendix 2   Suggested sterile procedure

Before the lesson

1   Slides or any other glassware which might come into contact with the site from which a blood sample is taken should be sterilised by autoclaving at 121 °C (103.5 kN m^{-2}, 15 lbf in^{-2} above atmospheric) for 15 minutes or by heating dry at 160 °C for 2 hours.

2   A suitable disinfectant, able to kill viruses, should be freshly prepared. The recommended disinfectant is a solution of sodium chlorate(I) (sodium hypochlorite) containing 10 000 ppm available chlorine. This can be obtained by preparing a 10% dilution of a laboratory solution of sodium chlorate(I) containing not less than 10% (100 000 ppm) available chlorine. Concentrated sodium chlorate(I) is CORROSIVE. Note that domestic hypochlorite (bleach) solutions have already been diluted, often by an unspecified amount. It is difficult to make up accurate dilutions using such sources of the chemical.

During the lesson

3   Because of the risk of contamination through broken skin, the participation in this practical work of anyone with any sort of open wound, particularly on or near the face or hands, should be strictly limited. Depending on the nature and position of the wound, the student may need to be excluded from the work altogether.

4   Students and teachers must thoroughly wash both hands using soap and water. Those giving blood samples must pay particular attention to washing the site chosen for the sampling. Dry hands using only disposable towels.

If the teacher is taking the samples, he/she must wash and dry his/her hands before proceeding.

5   Using a cottonwool swab, wipe the chosen site with 70% alcohol [70% *v/v*, propan-2-ol (isopropanol) or ethanol] and allow it to dry.

6   Remove a new sterile disposable lancet from its packet (or detach the cap over the lancet tip) immediately prior to its use. Do not allow the sharp end to touch anything.

7   Puncture the skin of the chosen site using the lancet and immediately place the lancet into a 'sharps' container (see Annexe 3), small enough to fit in the autoclave. *Lancets must be used once only.*

8   Collect the blood by letting a drop or two fall in to a sterile tube or on to a sterile slide or sterile rod (see 1). There must be no contact between the area of the pinprick and any apparatus unless the apparatus has been sterilised.

9   Apply a sterile gauze dressing to the puncture site and press gently until bleeding has stopped. Once blood flow has stopped, place the dressing in the container used for the lancets or an autoclavable disposable bag.

10   Any blood spilt on the bench etc. must be wiped up at once using the freshly-prepared disinfectant (see 2). Hold the swab with forceps or wear rubber or plastic gloves.

11   The greatest care must be taken to avoid contamination of the skin with blood from another person. If this should occur, however, the contaminated area must be washed thoroughly with soap and water.

12   When students have finished with the slides and any other contaminated glassware that will be reused, these should be placed in a discard jar of the disinfectant referred to in 2 but diluted to produce a solution containing 25 000 ppm available chlorine. Note that sodium chlorate(I) is rapidly inactivated by the presence of organic matter, including blood. Sharp items for disposal should be placed in the 'sharps' container with the lancets. Non-sharp items (e.g. blood-grouping cards) should be placed in the disposal bag with the swabs and dressings.

13   At the end of the practical, wash hands again using soap and water and dry thoroughly using only disposable towels.

After the lesson

14   The disposal bag with the contaminated swabs, etc., should be closed, not sealed, and autoclaved (see 1), together with the slides and other contaminated glassware from the discard jar and the 'sharps' container. After autoclaving, the disposal bag should be sealed and, together with the 'sharps' container, ideally, incinerated. If this is impracticable, disposal can use the normal route for laboratory refuse. Autoclaved slides, etc., can be washed for reuse (particular care must be taken in handling any coverslips, which may cause cuts). Alternatively, if glassware has not been contaminated by too much blood, it could remain in the discard jar of disinfectant overnight before being washed in the normal way. Gloves should be used to protect the skin from the disinfectant.

Appendix 3   Sample letter and consent form

Dear Parent/Guardian

During the next few weeks we shall be studying blood during science lessons. Students usually find it very interesting to look at samples of their own blood under a microscope or to carry out other investigations with it.

This letter is to ask your permission for a sample of blood to be taken from your son/daughter. Please note the following points.

1   Only one or two drops will be taken from a prick in a finger.

2   A Community Health Physician has approved the sterile procedure we will use.

3   The sample will be taken only if your son/daughter wants it to be done and you also have agreed.

Please complete the form below and return it to me as soon as possible.

Yours sincerely

Science Teacher

****

For the parent

I am *willing/not willing** for a sample of blood to be taken from my child for use in a science lesson.

Signed:...   (Parent or Guardian)

Date:...

**Please cross out the one that does not apply.*

For the student

(*This section need not be completed until the lesson*)

I agree that the teacher may prick my finger to obtain a drop of blood.

Signed:...

Date:...

Appendix 4   Sundry items

1   Autoclavable 'sharps' containers

These are available from several suppliers including Philip Harris, Griffin and George, etc.

2   Automatic finger-pricking device

The *Autolet Lite* lancing device, platforms and *Unilet Superlite* or *ComforTouch* lancets are available from:

Medical Shop
Owen Mumford
Brook Hill
Woodstock
Oxford OX20 1TU

Tel: 01993 812021; *Fax*: 01993 813466;
E-mail: owenmumford.co.uk

A variety of finger-lancing devices, including *Autolet* and *Glucolet*, is available from:

DEPTH. Diabetic Care Centre
7 Spurway Parade
Woodford Avenue
Gants Hill
Ilford IG2 6UU

Tel: 020 8551 6263

MICROBIOLOGY AND BIOTECHNOLOGY

This Topic replaces Chapter 5a 'Microbiology' and Chapter 5b 'Biotechnology' in the second edition of Topics in Safety. *It is an updated version of the section on microbiology and biotechnology in* Safety in Science Education *(DfEE, 1996) produced as a result of a safety conference convened by the ASE in 1997. The Appendixes are retained from the second edition of* Topics in Safety.

1 Introduction

The nature of the growth, reproductive capacity and biochemistry of many microorganisms makes them of great economic, social and medical importance. The fundamental rules of personal, public and domestic hygiene rely on an understanding of the characteristics of these organisms. Microorganisms possess many obliging features that make them ideal subjects for safe practical exercises in schools. Unlike many organisms, they do not necessarily have to be maintained over long periods, and do not have to be fed and watered at weekends! Staff in schools and colleges should be in no doubt of the considerable educational value of thoughtful, practical microbiological work and of the need for every pupil to possess a basic knowledge of the biology of these organisms.

Work in microbiology and biotechnology in schools is categorised into three levels which are described in outline below. Although appropriate for use in schools, these levels are **not** the same as 'levels of containment' used by professional microbiologists. Further detailed guidance for each is provided in Tables 1 and 2.

■ **Level 1 (L1)**: work with organisms which have little, if any, known risk and which can be carried out by teachers with no specialist training. The organisms will be observed in the closed containers in which they were grown.

■ **Level 2 (L2)**: work where there may be some risks of growing harmful microbes but these are minimised by a careful choice of organisms or sources of organisms and by culturing in closed containers which are taped before examination and remain unopened unless the cultures within have been killed. Once a culture, prepared by students, has been grown, subculturing or transfer of organisms from one medium to another is not normally done. L2 work may be carried out with students between the ages of 11 and 16 years and by science teachers who may require training and some supervision, which can be provided through a short in-service course or in school by a knowledgeable biology teacher.

■ **Level 3 (L3)**: work where cultures of *known* fungi and bacteria are regularly subcultured or transferred. This work is normally confined to students over the age of 16 and institutions where facilities are appropriate. Teachers should be thoroughly trained and skilled in aseptic technique. This is a higher level of training than required for L2 work. Non-specialist teachers should not carry out or supervise this work.

A significant risk associated with work in microbiology or biotechnology is the generation of microbial aerosols, where fine droplets of water containing cells and/or spores of microbes are released into the air. Aerosols can be formed whenever liquid surfaces are broken or material is crushed or ground. The particles are so small that they are easily carried by air currents and can be inhaled into the lungs. Many of the safety measures detailed below are designed to minimise the risk of aerosol formation.

Although microbiology and biotechnology are considered separately in the following sections, they share many safety requirements. However, a major difference is one of scale with a corresponding increase of risk with larger volumes of microorganisms. Some additional precautions for biotechnology are described.

Before work with microbes is started, students should wash their hands with soap and water (except for L2 and L3 work investigating microbes on unwashed hands) and cover any cuts with waterproof plasters. Hands should also always be washed after working with microbes.

Table 1 Microbiology.

Source of hazard(s)		Guidance
Organisms	L1	Limited to algae, yeasts, moulds and bacteria used for culinary purposes, some moulds and commonly-occurring bacteria where they grow naturally on decaying vegetable material.
	L2	Care in the choice of suitable cultures (see Table 3) must be taken by obtaining them from recognised specialist suppliers which would include culture collections and, for live yeast, reputable bakers and health food shops. Where possible, organisms with unusual growth requirements, e.g., high salt, low pH, low temperature, should be chosen but these may not grow well on standard media.
		Organisms may be cultured from the environment but not from environments which are likely to contain harmful organisms, for example, lavatory seats or body surfaces other than fingers or hands. Containers of such cultures, once they have been incubated, must then be sealed before examination.
	L3	Known cultures from reputable specialist suppliers. Organisms may be cultured from the environment or from body surfaces if the work is appropriate to the course and if cultures are not opened by students.
		Teachers wishing to use organisms at L2 and L3, not listed as minimum risk, must have had suitable training in microbiological techniques and should consult an appropriate advisory body; see section 3 for details. Proficiency in aseptic technique and the ability to recognise when a culture has or has not become contaminated are key skills in minimising risk as well as providing reasonable certainty that the intended organism is the one that is being studied.
Culture media	L1	Organisms can only be cultured on the substances on which they grow naturally, for example, bread, fruit, vegetables, milk, cheese, yoghurt, hay or grass and other plants, in the case of rusts and mildews.
	L2	Agar-based culture media generally with a simple nutrient base, low pH or high salinity, but **not** those which select for organisms which are potentially pathogenic to humans, for example, blood agar, MacConkey's agar, dung or faecal agar.
		Similar restrictions apply to broth media.
	L3	As for L2, unless strict precautions are taken to prevent any release of microbes.
Storage of organisms and media		It is unwise to maintain bacteria and fungi for long periods, in case they become contaminated, except perhaps for some work at L3. Such organisms should be subcultured and checked for purity every 3 months or so but only if aseptic technique can be guaranteed. Mixed cultures of protozoa from reputable suppliers can be maintained indefinitely without risk.
		Cultures, other than those requiring light for their growth and survival, are best stored *in the dark* at 10–15 °C. If it is impossible to achieve a constant, cool temperature, a refrigerator may be used but never one in which human foodstuffs are kept.
		Media should be stored as dry powder or tablets. Once sterilised, media can be stored for several months in tightly-sealed, screw-topped bottles away from direct sunlight.
Contamination of teachers and students		Before beginning practical work, hands should be washed with soap and warm water, and all should be washed again after the activities are finished. There must be no hand-to-mouth operations such as chewing, sucking, licking labels or mouth pipetting.
	L3	Teachers, technicians and students should wear lab coats or aprons which can be relatively easily disinfected (as necessary) and cleaned. Teachers should consider the use of lab coats or aprons for L2 work.
Inoculation of cultures		Inoculation should involve precautions to prevent contamination of the person and work surfaces. It should also avoid the contamination of culture media with unwanted microbes. Media and Petri dishes, etc., should be either purchased pre-sterilised or sterilised by the user before agar plates are poured.
		Media must not be deliberately inoculated with material likely to be sources of human pathogens.
	L3	For the aseptic transfer of cultures, work surfaces should be swabbed with a suitable disinfectant before and after *all* operations *and sufficient time allowed for disinfection to occur*. Arrangements should be made to sterilise inoculating loops and spreaders before and after inoculation, and to provide discard pots for pipettes and syringes. The mouths of all containers, tubes, flasks, McCartney bottles, etc., should be flamed after removing caps and before their replacement. Lids of Petri dishes should be opened only just enough to allow the inoculating tool to be introduced and for as little time as possible.
Bench surfaces		For practical work by students, benches should be wiped down with a cloth soaked in a suitable disinfectant, *preferably before*, but *always after* practical work, *and sufficient time allowed for disinfection to occur.*

Source of hazard(s)	Guidance

Incubation

L1 Incubation should be limited to ambient conditions in the classroom. The only exception will be yoghurt-making at 43 °C, which, by using a starter culture and a special medium, is less likely to encourage unwanted, possibly harmful, growths.

Yeast cultures generate considerable quantities of carbon dioxide gas. Incubation containers should be plugged with cotton wool, or closed with plastic caps or fermentation locks, which will allow excess gas to escape.

L2/3 The upper limit for general school-based work should be 30 °C because in this temperature range, (a) cultures of microorganisms suitable for school use grow well and (b) although some pathogens can grow on certain culture media, there is unlikely to be a hazard when conducting investigations using material derived from suitable environments, e.g. soil, water and appropriate culture media and incubation conditions. Exceptions to this will include yoghurt making (43 °C), the culturing of *Streptococcus thermophilus* (50 °C) and *Bacillus stearothermophilus* (60 °C), and debilitated strains of *E. coli* for work with DNA.

Agar plates should be incubated inverted to avoid condensation dripping onto cultures. During incubation, the lid of the Petri dish should be taped to the base with two or four small pieces of tape so that the lid cannot be accidentally removed and conditions inside cannot become anaerobic.

Unless cultures are known to be minimum risk, teachers should consider taping incubated dishes closed around their circumferences before examination by pupils or students.

Spills

All spills should be reported to and dealt with by the teacher, who should record all incidents. All spills carry a risk of aerosol formation and procedures for dealing with them must reduce this as far as possible. Spills should be covered with towels or a cloth soaked in a suitable freshly-prepared disinfectant, preferably one that is not appreciably degraded by contact with organic matter or, alternatively, freshly-prepared sodium chlorate(I) (hypochlorite) solution with a concentration preferably greater than 1%, and left for at least 15 minutes. The spill debris should then be swept up using disposable paper towels. Disposable plastic gloves should be worn. Seriously contaminated clothing should be disinfected before laundering. Contaminated skin should be carefully washed with soap and warm water. Lysol and other cresolic disinfectants are caustic and toxic by skin absorption and should not be used. Clear phenolics are suitable but are no longer so readily available to schools in sensible quantities at reasonable prices. *MicroSol (VirKon)* is a relatively stable alternative.

To prevent breakages and spills, cultures must be centrifuged in *capped*, plastic tubes.

Observation of cultures of bacteria and fungi

L1 Cultures should be viewed in the unopened containers in which they were grown.

L2 Cultures should be examined by pupils in containers which have been taped closed. If cultures may contain pathogens and there is a risk that students may open them, even though instructed not to do so, it will be prudent for the cultures to be completely sealed with tape before examination. If it is necessary for students to open cultures for examination, special precautions may be necessary. Other than for pure, non-pathogenic, cultures prepared by teachers or technicians under aseptic conditions, and especially for cultures originating from environmental samples in which pathogens may be present, these must be killed by the teacher or technician as follows. A filter paper is placed in the lid of an inverted agar plate and moistened with 40% methanal solution (formalin). After 24 hours, the filter paper is removed. (Take care with methanal; eye protection, gloves and use of a fume cupboard to avoid breathing fumes are necessary.)

L3 Cultures of known and non-pathogenic microbes can be examined using a variety of techniques. Organisms cultured from body surfaces or any environmental source must be examined in unopened containers, or killed before examination as described above.

Sterilisation and disposal

All cultures must be heated to kill microorganisms before disposal. This is best done using a pressure cooker or autoclave, in conjunction with autoclavable bags. The caps of all screw-topped bottles must be loosened before cultures and media are sterilised. It is very important that instructions for use of the autoclave are followed in order to achieve and maintain sufficiently high temperatures for a long enough time. Pressure cookers are unlikely to be equipped with appropriate instructions for sterilisation and those for some autoclaves, designed for use with surgical instruments, state that the equipment is unsuitable for sterilising liquid media. Such autoclaves can be used for microbiological preparations but advice on their correct operation should be sought. Teachers and technicians should be trained to follow safe working practices. Seals and safety valves should be checked before each use. Heating autoclaves or pressure cookers with Bunsen burners is not recommended. Rapid cooling and the release of steam to lower the internal pressure quickly to atmospheric pressure is dangerous because it may shatter glassware and/or cause liquid media to boil over. Equipment should be allowed to cool unaided before opening. Further information may be sought from the organisations listed in section 3.

Sterilisation cannot be achieved by the use of chemical disinfectants. If, in exceptional circumstances, chemical disinfection of cultures is contemplated prior to disposal, use a freshly-made solution of a disinfectant that is not degraded when in contact with organic matter (see 'Spills' above). Cultures and

(continued)

Source of hazard(s)	Guidance
	equipment must be opened under the surface of the solution and left for at least 12 hours. Again it is essential to follow disinfectant instructions carefully. Chlorate(I) solution is inactivated by large amounts of organic matter, although if a culture might contain viruses this is often the preferred disinfectant.
	Microwave ovens are not suitable for sterilisation of most items, though they are sometimes used for liquefying prepared agar media. Beware of explosions which have occurred when solid medium has blocked the opening of a container.
	After sterilisation, solid cultures can be disposed of, in tied autoclave bags or similar, through the refuse system; liquid cultures can be flushed away down the lavatory or the sink with lots of water. Sterilised culture material should not be allowed to accumulate in open or closed waste traps.
	Incineration is an acceptable alternative to autoclaving. (Note, however, that polystyrene Petri dishes will generate harmful fumes when incinerated; a purpose-built incinerator with a tall flue should be used.)
	Clean glass equipment can be sterilised by dry heat in an oven (165 °C for at least 2 hours) or, in the case of wire loops, by heating to red heat in a Bunsen burner flame.
Radiation	Use to induce mutations in yeasts only; ensure that eyes are protected from UV radiation.

Table 2 Biotechnology.

Source of hazard(s)	Guidance
Organisms	The level restrictions which apply for microbiology also apply to biotechnology work.
	L1 Particularly suitable organisms include yoghurt bacteria, yeasts such as for the production of wine or bread and some unicellular algae.
	L2 Other than L1 organisms, it is recommended that organisms with unusual growth requirements are used, e.g. high salt, low pH, low temperature. Some examples of minimum risk organisms include *Vibrio natriegens (Beneckea natriegens), Photobacterium phosphoreum* and *Acetobacter aceti*.
	Avoid the large-scale culture of organisms which produce antibiotics, particularly penicillin.
	Cultures of organisms should only be obtained from recognised suppliers, including culture collections.
	L3 As for L2.
Culture media	The solutions generally used in biotechnology work present few problems other than those associated with quantity and the potential for contamination. Scaling up is often a necessary activity in biotechnology but keep quantities to a sensible minimum to make handling easier and reduce the quantities of enzymes, antibiotics, etc., which may be generated. All media should be sterilised prior to use. The use of animal dung for investigations of biogas generation is not recommended; use grass clippings inoculated with well-rotted garden compost.
Incubation/ Fermentation	To minimise the risks from contaminating pathogenic organisms, incubation temperatures should normally be no more than 30 °C. However, for yoghurt making, 43 °C may be used if hygienic preparation is followed; and for work with DNA using K 12 strains of *E. coli*, incubation at 37 °C is permissible assuming good aseptic technique.
	L2, 3 Use of fermenters is limited to these levels.
	The generation of large volumes of gas (carbon dioxide or methane) is a risk associated with many fermentations. Vessels must be suitably vented to allow the gas to escape but prevent aerosol formation or the entry of unwanted organisms. In the case of methane, the gas must be kept away from naked flames and electrical equipment which can cause sparks.
	Other than for work with yeasts and small-scale biogas generation using plant material, wholly anaerobic fermentations should not be used in schools. Investigations which are partially anaerobic, e.g. setting up a Winogradsky column, may, however, be attempted.
Contamination	Cultures should be started by inoculation with a significant volume of actively-growing inoculum (for example 20% of total volume).
	All equipment and materials (other than the inoculum) should be sterilised prior to use.
Spills	Routines for dealing with spills are the same as for microbiology. With fermenters there is the risk of spills of large amounts of liquid culture. All possible steps should be taken to guard against this, for example, by using equipment within a spills tray. In the case of gross spills, unless the organism is known to be safe, the lab should be cleared before attempting to deal with the spill.

Source of hazard(s)	Guidance
Electrical hazards	Keep all electrical leads, especially mains leads, tidy and site electrical equipment so as to minimise the risk of water entering.
Disposal	All cultures should be sterilised before disposal, preferably in an autoclave. If a fermenter cannot be sterilised complete, add a freshly-prepared disinfectant that is not appreciably degraded by contact with organic matter to the culture and leave for sufficient time to enable disinfection to occur before pouring the contents into containers which can be autoclaved.
Enzymes	Handle all enzymes, whether solid or liquid, or cultures which may produce them, with due care. Problems with enzymes increase with quantity as well as variety. Minimise skin contact and use eye protection and disposable gloves for solid or concentrated solutions of lipolytic and proteolytic enzymes. Avoid the release of powders into the air.
Plant growth substances	Often, wrongly, called plant hormones; many are toxic and some may be carcinogenic. Teachers and technicians should handle solids or concentrated solutions with appropriate care. The very low concentrations used in solutions by students present no significant risk.
Animal cell culture	Work with animal tissue culture is not recommended for use in schools. If teachers wish to do such work they should ensure that cultures are obtained from suppliers which can guarantee that their cell lines are pathogen-free.
Practical work with DNA	Practical work with DNA is restricted to that which does not result in the formation of nucleic acid molecules combining genetic material from different species of organism. Acceptable work includes: plasmid transfer (if the plasmid DNA is returned to its natural host), the induction of certain types of plant tumour, the induction of mutations in yeast using UV radiation and the fragmentation of DNA with enzymes, followed by separation of the fragments using electrophoresis. The majority of hazards associated with such work, including those that arise from the construction of DIY equipment (such as electrophoresis apparatus), are with well-known and well-documented chemicals, organisms and procedures for which advice on their safe use is readily available. Risks associated with the genetic material itself are considered to be negligible as long as this is obtained from reputable schools' suppliers. However, this does not apply to materials and kits imported from abroad (especially the USA), some of which may include substances or procedures that could be illegal in the UK or are not considered safe or appropriate here. This advice supersedes that given in *Microbiology: an HMI guide for schools and further education*. It may change with the implementation of the Genetically Modified Organisms (Contained Use) Regulations, 2000; see Topic 16 for more details.

2 Suitable and unsuitable microorganisms

Table 3 lists selected microorganisms which present minimum risk given good practice. Following changes to the hazard categorisation of certain microorganisms by the Advisory Committee on Dangerous Pathogens[1], these tables supersede the existing lists found in the CLEAPSS *Laboratory Handbook* (1992), *Microbiology: an HMI guide for schools and further education* (1990), *Topics in Safety* (1988) and *Safety in science education* (1996). It is not a definitive list; other organisms may be used if competent advice is obtained. It should be noted that strains of microorganisms can differ physiologically and therefore may not give expected results. Where possible, fungi that produce large numbers of air-borne spores should be handled before sporulation occurs, so that the spread of spores into the air and possible risks of allergy or the triggering of asthmatic attacks are minimised. *This is particularly important for some species, such as* Aspergillus *and* Penicillium, *which produce very large numbers of easily dispersed spores.* It should be noted that certain species of these two fungi, previously listed as unsuitable for use in schools, are now not thought to present such a serious risk to health, *given good practice in culture and handling.*

[1] Advisory Committee on Dangerous Pathogens (1995) *Categorisation of biological agents according to hazard and categories of containment* (4th edn). HSE Books. ISBN 0717610381.

Table 3 Selected microorganisms.

Bacterium	Educational use/interest/suitability	Ease of use/maintenance
Acetobacter aceti	Of economic importance in causing spoilage in beers and wines. Oxidises ethanol to ethanoic (acetic) acid and ultimately to carbon dioxide and water.	Needs special medium and very frequent subculturing to maintain viability.
Agrobacterium tumefaciens	Causes crown galls in plants; used as a DNA vector in the genetic modification of organisms.	Grows on nutrient agar, but requires 2–3 days' incubation.
Alcaligenes eutrophus	In the absence of nitrogen, it produces intracellular granules of poly-ß-hydroxybutyrate (PHB); was used in the production of biodegradable plastics.	Grows on nutrient agar.
Azotobacter vinelandii	A free-living nitrogen fixer, producing a fluorescent, water-soluble pigment when grown in iron (Fe)-limited conditions.	Grows on a nitrogen-free medium.
Bacillus megaterium	Has very large cells; produces lipase, protease and also PHB (see *Alcaligenes*); Gram-positive staining.	Grows on nutrient agar.
Bacillus stearothermophilus	Thermophilic species which grows at 65 °C; produces lipase and protease. Also used to test the efficiency of autoclaves.	Grows on nutrient agar.
Bacillus subtilis†	General-purpose, Gram-positive bacterium. Produces amylase, lipase and protease.	Grows on nutrient agar.
Cellulomonas sp.	Produces extra-cellular cellulase.	Grows on nutrient agar but also used with agar containing carboxymethylcellulose.
Chromatium species	A photosynthetic, anaerobic bacterium.	Requires special medium and light for good growth.
Erwinia carotovora (= *E. atroseptica*)	Produces pectinase which causes rotting in fruit and vegetables. Useful for studies of Koch's postulates.	Grows on nutrient agar.
Escherichia coli†	K12 strain: general-purpose, Gram-negative bacterium. B strain: susceptible to T4 bacteriophage.	Grows on nutrient agar.
Janthinobacterium (=*Chromobacterium*) *lividum**	Produces violet colonies. Grows best at 20 °C.	Needs frequent subculture and is best grown on glucose nutrient agar and broth.
Lactobacillus species	Ferment glucose and lactose, producing lactic acid; *L. bulgaricus* is used in the production of yoghurt.	Requires special medium containing glucose and yeast extract and frequent sub-culturing to maintain viability.
Leuconostoc mesenteroides	Converts sucrose to dextran: used as a blood plasma substitute.	Requires special medium as for *Lactobacillus*.
Methylophilus methylotrophus	Requires methanol as energy source; was used for the production of 'Pruteen' single-cell protein.	Requires special medium containing methanol.
Micrococcus luteus (= *Sarcina lutea*)	Produces yellow colonies; useful in the isolation of the bacterium from impure cultures. Also used to simulate the effects of disinfectants, mouthwashes and toothpastes on more harmful organisms. General purpose Gram-positive bacterium.	Grows on nutrient agar.
Photobacterium phosphoreum	Actively-growing, aerated cultures show bioluminescence; grows in saline conditions.	Requires a medium containing sodium chloride.
Pseudomonas fluorescens	Produces a fluorescent pigment in the medium.	Grows on nutrient agar.
Rhizobium leguminosarum	A symbiotic, nitrogen fixer; stimulates the formation of nodules on the roots of legumes. Only fixes nitrogen in plants.	Grows on yeast malt agar; some authorities recommend buffering with chalk to maintain viability.

† Some strains have been associated with health hazards. Reputable suppliers should ensure that safe strains are provided.
* Can be chosen for investigations that once required the use of *Chromobacterium violaceum* or *Serratia marcescens*.

Bacterium	Educational use/interest/suitability	Ease of use/maintenance
Rhodopseudomonas palustris	A photosynthetic, anaerobic, red bacterium. Also grows aerobically in the dark.	Requires light and a special medium, growing atypically on nutrient agar.
Spirillum serpens	Of morphological interest.	May grow on nutrient agar but requires **very** frequent subculturing to maintain viability.
*Staphylococcus albus (epidermidis)**	A general-purpose, Gram-positive bacterium, producing white colonies.	Grows on nutrient agar.
Streptococcus (= Enterococcus) faecalis	Of morphological interest, forming pairs or chains of cocci.	Nutrient agar with added glucose can be used but grows better on special medium, as for *Lactobacillus*.
Streptococcus (= Lactococcus) lactis	Of morphological interest, forming pairs or chains of cocci. Commonly involved in the souring of milk; also used as a starter culture for dairy products.	Can grow on nutrient agar with added glucose; some authorities recommend buffering with chalk to maintain viability.
Streptococcus thermophilus	Ferments glucose and lactose, producing lactic acid; used in the production of yoghurt. Grows at 50 °C.	Can grow on nutrient agar with added glucose; some authorities recommend frequent subculturing to maintain viability.
Streptomyces griseus	Responsible for the earthy odour of soil. Grows to form a fungus-like, branching mycelium with aerial hyphae bearing conidia. Produces streptomycin.	Grows on nutrient or glucose nutrient agar but better on special medium which enhances formation of conidia.
Thiobacillus ferrooxidans	Involved in the bacterial leaching of sulfur-containing coal. Oxidises iron(II) and sulfur. Demonstrates bacterial leaching of coal samples containing pyritic sulfur.	Requires special medium.
Vibrio natriegens[+] *(= Beneckea natriegens)*	A halophile, giving **very** rapid growth. Prone, however, to thermal shock with a sudden drop in temperature.	Requires medium containing sodium chloride.

Fungus	Educational use/interest/suitability	Ease of use/maintenance
Agaricus bisporus	Edible mushroom; useful for a variety of investigations on factors affecting growth.	Grows on compost containing well-rotted horse manure; available as growing 'kits'.
Armillaria mellea	The honey fungus; causes decay of timber and tree stumps. Produces rhizomorphs.	Grows very well on malt agar. Some authorities recommend carrot agar.
*Aspergillus nidulans***	For studies of nutritional mutants. Produces abundant, easily dispersed spores – may become a major laboratory contaminant!	Grows on Czapek Dox yeast agar. Special media required for studying nutritional mutants.
*Aspergillus niger***	Useful for studies of the influence of magnesium on growth and the development of spore colour. Used commercially for the production of citric acid. Produces abundant, easily dispersed spores – may become a major laboratory contaminant!	Requires special sporulation medium for investigations.
*Aspergillus oryzae***	Produces a potent amylase; useful for studies of starch digestion. Also produces protease. Used by the Japanese in the production of rice wine (saki).	Grows on malt agar; add starch (or protein) for investigations.

* This organism has been known to infect debilitated individuals and those taking immuno-suppressive drugs. Some authorities advise against its use.

[+] A well-known supplier currently lists an unspecified species of *Vibrio* because of its morphological interest. This has a typical shape, better shown than by *V. natriegens*. However, this species is a Hazard Group 2 organism which may cause human disease. This bacterium should only be used in establishments that have containment facilities suitable for work with Hazard Group 2 microorganisms.

** Possible risk of allergy/asthma if large numbers of spores are inhaled.

Fungus	Educational use/interest/suitability	Ease of use/maintenance
Botrytis cinerea	Causes rotting in fruits, particularly strawberries. Useful for studies of Koch's postulates with fruit, vegetables and *Pelargonium* sp. Important in the production of some dessert wines ('noble' rot). Used in ELISA protocols.	Can be grown on malt agar or agar with oatmeal.
Botrytis fabae	Causes disease in bean plants.	Requires agar with oatmeal.
Candida utilis	Simulates behaviour of pathogenic *Candida spp.* in investigations of fungicidal compounds.	Grows in malt agar or glucose nutrient agar.
Chaetomium globosum	Useful for studies of cellulase production; thrives on paper.	Can be grown on V8 medium but survives well just on double thickness wallpaper, coated with a flour paste.
Coprinus lagopus	For studies of fungal genetics.	Grows on horse dung.
Eurotium (= *Aspergillus*) *repens*	Produces yellow cleistocarps (cleistothecia) embedded in the medium and green conidial heads in the same culture.	Requires special medium.
Fusarium graminearum	Causes red rust on wheat; used in the manufacture of 'Quorn' mycoprotein.	Can be grown on V8 medium.
Fusarium oxysporum	A pathogen of many plants. Produces sickle-cell shaped spores, a red pigment and pectinase.	Grows well on several media including malt, potato dextrose and Czapek Dox yeast agar.
Fusarium solani	Digests cellulose; macroconidia have a sickle shape.	Grows on potato dextrose agar.
Helminthosporium avenae	A pathogen of oats.	May not grow easily in laboratory cultures.
Kluyveromyces lactis	A yeast, isolated from cheese and creamery products. Ferments lactose and used to convert dairy products to lactose-free forms. Genetically-modified strains are used to produce chymosin (rennet).	Grows on malt agar or glucose nutrient agar.
Leptosphaeria maculans	For studies of disease in brassica plants.	Requires cornmeal agar or prune yeast lactose agar to promote sporulation in older cultures.
Monilinia (= *Sclerotinia*) *fructigena*	For studies of brown rot in apples. Useful for studies of Koch's postulates.	Grows on malt agar or potato dextrose agar.
Mucor genevensis	For studies of sexual reproduction in a homothallic strain of fungus.	Grows on malt agar.
Mucor hiemalis	For studies of sexual reproduction between heterothallic + and – strains and zygospore production.	Grows on malt agar.
Mucor mucedo	Common black 'pin mould' on bread. For sporangia (asexual), mating types and amylase production.	Grows on malt agar.
Myrothecium verucaria	For studies of cellulose decomposition but *Chaetomium globosum* is preferred.	Grows on malt agar.
*Neurospora crassa**	Red bread mould. Produces different coloured ascospores. Can be used in studies of genetics. Beware – readily becomes a major laboratory contaminant!	Grows on malt agar.
*Penicillium chrysogenum**	Produces penicillin; useful for comparative growth inhibition studies in liquid media or when inoculated onto agar plates seeded with Gram-positive and negative bacteria. Produces yellow pigment.	Grows on malt agar, though some authorities indicate that it thrives better on liquid media.
*Penicillium expansum**	Does not produce penicillin; causes disease in apples. Useful for studies of Koch's postulates.	Grows on malt agar.

* Possible risk of allergy/asthma if large numbers of spores are inhaled.

Fungus	Educational use/interest/suitability	Ease of use/maintenance
*Penicillium notatum**	Produces penicillin; useful for comparative growth inhibition studies in liquid media or when inoculated onto agar plates seeded with Gram-positive and negative bacteria.	Grows on malt agar.
*Penicillium roqueforti**	Does not produce penicillin; familiar mould of blue-veined cheese.	Grows on malt agar.
*Penicillium wortmanii**	Produces wortmin rather than penicillin.	Grows on malt agar.
Phaffia rhodozyma	A fermenting red yeast. Used to colour the food supplied to fish-farmed salmon.	Grows on yeast malt agar.
Phycomyces blakesleanus	Produces very long sporangiophores which are strongly phototropic.	Grows on malt agar.
Physalospora obtusa	An ascomycete fungus that grows on apple. Thought to produce pectinase.	Grows on potato dextrose agar.
Phytophthora infestans[+]	Causes potato blight. Produces motile zoospores.	Can be grown on V8 medium.
Plasmodiophora brassicae	For studies of disease in brassica plants, particularly club root. Useful for studies of Koch's postulates.	May not grow easily in culture.
Pleurotus ostreatus	Edible oyster cap mushroom.	Can be grown on rolls of toilet paper!
Pythium de baryanum[+]	Causes 'damping off' of seedlings; cress is best to use.	Grows on cornmeal agar.
Rhizopus oligosporus	Used in the fermentation of soya beans to make 'tempe', a meat-substitute food in Indonesia.	Grows on potato dextrose agar, Czapek Dox yeast agar and other fungal media.
Rhizopus sexualis	Produces rhizoids and zygospores. Useful for studies of the linear growth of fungi.	Grows on potato dextrose agar and other fungal media.
Rhizopus stolonifer	Produces rhizoids. Produces lipase.	Grows on potato dextrose agar, potato carrot agar, Czapek Dox yeast agar and other fungal media.
Rhytisma acerinum	An indicator of air pollution: less common in industrial areas. On sycamore leaves, it forms 'tar' spot lesions, the number or diameter of which can be compared at different sites.	Difficult to maintain but laboratory cultures are not likely to be needed.
Saccharomyces cerevisiae	Valuable for work in baking and brewing, showing budding, for spontaneous mutation and mutation-induction experiments, and for gene complementation using adenine- and histidine-requiring strains.	Grows on malt agar or glucose nutrient agar.
Saccharomyces diastaticus	Able to grow on starch by producing glucoamylase.	Grows on malt agar and nutrient agar + 1% starch.
Saccharomyces ellipsoideus	Used in fermentations to produce wine; can tolerate relatively high concentrations of ethanol.	Grows on malt agar.
Saprolegnia litoralis[+]	Parasitic on animals. Produces zoospores. Good illustration of asexual and sexual stages.	Culture by baiting pond water with hemp seeds.
Schizosaccharomyces pombe	Large cells, dividing by binary fission. Good for studies of growth, using a haemocytometer for cell counts. Prone to thermal shock.	Grows on malt agar. For studies of population growth, a malt extract broth can be used.
Sordaria brevicollis	For studies of fungal genetics, including inheritance of spore colour and crossing over in meiosis.	Requires special medium for crosses between strains.
Sordaria fimicola	For studies of fungal genetics, including inheritance of spore colour and crossing over in meiosis.	Grows on cornmeal, malt and other agars but may not transfer readily from one medium to another. White-spore strain may not always grow normally on standard cornmeal agar.
Sporobolomyces sp.	Found on leaf surfaces. Spores are ejected forcibly into the air from mother cells.	Grows on malt, yeast malt and glucose nutrient agar but laboratory cultures may not be needed.
Trichoderma reesei	Commercial production of cellulase.	Grows on malt agar.

* Possible risk of allergy/asthma if large numbers of spores are inhaled.
[+] Now classed as a protoctist, so may not be listed under fungi by some suppliers.

Viruses

These are rarely used in schools and colleges but a selected list of those which might be considered is given below.

> Bacteriophage (T type) (host *E. coli*)
> Cucumber Mosaic Virus
> Potato Virus X
> Potato Virus Y (not the virulent strain)
> Tobacco Mosaic Virus
> Turnip Mosaic Virus

Algae, protozoa (including slime moulds) and lichens

Though some protozoa are known to be pathogenic, the species quoted for experimental work in recent science projects and those obtained from schools' suppliers or derived from hay infusions, together with species of algae and lichens, are acceptable for use in schools.

Unsuitable microorganisms

A number of microorganisms have in the past been suggested for use in schools but are no longer considered suitable; these are listed below. Some fungi previously considered unsuitable have been reinstated in the list of selected organisms now that it is thought that they do not present a major risk, *given good practice*.

Bacteria

Chromobacterium violaceum
Pseudomonas tabaci
Clostridium perfringens (welchii)
Serratia marcescens
Pseudomonas aeruginosa
Staphylococcus aureus
Pseudomonas solanacearum
Xanthomonas phaseoli

Fungi

Rhizomucor (Mucor) pusillus

3 References and materials

For addresses of CLEAPSS and SSERC, see 'Introduction' page 2.

1 Organisations which can be consulted about the suitability of microorganisms:
ASE (members only)
CLEAPSS School Science Service (school and college members only)
Microbiology in Schools Advisory Committee (MISAC) (see page 105)
National Centre for Biotechnology Education (NCBE) (see page 104)
SSERC (Scottish school and college members only)

2 HSE (2000) L29 *A guide to the genetically-modified organisms (contained use) Regulations 2000*. HSE Books. ISBN 0 7176 1758 0.

3 Kits from the Culture Collection of Algae and Protozoa are available from Philip Harris and the National Centre for Biotechnology Education (NCBE).

Appendix 1   Steam sterilisation

This is the preferred method of sterilisation for both preparation and disposal.

Liquids and articles which would be damaged by dry heat at 160 °C are sterilised by steam at 121 °C (103 kN m^{-2} or 15 lbf in^{-2} steam pressure). The holding time under these conditions should be at least 15 minutes. In schools, autoclaves are invariably of the non-jacketed, 'pressure-cooker' type. Indeed the 'autoclave' may actually be a domestic pressure cooker. These vertical, portable laboratory autoclaves are adequate for all normal school work but their limitations should be recognised. Their main disadvantages are that there may be inefficient removal of air and their small size is a temptation to overloading.

Air has an important influence on the efficiency of steam sterilisation. For example, if all the air is removed from the vessel, saturated steam at 103 kN m^{-2} (15 lbf in^{-2}) has a temperature of 121 °C. With only half the air removed, the temperature of the air-steam mixture is only 112 °C.

In order to arrive at the full 'cycle' time for a vertical autoclave, we must add to the minimum 15 minute holding period at 121 °C:

a)   a heating up period to allow the water to come to the boil;

b)   a period of vigorous free steaming to expel air from containers;

c)   an addition to the holding period, possibly but exceptionally as much as an extra 20 minutes if the load includes certain 'difficult' materials (see below);

d)   a cooling period (rapid cooling under a tap or by other means being inadvisable).

The cooling period increases the time of exposure to steam and may be necessary for the effective sterilisation of some materials. In any case rapid cooling may lead to glassware cracking or liquids boiling over and being wasted. It can be very dangerous to open an autoclave before the pressure has dropped to atmospheric (when the temperature inside will be about 80 °C). The sudden change in temperature caused by opening before the pressure has been allowed to fall has been known to cause violent cracking of glass containers. Serious scalds and burns have occurred because this hazard was not appreciated.

'Difficult' materials referred to under (c) would not be met frequently in normal school work. Materials such as dry soil will contain heat-resistant spores and will allow steam to penetrate only very slowly. Contaminated cloth can also be difficult because the displacement of air can be a problem.

However, even very exacting samples such as soil caked on tightly rolled and packed lint have been shown to be reliably sterile after a 35 minute holding time in a domestic pressure cooker. For standard media and recommended 'non-pathogenic' organisms, a 15–20 minute holding period will be effective. Should there be any doubt, the holding time should be increased.

Appendix 2   Subculturing and transfer work at level 3

Work at this level may involve subculturing and transfer work and more sophisticated aseptic techniques are required. In addition to the safety precautions appropriate for level 2, the following points should be noted.

1   The work area should ideally be on an impervious bench surface such as plastic laminate and away from doors, windows and other direct sources of draughts. Before work is started, the bench should be cleaned with a suitable disinfectant, e.g. a clear phenolic or *MicroSol* (*VirKon*).

2   Working close to a Bunsen burner, where the updraught will prevent organisms falling onto apparatus, gives protection to both work and worker.

3   A good deal of technique is associated with the use of the inoculating loop. Loops can be easily made by bending 24 s.w.g. nichrome wire round a match stick, with care to ensure that the loop so formed is fully closed. The overall length of the wire including the loop should be no more than 50 mm. This is to minimise vibration and flicking of material from a charged loop. Loops should be attached to a metal 'chuck' type holder and not to glass rods. This is because flame sterilisation should include the lower part of the handle. When the handle is a glass rod it is likely to shatter.

4   Any instrument introduced into a culture must first be sterilised. Loop and lower handle are heated to red heat whilst held almost vertically in a roaring Bunsen burner flame. Before use, the wire is allowed to cool, or can be quenched in sterile water or the medium to be used. Alternatively, the wire can be dipped in ethanol and passed through the flame to burn off any excess. Direct flaming of a wet loop can cause spluttering. Material which spits from an overcharged loop may not have been sterilised. This can be avoided by immersing the contaminated loop in a beaker of boiling water before flaming.

5   The mouths of culture tubes, McCartney bottles, etc., should be flamed when removing caps or plugs, and the flaming should be repeated before replacement. Plugs and caps should not be placed on the bench. With practice it is possible to manipulate tubes, plugs and loop without any of them leaving the hands. If tubes or caps cannot be handled conveniently, they may be placed on a ceramic tile which has been swabbed with a suitable disinfectant. Culture tubes and similar glassware should always be supported in a rack, preferably a plastic coated wire one; they should never be propped up or laid down on the bench.

6   Lids of Petri dishes should be opened just enough to allow the inoculating tool to enter and be manipulated. Lids should be opened for the minimum amount of time necessary for the particular operation to be performed. The lid should be held open at an angle, the opening facing away from the worker. Occasionally, for certain operations, a lid may have to be removed completely. It should be placed, inner surface down, on a clean surface such as a disinfected ceramic tile or on a piece of lint moistened with disinfectant. The lint should only be moist, when fallen drops will diffuse into it. If it is saturated then an aerosol may be produced.

7   Where 'transfer chambers' are used their limitations should be realised. The chambers on the schools market can help to cut down the general level of contamination of a laboratory by microorganisms from the air and dust. They can also provide a clearly delineated 'clean' area for sixth-year work in laboratories that have to be used by other forms. However they are not designed to give protection against potential pathogens. The use of such a chamber does not give protection against the consequences of poor technique. In the event of a spillage, any aerosol or spore cloud formed may be concentrated right under the nose of the operator.

8   Pipettes, including Pasteur pipettes, have their wide ends plugged with non-absorbent cotton wool in an attempt to keep them dust and microbe free. Plugs are easily penetrated by organisms in liquid suspension. A wet plug will obstruct air flow and can be pushed out by air pressure followed by a gush of liquid. For this reason, pipettes are never used in the mouth. A variety of simple devices is available for drawing fluid into a pipette. For quantitative work either sterile disposable syringes or graduated glass pipettes, heat sterilised in aluminium foil and operated by an autoclavable rubber bulb or similar device, should be used. For some applications, inexpensive micropipettors and autoclavable tips are appropriate.

9   Where 'stock cultures' are kept, they should be checked for contamination before use by plating out a subculture and examining it for mixed growth. Whenever mixed cultures are found, the stock should be destroyed by autoclaving it and a fresh culture obtained. The long term maintenance and storage of cultures in schools is not generally recommended.

10   At the end of practical work, the bench should again be disinfected (see **1**).

16   WORKING WITH DNA

This is a new Topic.

IMPORTANT NOTE   This guidance has been prepared to provide advice on the Genetically Modified Organisms (Contained Use) Regulations 2000[1]. At the time of publication, the new Regulations have just been considered by ministers so this Topic may be subject to amendment when the Regulations are published and implemented. *If amendments to the Regulations are made in the future, details will be provided on the National Centre for Biotechnology Education (NCBE) website: www.ncbe.reading.ac.uk, and also on the ASE website.*

1 Introduction

Work with DNA is central to much current research in the biological sciences and to developments in modern biotechnology. There is growing public awareness of DNA technologies, their current and potential applications and the wider issues that they engender.

The science upon which these technologies are founded, and the wider concerns associated with them, feature in nearly every UK course specification in biology or science. Surveys have repeatedly shown support from both parents and pupils alike for the inclusion of modern DNA technology in the science curriculum [1, 2] (see page 105).

Despite the incorporation of the basic concepts of genetic modification into both the National Curriculum of England and Wales [3] and post-16 biology specifications for well over a decade, pupils' understanding of modern genetics generally remains poor [4, 5]. The controversy surrounding DNA technology often centres on disagreement about its potential consequences, which demands an understanding of the relevant sciences [6]. Thus Lewis *et al.* [7] found that while students of school age were able to discuss issues arising from the use of DNA technology, their misunderstandings of the underlying science made it difficult for them to come to well-reasoned and informed opinions. More recent research by Hill *et al.* [8] has hinted that students may respond negatively to teaching about genetic modification if its implications are not considered alongside the science.

Clearly, given its potential impact, there is a need for better all-round education about DNA technology. The role of practical work in developing students' understanding is complex and poorly understood. It is nevertheless accepted as an essential feature of school-based science education in most developed countries and has been strongly advocated by educationalists in the UK.

In the UK, both *Science and Plants for Schools* (SAPS) and the *National Centre for Biotechnology Education* (NCBE) have been active in promoting practical biotechnology in schools [9, 10, 11, 12]. However, practical work involving DNA has been slow to catch on in UK schools compared with several other northern European countries and the USA [13, 14, 15]. There are numerous reasons for this, a key one being uncertainty over health and safety. This has not been helped by ambiguous and inconsistent advice from school health and safety publications [16, 17].

This Topic is part of an attempt to put the record straight. Readers should be aware that policy in this area is developing. In cases of doubt, teachers should follow guidance from their employers and, if necessary, also consult one of the recognised school science health and safety organisations.

2 Naked DNA

DNA only gains a biological function by being inserted into a living cell. Hence work with DNA itself ('naked' DNA) is not generally thought to constitute a health hazard even if new nucleic acid molecules are formed. Risks associated with most activities that might foreseeably be undertaken with naked DNA in school laboratories, such as gel electrophoresis, cutting with restriction enzymes, ligation and the polymerase chain reaction (PCR) can therefore be controlled by normal good laboratory practice.

The one exception to this is full-length copies of viral DNA that are infectious in their own right. These are legally regarded as microorganisms even when they are not encapsulated or enveloped [18]. This means that if full-length viral DNA (such as DNA from phage lambda) were to be combined with DNA from other

---

[1]   HSE (2000) L29 *A guide to the genetically-modified organisms (contained use) Regulations 2000.* HSE Books. ISBN 0 7176 1758 0.

sources, a genetically-modified organism would have been created. For such work to be undertaken legally, the premises would have to be registered with the Health and Safety Executive (HSE). A brief summary of the regulations governing such work is given in section 3.4.

2.1 DNA extraction

Simple practical tasks such as the extraction of DNA from microorganisms, plant or animal tissue, e.g. fish roe, may all be carried out, adopting relevant laboratory health and safety precautions. For instance, where microorganisms are involved, it is important to observe good microbiological practice. If DNA is to be extracted from human tissue, e.g. cheek cells, for amplification by the PCR, the sampling procedure must be designed to minimise the risk of the transmission of infective agents between participants (for example, students should only work with their own DNA samples). It should also be borne in mind that crude extracts of DNA may still contain allergens or toxins present in the source material and must therefore be handled appropriately, e.g. if the seeds of a plant that contains a toxic alkaloid have been used.

The extraction of DNA from calf thymus tissue is sometimes referred to in school texts, although since the advent of BSE and variant CJD, there is a risk (albeit small) of accidental exposure to the infectious agent while the extract is being prepared. Beef thymus is, however, now classified as 'specified offal' under the *Specified Bovine Offal Order* 1995, which means that butchers and abattoirs are most unlikely to supply this tissue for schools to use in practical studies.

2.2 DNA from laboratory suppliers

DNA from a variety of organisms is available from molecular biology and school suppliers. Sources include bacteriophage lambda, salmon sperm and even cloned human DNA. While these can generally be regarded as safe, DNA from mammalian sources may not have been screened to ensure that it is free from contaminating viruses. It is therefore recommended that such material is not used in schools. In addition, full-length viral DNA that may have been genetically modified must not be used without prior registration with the HSE (see section 3.4).

2.3 Manipulation of DNA *in vitro*

With the exception of full-length viral DNA mentioned above, restriction and ligation of plasmid or other DNA with enzymes, DNA gel electrophoresis and the polymerase chain reaction (PCR) may all be performed in a school laboratory.

2.4 Ethical considerations

Wider issues, including ethical concerns associated with the use of human DNA that may be construed as 'genetic tests', are beyond the scope of this Topic. Teachers should be aware that such issues may arise and ensure that any relevant practical procedure addresses these concerns by, for example, the random mixing of samples or the judicious selection of the DNA sequence to be investigated. Where appropriate, the relevant authorities should be consulted (e.g. the UK Human Genetics Commission: www.hgc.gov.uk).

3 Genetic modification

3.1 What is 'genetic modification'?

Genetic modification is officially defined as 'the alteration of genetic material (DNA or RNA) of an organism by means that could not occur naturally through mating and/or recombination' [18].

3.2 EU Directives and UK Regulations

Throughout most of the world, the use of all live genetically-modified organisms (GMOs) is controlled by law. There are currently two relevant sets of directives governing genetic modification throughout the European Union. Laws in the United Kingdom have been enacted to comply with these directives. In England, Wales and Scotland, genetic modification of organisms in containment, e.g. work in a laboratory, is governed by the *Genetically Modified Organisms (Contained Use) Regulations, 2000* [18]. Northern Ireland has its own separate but virtually identical legislation. Similarly, within Great Britain and Northern Ireland there are separate regulations covering deliberate releases of GMOs into the environment, e.g. field trials of genetically-modified crops. It is important to note that it is not the *techniques* of genetic modification that are controlled, but rather *activities with living organisms that are produced by these techniques.*

3.3 Microbial transformation

In the school context, work falling within the scope of these Regulations is most likely to involve the 'transformation' of microorganisms, that is, the introduction of DNA into microorganisms by 'artificial' means. For pre-university educational work, this almost always involves the use of plasmid DNA. Plasmids are small rings of DNA comprising just a few genes, that are found in bacteria and yeasts. They are not normally essential for the microbes, but they may help them to survive in rare and exotic environments. For instance, some plasmids enable the bacteria that carry them to resist the toxic effects of heavy metals or antibiotics, or

Table 1 Analysis of some educational activities involving DNA for the hazards and risks, and the preventative or protective measures required to limit risks. Adapted from Richardson, J. (1995) [19].

Type and source of hazard	Nature of the risk	Type of activity in which risks may arise	Means of limiting risks
CHEMICAL HAZARDS			
Antibiotics	Toxicity	Preparation and use of media for maintaining microbial cultures that harbour plasmids; selective media for transformation experiments.	Selection of appropriate antibiotics. Scale of use and dilution. Care in handling powdered antibiotics when preparing solutions to avoid contact and raising dusts, e.g. use a fume cupboard and wear eye protection and suitable gloves. Destruction before disposal by autoclaving.
Buffer solutions	Toxicity; irritancy	Making up solutions for extracting or dissolving DNA or for gel electrophoresis.	Choice of buffer type; use of prepared solutions needing only dilution; limited scale of use. Precautions such as the use of a fume cupboard and gloves where appropriate.
Detergents	Allergenic reactions	Making up solutions from concentrates or powders. Use to break down membranes when extracting DNA, etc.	Detergent type SDS (sodium dodecyl sulfate (also known as sodium lauryl sulfate)) as used in domestic detergents, shampoos, etc.); dilution; limited scale of use.
DNAs	Infection from certain types of viral DNA or from contaminants	Making up and handling DNA solutions and digests.	With the types of DNA used in the kits designed for schools, e.g. plant and phage lambda, the risks are insignificant. Avoid potentially hazardous sources.
DMF (N,N-dimethyl formamide)	Toxicity	DMF is a solvent for X-Gal which is often employed as an indicator in microbiological media used for transformation experiments.	Prepare solutions in a fume cupboard. Wear eye protection and gloves. Limit the scale of use. Store DMF in appropriate conditions.
Dyes and stains	Toxicity; allergenic reactions	Staining DNA fragments on electrophoresis gels.	School kits typically use thiazin dyes such as methylene blue or Azure A and B, or Nile blue sulfate for staining DNA. Avoid breathing in the powders when making up solutions, e.g. use a fume cupboard and control spills. Keep dyes off the skin – gloves of an appropriate type may be needed. Avoid the use of other stains such as ethidium bromide (which is a mutagen).
Enzymes	Allergenic reactions	Restriction enzymes used to cut DNA. Proteases used when extracting DNA.	Scale and containment: only very small quantities of restriction enzymes are used. Spills of protease should be rinsed with water and wiped up promptly.
Ethanol	Toxicity and fire Explosion	Stains such as methylene blue used in ethanolic solution.	Limited scale – small volume technique. Keep off skin – use gloves of a suitable type.
		Precipitating DNA extracts.	When preparing cold ethanol, ensure that it is placed in a sealed, vapour-tight container to avoid explosions in non-spark-proof freezers.

(continued)

Type and source of hazard	Nature of the risk	Type of activity in which risks may arise	Means of limiting risks
Electrophoresis gels	Toxicity (if polyacryl-amide gels are cast) Burns or scalds from molten gels	Making up and using gels.	Make agarose gels only and follow good practice in preparation. Exercise caution if using a microwave oven to liquefy gel – do not use sealed containers and beware of superheated liquids which may froth up unexpectedly. If polyacrylamide gels are used, do not make up or cast your own – buy them ready-made.

MICROBIAL HAZARDS

Type and source of hazard	Nature of the risk	Type of activity in which risks may arise	Means of limiting risks
Bacteria, fungi	Infection; genetic transfer; accidental release of a GMO into the environment	Transformation.	The use of appropriate non-pathogenic strains, and non-mobile genetic elements, coupled with good micro-biological practice. All cultures must be destroyed by autoclaving after use. **IMPORTANT!** Non-self cloning work requires registration with the HSE and the establishment of a GMSC; see section 3.4.
Pathogenic microorganisms including viruses	Infection	Collection and handling of human DNA samples, e.g., from cheek cells for amplification by the PCR.	Ensure that the sampling method is non-invasive and the procedure is explicitly designed to prevent cross-infection.
		Preparation of DNA extracts from bovine thymus glands.	Since the occurance of BSE and variant CJD, bovine thymus tissue should no longer be available and should not be used in schools.
DNAs other than those provided in school kits, especially if unknown or incompletely characterised	Infection (more likely – transfection) via skin with viral DNA contaminants	Extraction of DNA	Use only UK school kits. Good microbiological practice should reduce risks from other material to an acceptable minimum.

ELECTRICAL HAZARDS

Type and source of hazard	Nature of the risk	Type of activity in which risks may arise	Means of limiting risks
Gel electrophoresis tanks and power supplies	Electrical shock, burns and fire	Connecting and disconnecting power supplies and using gel tanks. The buffer solution is highly conductive and gels are directly handled within it. Gels may have to be run unattended overnight.	Use low voltage (< 50 V) supplies from dry cells or a well-designed mains-to-low voltage and low-current device. If higher voltages are used to shorten run times, professionally-designed apparatus must be employed (e.g., *interlocked* tank terminals; current limited; *shrouded* leads). Teachers' use only, unless pupils are aged over 16 years and trained.

OTHER PHYSICAL HAZARDS

Type and source of hazard	Nature of the risk	Type of activity in which risks may arise	Means of limiting risks
Centrifuges	Physical injuries	Centrifuging extracts and DNA, e.g. in the extraction of plasmid, nuclear and chloroplast DNA.	Proper use of a centrifuge of an appropriate design, with the correct type of tubes, observing the usual precautions.
Microwave ovens	Explosion of sealed containers; burns and scalds from hot containers and liquids	Preparation of microbiological media and agarose gels.	Ensure that containers are not sealed and that hot containers and liquids are handled with great care, e.g. wear heat-proof gloves.
Ultraviolet radiation (UVR)	Carcinogenic effects on skin. Damage to eyes	Examining stained gels using short-wave UVR.	If the use of ethidium bromide (mutagenic) is avoided, short-wave UVR will not be needed.

to live on particular nutrients. Sequences of DNA can be 'spliced' into plasmids, allowing them to be used as vectors for transferring genes between organisms.

Numerous practical kits have been developed for demonstrating microbial transformation. These are particularly common in the USA where they have become a routine part of high school biology courses. A search of the World Wide Web will unearth many sites describing practical exercises for schools.

IMPORTANT NOTE

Although many of these procedures may be freely used in the USA, within the European Union such work is more strictly regulated, and teachers could easily be in breach of the law were they or their students to carry out the majority of the genetic modification exercises that are currently described on the Web.

3.4 Working with DNA in the UK

Under the UK Regulations referred to in section 3.2, before genetic modification (other than 'self cloning', as defined in section 3.5) is undertaken, the premises involved must be registered with, and approved by, the HSE. There is a fee for this and, in addition, a local 'Genetic Modification Safety Committee' (GMSC) will need to be established, consisting of individuals who are suitably qualified to advise on any risks to human health and the environment of all activities before they begin. Records of such risk assessments must be retained for at least 10 years after the relevant activity has ceased. **Schools wishing to undertake such work are advised to contact the HSE for further details.**

These stringent requirements would seem to preclude most schools from carrying out practical genetic modification. There is, however, one important exception to this rule, namely, 'self cloning'.

3.5 'Self cloning'

Microbial transformation in which DNA (or RNA) is returned to a species in which it could naturally occur is known technically (and rather confusingly) as 'self cloning'. In this context, 'cloning' means making copies of plasmid DNA within an organism. Because the plasmids used are made entirely from DNA that could occur naturally within the species involved, the work is called 'self cloning'.

The official definition of self cloning runs as follows:

... the removal of nucleic acid sequences from a cell ... followed by the re-insertion of all or part of that nucleic acid ... into cells of the same species or into cells of phylogenetically closely-related species with which it can exchange genetic material by homologous recombination.' [18]

In other words, if the transfer of genetic information is largely confined to that which could naturally occur within a single species, the work is regarded as 'self cloning'. The nucleic acid may have been subject to modification by enzymic, chemical or mechanical steps so as to produce a novel order of genes or bases, to remove sequences, to produce multiple gene copies, etc.

Self cloning, *where the resulting organism is unlikely to cause disease in humans, animals or plants*, is *exempt* from the 'Contained Use' Regulations. Schools and others may therefore undertake such work without licensing their premises or setting up a GMSC. However, somewhat unusually (since these microbes could in theory be found in nature), the organisms produced *are* covered by the 'Deliberate Release' Regulations.

3.6 Containment

Under current legislation it is an offence to release any GMO into the environment or to allow it to escape without prior consent of the Secretary of State. It is therefore essential that even 'self-cloned' organisms are adequately contained and that a 'release' does not occur. A key point is that an accidental release of a GMO might be considered to be deliberate if the steps taken to ensure containment are deemed to have been inadequate. Note that if a GMO cannot survive in, or transmit genes to, other organisms in the environment, it is regarded as being 'biologically contained', and an accidental escape is *not* regarded as a 'release'.

Fortunately, containment can be ensured simply by following good microbiological practice (e.g. effective aseptic technique and autoclaving materials before disposal) and good occupational safety and hygiene, coupled with the careful selection of suitable host organisms and plasmids. The latter would usually involve, for example, using host strains that are weakened and 'non-mobilisable' plasmids that cannot transfer their genes into the host's chromosome, or be transferred into other organisms by natural means such as bacterial conjugation.

Kits from reputable suppliers (e.g. from the NCBE), that have been designed for use in UK schools, should comply with these requirements.

3.7 Host strains

The species of bacterium that is most commonly used for cloning work is *Escherichia coli,* strain K 12. Unlike the wild type, K 12 strains of *E. coli* are usually unable to inhabit the mammalian gut. This strain's origins can be traced back to work in the USA in 1922. Biochemical and genetic studies by Edward Tatum in the 1940s made the strain popular with researchers and, after many millions of generations of laboratory cultivation, it is now known to have undergone significant changes. These have altered the lipopolysaccharides that comprise the outer membrane of the bacterial cell, so that it can no longer infect mammals.

Many strains of *E. coli* K 12 have been specially selected for transformation work. Usually these do not harbour any extra-chromosomal DNA of their own, but can be transformed efficiently by plasmids. Compared to the wild type *E. coli*, these 'cloning strains' are severely weakened and would find it difficult to thrive outside the laboratory. They may have unusual nutritional requirements, and are often susceptible to damage, e.g. from the ultraviolet component of sunlight.

3.8 Plasmids

Plasmids can pass from one bacterial cell to another of the same or a related species by a natural 'mating' process called conjugation. During conjugation, a tube (pilus) is formed between adjacent cells, through which the plasmid passes. The genes required for the formation of the pilus are also carried on a plasmid (an F or fertility plasmid). Host strains used for transformation experiments in schools usually have no F plasmid, so that they cannot pass on genetic material by conjugation. They often also lack phages, so that DNA cannot be picked up and passed on by viral infection (transduction).

The use of non-conjugative strains of bacteria that lack phages, coupled with the use of non-mobilisable plasmids (see section 3.9), significantly reduces the risk of DNA being transferred between microorganisms, and hence the unwanted transfer of characteristics such as antibiotic resistance [20].

The transformation of bacterial cells with plasmid DNA is very inefficient and only a small proportion of the cells treated will take up the DNA. Therefore a means of selecting those cells that have been transformed is needed. The incorporation of one or more antibiotic-resistance genes into the plasmid DNA used to transform cells is the commonest method of achieving this. In the presence of appropriate antibiotics, such plasmid-bearing cells thrive while their less well-endowed (untransformed) neighbours perish. In this way, selection pressure is applied to maintain the plasmid in the population of cells. Without that pressure, the few transformed cells would be swamped by their untransformed neighbours.

3.9 Missing genes

For a plasmid to travel through a pilus, two additional requirements must be met. The plasmid must possess a gene encoding a mobility protein *(mob)* and have a *nic* site. The mobility protein nicks the plasmid at the *nic* site, attaches to it there and conducts the plasmid through the pilus. Plasmids for school demonstration

experiments usually have neither a *nic* site nor the *mob* gene. This means that once a plasmid has been introduced into a bacterial cell by artificial means (transformation), it cannot naturally transfer (by conjugation) into other cells that do not possess it.

3.10 Incubation at 37 °C

Although model risk assessments for microbiological work normally warn against incubating cultures at 37 °C to avoid the growth of contaminating pathogens, the delicate strains of *E. coli* used for cloning work often will not grow quickly or reliably unless maintained at this temperature. Good microbiological practice, coupled with the use of selective growth media, will ensure that contaminating human pathogens are not inadvertently cultivated at this temperature.

3.11 Physical and chemical containment

In addition to the biological containment measures described above, good microbiological practice must be followed to ensure that the microorganisms are physically and chemically contained during the investigation and destroyed afterwards. UK law requires that genetically-modified microorganisms must be inactivated after use by a *validated* means. In practice in a school, this means that any cultures must be destroyed by autoclaving them.

The containment and the destruction of cells when such work is undertaken will prevent the spread of antibiotic-resistant populations. In addition, most of the antibiotics used for such work are heat-labile and readily break down when media are autoclaved after use.

Together, these methods of physical, chemical and biological containment will ensure that educational exercises which demonstrate the principles of genetic modification are as safe as possible.

4 Useful addresses

For addresses of CLEAPSS and SSERC, see 'Introduction' page 2.

National Centre for Biotechnology Education (NCBE)
The University of Reading, Whiteknights, PO Box 228, Reading RG6 6AJ.
Tel: 0118 987 3743
Fax: 0118 975 0140
E-mail: NCBE@reading.ac.uk
Website: www.ncbe.reading.ac.uk

Microbiology in Schools Advisory Committee (MISAC).

c/o Society for General Microbiology (SGM)
Marlborough House, Basingstoke Road, Spencer's
Wood, Reading RG7 1AG.
Tel: 0118 988 1835
Fax: 0118 988 5656
E-mail: education@sgm.ac.uk
Website: www.biosci.org.uk/MISAC

Science and Plants for Schools (SAPS)

Homerton College, Hills Road, Cambridge CB2 2PH
Tel: 01223 507168
Fax: 01223 215004
E-mail: hom-saps@lists.cam.ac.uk
Website: www-saps.plantsci.cam.ac.uk

5 Suppliers of plasmids, cultures, etc.

Plasmids and cells for transformation experiments
should only be obtained from recognised suppliers.

Some bacterial strains that are commonly used for
transformation experiments lack an enzyme required for
DNA repair, and this means that they can be subject to
mutations if they are maintained on slope cultures.
Fresh cultures should therefore be obtained as required
from suppliers, rather than being maintained in school.
This will ensure that the host cells are the correct
species and strain and thereby avoid disappointment or
the inadvertent transformation of contaminating
microorganisms.

As noted above, many of the kits and protocols supplied
by US firms may not be appropriate for use in UK
schools. Even if a school was to register with the HSE
so that it could undertake non-self cloning work, most
of the US school kits currently provide insufficient
information about the host strains and/or plasmid
construction for an adequate risk assessment to be
made.

6 References

1. IGD (1997) *Consumer attitudes to genetically-modified foods.* Institute of Grocery Distribution, Watford.

2. Osborne, J. and Collins, S. (2000) Pupils *and parents' views of the school science curriculum.* A study funded by The Wellcome Trust. King's College London.

3. Department for Education and Employment and the Qualifications and Curriculum Authority (1999) *The National Curriculum. Key Stages 3 and 4.* Stationery Office. Website: www.nc.uk.net

4. House of Commons Science and Technology Committee (1995) *Third Report – Human Genetics: The Science and its Consequences, Volume 1.* HMSO.

5. Lock, R., Miles, C. and Hughes, S. (1995) The influence of teaching on knowledge and attitudes in biotechnology and genetic engineering contexts: implications for teaching controversial issues and the public understanding of science. *School Science Review,* 76(276), 47–59.

6. Straughan, R. and Reiss, M. (1996) *Improving Nature? The science and ethics of genetic engineering.* Cambridge: Cambridge University Press.

7. Lewis, J. M., Driver, R. H., Leach, I. T. and Wood-Robinson, C. (1997) *Opinions on and attitudes towards genetic engineering. Acceptable limits: a discussion task. Working Paper 7 of the Young People's Understanding of, and Attitudes to, 'The New Genetics' Project.* Centre for Studies in Science and Mathematics Education, The University of Leeds.

8. Hill, R., Stanistreet, M. and Boyes, E. (2000) What ideas do students associate with 'biotechnology' and 'genetic engineering'? *School Science Review.* 81(297), 77–83.

9. Madden, D. (ed) (1995) *Investigating plant DNA* (2nd edn). National Centre for Biotechnology Education, The University of Reading. Web site: www.ncbe.reading.ac.uk.

10. Madden, D. (1996) *The Lambda Protocol* (2nd edn). National Centre for Biotechnology Education, University of Reading. Website: www.ncbe.reading.ac.uk.

11. Madden, D. (2000) *Illuminating DNA.* National Centre for Biotechnology Education, University of Reading. Website: www.ncbe.reading.ac.uk.

12. Madden, D. (2000) *The Transformer Protocol.* National Centre for Biotechnology Education, University of Reading. Website: www.ncbe.reading.ac.uk.

13. Micklos, D. and Freyer, G. (1990) *DNA Science. A first course in recombinant DNA technology.* Carolina Biological Supply Company/Cold Spring Harbor Laboratory Press.

14. Bloom, M., Freyer, G. and Micklos, D. (1996) *Laboratory DNA Science. An introduction to recombinant DNA techniques and methods of genome analysis.* The Benjamin/Cummings Publishing Company.

15. Agensen, H. *et al.* (1992) *Experimental gene technology in education* [English edition]. Nucleus Forlag ApS, Studsgade 28, 8000 Arhus C, Denmark.

16. DES (1985; 1990) *Microbiology. An HMI guide for schools and further education.* HMSO.

17. DfEE (1996) *Safety in science education.* Stationery Office.

18. HSE (2000) L29 *A guide to the genetically-modified organisms (contained use) Regulations 2000.* HSE Books. ISBN 0 7176 1758 0.

19. Richardson, J. (1995) Practical work with DNA. *Education in Science,* 162, 16–18.

20. Timms-Wilson, T. M, Lilley, A. K. and Bailey, M. J. (1999) *A review of gene transfer from genetically-modified microorganisms.* Stationery Office. [Health and Safety Executive Contract Research Report 221/1999]

21. *ACGM Compendium of Guidance. Guidance from the Health and Safety Commission's Advisory Committee on Genetic Modification* (2000). Stationery Office. Website: www.hse.gov.uk.

This topic replaces Chapter 3 of the second edition. It was retained mainly because the HSE Guidance Note GS 23, Electrical Safety in Schools (see Appendix 3) is no longer in print (although the HSE considers its guidance is still valid) and is unlikely to be revised in the near future. The Topic, which owes much to GS 23, may be superseded if new HSE guidance becomes available.

1 Electrical hazards

An electric current flowing through a human body presents a hazard in two ways. Small currents interfere with the electrochemical mechanisms of the nervous system and produce the effects known as *electric shock*. A large current, in addition, causes a heating effect and destroys tissue as in a *burn* caused by contact with a hot object.

The skin of adults provides a layer of insulation which is remarkably effective when hard and dry. The soft skin of a child, especially when wet, provides a much lower resistance. If the skin is cut and in contact with a conducting liquid (such as salt water), the resistance becomes low and dangerous currents can flow with quite low voltages. Because of the variation of electrical resistance between persons (and for the same person under different conditions), it is very difficult to define a dangerous voltage. While lower voltages can be dangerous in exceptional circumstances, only supplies greater than 40 V dc (or peak ac) are normally regarded as sufficiently dangerous in schools to warrant protection[1].

An electric current which flows, say, from one finger to another on the same hand is unlikely to prove fatal, although a serious burn could result. A current which flows through the brain, or which interferes with the nerve centres controlling the heart or breathing, may easily be fatal. In any accident where a current passes from one hand to the other or via the trunk to a foot, it is likely that breathing and the heart will be arrested and first aid[2] required while an ambulance is awaited.

1.1 Overheating of cables

Another hazard is the overloading of the electrical supply, a situation which is unlikely to occur in a school laboratory. This could happen if the heating failed and a large number of electric fires were brought into one room. This should cause the overload circuit breaker (either a fuse or an electromagnetically-operated switch) to operate before any damage can occur. Overloading of the **supply** is unlikely to be caused by an internal fault within a power unit, for example, but it could cause the unit to draw so much current from the supply that its lead became hot. This condition should be prevented by the fuse in the plug but, all too often, one finds a 13 A plug fitted with a 13 A fuse when a 3 A one would be correct. (See section 7.3 for advice on fuses.)

2 Batteries

Strictly, a **battery** is a number of separate **cells** connected together; so that a 12 V car battery (for example) consists of six 2 V cells in series. However, to most users, it is not significant whether the source of electrical power contains a number of cells or only one. All batteries produce a voltage when delivering very little current which is characteristic of the electrodes used in their construction. For example, zinc and carbon electrodes give a characteristic 1.5 V, while nickel and cadmium electrodes give 1.2 V.

All batteries have an internal resistance, which means that when they are delivering a current the terminal voltage is reduced by an amount equal to the product of that current and the internal resistance. This also means that some of the power is used inside the battery so increasing its temperature. The battery manufacturers have made tremendous efforts to control the internal resistance and so to minimise the wasted power. However, this means that there is now a wide choice of battery type to suit different applications.

All batteries convert chemical energy to electrical energy but the details of the chemistry used in commercial cells is often a closely-guarded trade secret. However, there

---

[1] The definition of 'hazardous live' used in British (and other) Standards is much more complicated than this, allowing for the differing effects of ac and dc and capacitative sources. While a physicist should have no difficulty with such detail, other science teachers could find it confusing and the simpler approach adopted here is likely to be accessible to all.

[2] First-aid posters are available from the local offices of The Red Cross, St John Ambulance Brigade, St Andrews Ambulance Association or The Royal Society for the Prevention of Accidents. Reminders are given in *Safeguards in the School Laboratory,* Chapter 17.

are some general principles which are in most school texts. Primary cells are designed so that once a particular chemical has all reacted, the cell ceases to work and it must be thrown away. Secondary cells are designed so that the essential chemical reaction is reversible, so that the cell may be re-charged by passing an electric current through it in the direction opposite to that which flows when the cell is delivering power. It is unwise to attempt to recharge a cell which is not designed to have a reversible chemical reaction; to do so may cause a build-up of pressure (see 2.1). There are ways of forcing the reaction in a primary cell to reverse but this presents a risk of pressure rise unless the cell is vented as discussed below.

2.1 Hazards

Batteries are unlikely to produce a high enough voltage to give rise to shocks or burns but they do present particular hazards of their own.

The electrodes are in electrical contact with an electrolyte which, in most cases, is a paste rather than a liquid. Nevertheless, if the cell is heated (perhaps because it is delivering a large current) some water from the paste will evaporate. In some cells, whether they are driving a current or not, electrolysis occurs causing some gas to be generated. For both of these reasons there can be a build-up of pressure inside the cell and, where this is anticipated by the manufacturer, a vent may be provided to release gases to the atmosphere and allow the pressure to fall again.

When there is no vent or the pressure builds up too quickly for the vent to cope, the cell or cells may burst explosively. The electrolyte in many cell designs is alkaline and if a drop of this paste enters the eye it must be washed out thoroughly to prevent injury[3]. The bang of the explosion can be quite frightening but is not likely to expel parts with sufficient force to cause injury.

2.2 Minimising the risks

Clearly, the risks of an explosion will be minimised if a build-up of pressure is unlikely. The oldest type of dry battery, based on the Leclanché cell, uses zinc and carbon electrodes with an ammonium chloride electrolyte. If this type of cell is placed in a circuit of low resistance (i.e. if it is short-circuited or just required to produce a large current), the electrolytic effects cause the cell to 'polarise' as hydrogen is produced. This causes the voltage to drop and the current to fall to a low level or even to zero. The manganese(IV) oxide (manganese dioxide) in the cell takes time to remove the hydrogen but then the cell will work again. Batteries using this type of cell are very unlikely to explode and are suitable for use by children under conditions where

short circuits are likely. They are sold for 'low current' or 'intermittent use'. EverReady cells of this type are coloured blue but they are not now readily available.

The zinc chloride cell uses different chemistry and depolarises more rapidly. It has lower internal resistance and can supply larger currents for longer than the 'blue' cell. Batteries of these cells are also unlikely to explode and are suitable for torches or other medium duties. EverReady call these cells 'silver seal' and they are widely available.

Alkaline manganese cells have a low internal resistance and depolarise very quickly, making them suitable for heavy duties such as driving motors as in cassette players. These cells are often labelled 'high power' and EverReady cells are coloured gold or have a gold line. Individual cells in batteries of this type have been known to explode but this probably happens only when the cells have not been used equally (by borrowing one or more of the group for use elsewhere).

If cells of different types or different histories are used in the same circuit, the risk of an explosion is greatly increased because the more powerful cells can force currents through the others, producing electrolysis and heating with the inevitable pressure build-up.

Finally, rechargeable cells, whatever their design, have the lowest internal resistance and do not suffer from polarisation. Consequently, they can supply really large currents; for example, it is possible to make a 1.5 V nickel-cadmium rechargeable cell drive a current of 40 A through a low resistance circuit for a short time. Such cells should never be used by children who are likely to create short circuits accidentally, although the hot connecting wires could provide a learning experience they are unlikely to forget! Some specially-designed alkaline manganese cells have a chemical reaction which is reversible and so they can be re-charged; a special charger is required.

3 Electrostatic machines

There are several designs of machines which produce electrostatic charges at very high potentials and which have been used in schools. Among these are frictional machines and the Wimshurst machine but the most commonly used one now is the van de Graaff generator.

3.1 Hazards

All of these machines can produce hundreds of thousands of volts but the quantity of charge (on a school-sized machine) is so small that the electric shock is not harmful to a normal healthy person. Someone who is about to suffer a heart attack anyway might have it brought on sooner by such a shock.

---

[3] This is the reason that no one should cut open cells using alkaline electrolytes.

3.2 Minimising the risks

Clearly, for the reason above, persons participating in experiments with a van de Graaff generator should, so far as is known, be in good health. Moreover, any attempt to increase the capacitance of the charged conductor could increase the charge and increase the risk. There has been a report that when **two** insulated children were holding hands and charged together from a van de Graaff generator, the shock experienced by the child who earthed the pair was distinctly unpleasant. It is therefore sensible to charge only one person at one time and other attempts to change the shock level would be unwise. It is considered inappropriate to attempt to repeat the experiments of Henry Cavendish, who gave himself shocks from systems of different capacitance and learned to judge the severity with sufficient accuracy to use himself as an ammeter and anticipate Ohm's Law by about a century.

4 Low-voltage power supplies

4.1 Hazards

The term 'low voltage' in schools is used to describe those sources of electrical power which are totally safe in normal use and cannot drive a current through a human body large enough to produce an electric shock or any other dangerous effect[4]. However, a low-voltage (or low-tension) power supply usually takes in power from the mains at 230 V and converts it to the safe low value required. The box therefore has a mains lead and contains several components at least parts of which are at mains voltage, presenting the hazards of the mains supply as below.

4.2 Minimising the risks

The risk of these hazards giving rise to harm result from either poor initial design or deterioration due to wear and tear. The ASE, CLEAPSS and SSERC have been working for many years to see that manufacturers who produce or import such goods of poor design are helped to improve them. In spite of this continuing effort, some items occasionally reach the market which are not designed to those high standards necessary to protect the students who will use them and those ordering equipment have a duty (under the Provision and Use of Work Equipment Regulations and other legislation) to check the safety and suitability of the items for their intended use.

Employers have a duty (under the Electricity at Work Regulations 1989) to ensure that the equipment is maintained in a safe condition. This is usually achieved by regular checks and tests as for other portable electrical appliances.

5 High-tension power supplies

High-tension or high-voltage power supplies are characterised by the ability to supply significant currents, perhaps up to 150 mA, at potentials of more than 40 V and up to about 500 V dc. These units are used for Millikan's experiment, certain discharge tubes (such as some Teltron tubes) and for high-voltage electrophoresis. They should be handled only by staff and A-level students and then with extreme care. They should never be used by more junior students even if only the low-voltage outputs are to be used.

5.1 Hazards

The output from such a supply can produce electric shocks just as lethal as the mains supply and must be treated with proper precautions. Again, the unit normally has a mains lead and contains several components at mains voltage, presenting the hazards of the mains supply.

5.2 Minimising the risks

The risks from the output are controlled by ensuring that the user is aware of the hazardous nature of the supply and by the use of shrouded connectors[5] to minimise chance contact with live conductors. No attempt to change the circuit should be made without first switching off the supply and students using such supplies must be instructed not to switch on initially until the circuit has been checked by staff. In some situations this may mean that the use of HT power supplies must be restricted to named members of staff[6].

Electrophoresis apparatus for high-voltage use should have suitable interlocks to prevent access to solutions or any other parts at dangerous voltages.

---

[4] On the other hand, to an electrical engineer, ordinary household mains voltage, nominally 230 V ac, is referred to as 'low voltage' compared with those used for power transmission namely, 66 000 V up to 400 000 V on the Supergrid. The electrical engineer would refer to our 'low voltage' as 'safety extra-low voltage' or SELV.

[5] There are two kinds of shrouded 4 mm plugs available: those with fixed shrouds which will only fit matching sockets and those with sprung shrouds which will fit standard 4 mm sockets. Since other devices, e.g. meters, in the HT circuit, will have standard sockets (even if the power supplies have fixed shroud-type sockets), sprung shrouds are advised (e.g. Philip Harris P71810/0 etc.).

[6] Experience shows that staff are much more likely to be injured by HT power supplies than students.

6 Extra-high-tension (EHT) power supplies

A supply which falls into this category has both a high voltage and a low current capability. For example, some school EHT power units are capable of generating over 5000 V dc but the maximum current is limited to less than 5 mA. The power supply for a GM tube is sometimes referred to as an EHT power supply, although it produces probably less than 400 V, because its output current is limited to only a milliamp or so.

6.1 Hazards

While 5 mA will produce an unpleasant shock, it will not be harmful to a normally healthy person. **Any supply without such a current limitation, perhaps obtained from the surplus market, must not be used at all**. Again, the unit normally has a mains lead and contains several components at mains voltage, presenting the hazards of the mains. Some very-low-current EHT units run from a 6 V battery so that even this hazard is avoided.

6.2 Minimising the risks

Provided unlimited supplies are not used, the only significant hazard is that of the mains supply which is minimised by good maintenance.

7 Mains supplies

The most common instance of a hazardous high voltage is, of course, the 230 V ac mains required as a power supply for many items of equipment and occasionally used directly (see section 9). Most school laboratories are now fitted with electricity supplies at mains voltage, some together with safety devices called 'school laboratory earth-leakage protection units' which may give a false sense of security to uninformed users. A standard ring main system is considered by the HSE to provide an appropriate laboratory installation in most cases[7]. In this case, the neutral wire remains close to earth potential, while the line (or live) wire alternates between a positive potential and a negative potential. A 30 A fuse provides adequate protection for the 15 A cable used in the ring because there are two parallel paths from any point on the cable back to the fuse.

NO SAFETY DEVICE CAN PROTECT THE USER AGAINST SHOCKS BETWEEN LINE AND NEUTRAL

In the *School laboratory earth-leakage protection unit*[8], as well as a sensitive residual current device, a transformer is used to separate the supply from the normal earth-referenced mains, and the mid-point (centre-tap) of the secondary of the transformer is connected to earth through a resistor giving two lines (instead of line and neutral). If line 1 is 115 V above earth potential, line 2 is 115 V below it and vice versa. Under normal (no-fault) conditions, the resistor carries no current and the centre tap is at earth potential. If there is a low resistance leak to earth from either line, a current flows through this resistor and, since it has a value of 12 000 Ω, most of the 115 V is developed across it. The leakage current is no greater than 115/12 000, i.e. 9.6 mA, during the fraction of a second before the RCD operates. The risk of injury from electric shock to earth is greatly reduced by the use of such devices. However, instead of one line at 230 V there are two lines each at 115 V. The chance of an earth leakage is therefore doubled but two chances of minor shocks are safer than one chance of a serious one! The HSE suggests that this sort of installation may be helpful where the situation is abnormal such as in special schools or where the rate of vandalism defeats the rate at which the system can be repaired.

NO SAFETY DEVICE CAN PROTECT THE USER AGAINST SHOCKS BETWEEN THE TWO LINES

Provided that the nominal tripping current of the RCD is not more than 5 mA, standard plugs and sockets may be used with this system, i.e. in which the centre tap of the isolating transformer is connected to earth through a resistor of at least 12 000 Ω. This is permitted both by the 16th Edition of the IEE Regulations and the HSE[9].

7.1 Hazards

The mains supply presents all three hazards discussed above: electric shock, burns and overheating of the supply.

7.2 Minimising the risks

There are four methods which are commonly used to minimise the risk of electric shock and electrical burns from the mains:

- the use of a physical barrier to prevent contact with live conductors which are usually separated from that barrier by an air gap

---

7 If further protection is advisable (because the students present particular risks), the HSE suggests the use of residual current devices (RCDs) which are discussed later.

8 Supplied by Blakley Electrics Ltd, Conington Rd, Lewisham, London SE13 7LJ (tel: 020 8852 4383). Originally designed at the request of Lancashire County Council.

9 Non-standard plugs and sockets are needed only in the rare cases when the centre tap is connected directly to earth or the tripping current is greater than 5 mA. There is an apparent conflict between recent amendments to the IEE Regulations and HSE guidance which has resulted in an optional reduction of the centre-tap-to-earth impedance from 12 000 ohm to 3900 ohm. Although such a system does not comply precisely with GS23 as published in February 1990, it is considered that standard socket outlets will not introduce any significant hazard and can be permitted.

- the use of one or more electrically-insulating layers on the conductors to prevent contact

- the use of a conducting cover which is connected to earth and some device (such as a fuse) to break the circuit

- the use of an isolating transformer to make the secondary circuit 'float' with respect to earth.

Each of these has its own particular application. The barrier method is used inside electrical distribution cabinets or boxes where bare conductors may be present. The door should be interlocked with switches such that it can be opened only when the power is off.

All mains leads should now be covered by two layers of insulation and many appliances also rely on this second method for protecting the users. It is frequently referred to as 'double insulation' although there may be only one thick or extra strong layer present. Such appliances have no need for an earth conductor for electrical protection and are often fed through a two-core cable. However, a fuse is still needed to protect against overloads causing the lead to be heated to the point where the insulation melts.

Many items of electrical equipment used in schools have metal cases for robustness. If a live wire inside one of these were to become loose and make contact with the metal, the case would also become live. If the user were then to make good electrical contact with the case, there is the possibility of an electric shock provided the circuit is completed. It is standard practice in the UK for one side of the supply (the 'neutral' wire) to be connected to earth. Consequently, if the user is connected to earth through the feet or a hand, then the circuit will be completed and a shock will result. If, however, the case is given a low-resistance connection to earth, when the wire makes contact with the case a large current will flow down this earth wire which should cause a fuse (or other device) to break the circuit and protect the user.

In a bathroom, the mains supply for shavers, electric-toothbrush chargers and similar appliances is fed through a transformer which isolates both sides of the mains from earth. In this case, a fault which allows the user to make contact with a live wire will not give rise to an electric shock even if the user is well-earthed through wet skin and plumbing because there is no circuit involving earth: the supply is 'floating'.

7.3 Choice of fuse

Many appliances have an input fuse inside the case as well as a fuse in the mains plug. The input fuse is to prevent (to some extent at least) damage to the appliance resulting from misuse or internal faults. The fuse in the mains plug may help in this (particularly if there is no input fuse) but is essentially there to protect the mains lead between the appliance and the plug.

Very few items of school laboratory equipment require more than a 3 A fuse in the plug. The following items may require a larger one:

- electrically-operated stills

- ovens and incubators

- hot plates

- colour television sets

- computer monitors

- projectors

Each of these items should be examined to see if the fuse required is stated on it. If the power is given in watts, the required fuse can be chosen from this table for ordinary (230 V) supplies.

Power	0 to 700 W	to 1.2 kW	to 1.6 kW	to 2.4 kW	to 3.1 kW
Fuse	3 A	5 A	7 A	10 A	13 A

To simplify the choice for the general public, only 3 A and 13 A fuses are on sale in most electrical shops. Any piece of domestic equipment requiring more than 3 A should now have a lead which is adequately protected by a 13 A fuse. This does not mean that all old equipment is so protected. Fuses of intermediate rating are still available from school suppliers.

Some items draw much more current on being switched on than when in normal use. These include some low-voltage power supplies, computer monitors, television sets and projectors. In these cases, the plug fuse will probably be at least twice the value expected from the above table, while the input fuse may be a 'slow-blow' or 'anti-surge' type.

7.4 Additional protection by earth-leakage circuit-breakers

A wooden or traditional tile floor, particularly when damp, provides a reasonable earth connection. A floor covered with plastic tiles or PVC sheet, as in many school laboratories, is a good insulator. A person holding the live case of a faulty instrument may, therefore, receive little or no shock since the current cannot flow to earth through the floor. Moreover, taps and sinks, which once gave good earth connections through the pipes buried in the earth, often no longer do so; waste pipes and supply pipes are now being installed which are constructed of non-conducting plastic materials. It is now quite difficult in many new laboratories to make an accidental connection to earth. This minimises the dangers of electric shocks.

Modern plumbing has a second consequence: water pipes once provided a good electrical earth at the premises of each consumer but, with plastic piping, the resistance of the earth connection back to the street transformer may be too high to allow currents as high as an amp or two to flow. It becomes impracticable, therefore, to rely on fuses or overload circuit-breakers to make the system safe. Earth-leakage circuit-breakers (ELCBs) have therefore been designed to sense these lower fault currents and cause the system to be switched off very rapidly: usually in less than 30 ms.

They are made in a variety of different sensitivities and are given a variety of different names. Those fitted in laboratories are usually of the current-operated type and are called residual current devices (RCDs) or residual current circuit breakers (RCBs[10] or RCCBs). All these units have a TEST button marked 'test often' or 'test monthly'. This button introduces a small earth leakage which tests the transformer and tripping mechanism. If this does not cause the unit to trip, expert attention is required.

A large variety of sensitivities is available. A unit, which trips at earth-leakage currents of 500 mA and above, protects against fires caused by hot connecting leads, etc. A unit which trips at 15 to 30 mA is appropriate for circuits where the impedance of the earth connection is moderate. A unit which trips at about 1 mA would give excellent protection against electric shocks caused by faults to metal cases but it is difficult to achieve this level of sensitivity without extra expense e.g. the *School laboratory earth-leakage protection unit* mentioned above.

However, the protection offered by a residual current device depends as much on the time taken to interrupt the supply as on the minimum current at which tripping will occur: 30 ms is the nominal time for most RCDs. An RCD cannot limit the fault current which flows during this interval: it could be several amperes.

The main disadvantage of fitting an RCD is nuisance tripping. This arises because the heat-proof insulation of some devices with heating elements, such as ovens, kettles and water-baths, permits leakage from line to earth even when in good condition. Further, switching on devices containing electric motors, such as refrigerators and floor polishers, can produce transient leaks due to the capacitors in the motors. These unavoidable leaks are usually a nuisance only if the RCD tripping current is set below 15 mA; unfortunately, some education authorities set lower tripping currents as a matter of policy. Then the only solution is to have some unprotected sockets for these devices, the justification for this being that the devices plugged in to

them are not handled by students. Unprotected sockets should be labelled suitably.

8 Portable appliance inspection and testing

In a modern laboratory with insulated floor and taps, etc., safety still depends on the maintenance of good earth connections to equipment. Consider what happens if the mains cable becomes worn where it enters a piece of apparatus and the live wire touches the case. A fault current flows in the circuit: live wire–case–earth wire–earth–local transformer neutral. (At the local transformer, which may be within the school boundary or in the street nearby, the neutral wire is connected to the earth by means of a metal rod or plate buried in the ground.) To provide safety, the current flowing when the fault occurs should be large enough to blow a fuse. If the instrument has a 3 A fuse in its plug, the current will rise to about 6 A in the fraction of a second before the fuse melts. This current will not produce a large enough heating effect to cause a fire but, if the resistance of the earth circuit is not quite zero, any person holding the case could receive a small electric shock caused by some current flowing through the hand–arm–body–leg–shoe circuit to the earth. It is more likely, however, that the circuit will be completed through the other hand which is holding a correctly earthed unit!

If a fault occurs and the earth connection is imperfect, perhaps because only one strand of the flexible wire remains, the resistance of the earth circuit may be too large to pass the current necessary to blow the fuse quickly. A user could then receive a more serious shock from the equipment. This fault condition is not immediately obvious since a check of the apparatus with an Avometer or a continuity tester would show a circuit from the earth pin on the mains plug to the instrument case. An electrical safety test set, often called an 'earth bond and insulation tester', provides a quick and easy test which fails any instrument with a less-than-adequate earth connection.

This simple pass/fail test can be applied by anyone with a little training in how to use the particular tester available but, much more important, is a **thorough inspection** of the appliance and its connection to the mains. Typically, 95% of the faults in school equipment are found by inspection with only the last 5% detected by the test set.

Much electrical equipment used in schools is now made to the 'double insulation' standard, usually by using a substantial plastic case, and is fitted with a two-core mains lead. It is impractical to subject this equipment to a meaningful test with the portable test equipment

---

[10] The principles used in residual-current circuit-breakers are discussed at length in Orton, R. J. J. (1992) Safety XI The principles of electrical safety. *School Science Review*, **74**(266), 7–17.

available to schools. Consequently, an inspection to check that the case and lead are undamaged is all that is really necessary to ensure its safety.

8.1 Who may do the inspection and test?

The Electricity at Work Regulations require the employer to set up a system to ensure that the electrical supply and the appliances powered by it are maintained in a safe condition. Some employers use a contractor to inspect and test both. Others use a contractor for the supply and their own employees, perhaps persons working in the school, to look after the appliances. It is up to the employer to decide and to provide any training which may be required as a result of that decision. (As with all safety training, the employer must see that it takes place but may require the establishment to pay for it, while employees have a legal duty to attend it.)

8.2 Frequency of inspection and testing

In general, inspection will be more frequent than testing. It is recommended that there should be two levels: informal and formal.

Informal inspection should take place every time equipment is used and it should only take a few seconds to check that there is no visible damage to the plug, the mains lead and the equipment itself.

The formal inspection should take place whenever experience indicates that it is necessary. For equipment like microscope lamps or low-voltage power supplies, which are used and moved frequently, a formal inspection should take place every term or half-term. For equipment which is rarely moved (even though it is used frequently) or rarely used, the inspection could be done only when a formal test is also done. This inspection should involve a check list and some sort of record (see Appendices 1 and 2).

The frequency of testing can again be flexible. Some employers have decided that it shall be done annually while others allow variation so that the items least at risk are only tested perhaps every five years while others are tested annually. This will depend to some extent on the availability of the 'earth bond and insulation test' set[11], on whether it is held by the establishment or has to be borrowed for a short period. The employer is expected to make the rules in order to satisfy the requirement of the Electricity at Work Regulations by ensuring that the appliances are safe to use.

8.3 Testing computer equipment

Many modern computers and monitors have plastic cases with a metal chassis inside. If there are no external conductors which are in electrical contact with the internal chassis, the item can be regarded as 'double-insulated' and be subjected to an inspection without a test. If there are metal screens around connections, perhaps carrying video signals between units, these should **not** be subjected to the ordinary earth continuity test – it could damage the connections to them. Some test sets have a special low-current test for this purpose but its value is debatable since these screens should never become live anyway.

If the metal chassis is accessible, then the ordinary earth-bonding test can be carried out to the chassis. Most computers will **fail** the insulation test, however, because there are mains interference filters built into them which allow small currents to flow between the line and earth. Clearly, the computer should not be regarded as unsafe because of this!

9 Special items

Many of these special cases are only done as teacher demonstrations because of their hazardous nature but teachers must remember that they have a duty to look after their own safety as well as that of students. Showing students how safety can be achieved in such cases is an important part of their education.

A draft of this advice was discussed with a Principal Electrical Inspector of the HSE and modified as a result. He stressed the importance of a safety screen between high-voltage conductors and students, and advised that the 230 V supply for the demonstrations described should be obtained either through a mains-isolating transformer or from a supply protected by a residual current device tripping at 30 mA or less (many laboratory supplies are so protected but, if necessary, protected plugs and adaptors are readily available for about £15). Finally, he emphasised that it was the duty of an education authority (or any other employer) to ensure that those responsible for constructing the apparatus were competent and capable of producing mains-operated apparatus that was safe so far as is reasonably practicable. (Many education authorities have rules governing those allowed to construct mains-operated equipment.)

---

[11] Many suppliers of school science teaching equipment also offer test sets with a range of facilities. The most important test is that of the connection to earth and the test set should be capable of delivering a test current of about twice the maximum load current for long enough to burn out any part of the earth circuit which forms a weak link. This means that the test set should be capable of supplying a current of about 25 A for a few seconds. The insulation test applied to earthed (Class 1) equipment is done to provide confidence that the item will still be safe until the next test. It can be done with an ac or dc voltage between 500 and 1250 V. The pass condition depends on the equipment being tested: items with mineral-insulated heating elements having lower insulation resistance than others. Some employers accept an insulation resistance of 0.5 MW for such items while requiring others to reach 2 MW.

9.1 Induction coils

School induction coils supplied by reputable firms since about 1970 cannot produce a current above 5 mA and so are electrically safe. Older induction coils or induction coils obtained from other sources should be regarded as potentially hazardous and not used.

9.2 Demountable transformers

These should be handled by students only if the equipment meets the normal earthing and insulation requirements for mains-operated equipment and there is no risk of any secondary coil producing over 25 V at 5 mA or more. If the coils do not meet normal earthing and insulation requirements for mains-operated equipment, they may be used by staff for demonstrations **only** if further precautions are taken to ensure their safety. These precautions will be similar to those described below for servicing equipment which might be 'live'.

9.3 Power-line demonstration

In 1987, a Health and Safety Executive (HSE) letter to education authorities expressed concern about the ac power-line demonstration and reminded them of the dangers of high voltages to both the demonstrators and their students. It stated:

'The experiments may continue if one of the following precautions, or any other equally effective precautions, are taken:

a) the voltage of the transmission line is limited to 50 V ac rms or 120 V dc;

b) the demonstration as a whole is located within an enclosure constructed, for example, in clear polycarbonate so that live conductors operating above 50 V ac rms or 120 V dc cannot be touched, or,

c) all conductors and terminations etc operating above 50 V ac rms or 120 V dc are fully insulated so that live conductors cannot be touched.'

Most would agree that these are very reasonable precautions and support the HSE policy of allowing potentially hazardous demonstrations to continue with appropriate precautions. Alternative ways of taking these precautions (and those in sections 9.5, 9.6 and 9.7) are described in detail in *Safety reprints*[12], SSERC Bulletin 158[13] and the CLEAPSS *Laboratory Handbook*[14].

9.4 Wiring 13 A plugs

Most science courses at secondary level include the correct wiring of standard 13 A plugs. This becomes hazardous if the students can insert their plugs into a live socket and there are bare wires on the end of the practice lead; or if the plug has been wired incorrectly and there is some item on the end of the lead.

There are three precautions which can be taken to protect the students and it is suggested that any two of them will be sufficient in any one exercise:

- the plug can be incompatible with the sockets in the room either because it is 'off-standard' (not quite the standard pin arrangement) or because it has been modified in school (by bending the earth pin or by fitting the earth pin with, for example, a pop-rivet)

- the power to all sockets can be switched off in such a way (e.g. by using a switch which is out-of-reach) that it cannot be accidentally restored.

- the unused end of the practice lead can be sealed so that no conductors are accessible (a risk assessment should show the nature of the seal required).

9.5 Ring-main models

Some courses involve the construction of models of ring mains. This useful exercise is usually run at a safe low voltage, e.g. 12 V but, for realism, uses 13 A plugs and sockets. The hazard arises because the 13 A plugs will be wired up with low-voltage lamps or motors (which would not necessarily be built to mains standards) and they could be plugged into 230 V mains. The best way to avoid this is to use for the model off-standard plugs and sockets[15], i.e. ones which look like 13 A ones to a casual inspection but have a small difference which prevents interconnection with the proper mains ones. (See *Safety Reprints*, the CLEAPSS *Laboratory Handbook* or SSERC Bulletin 158.)

9.6 The carbon arc lamp

Courses in the past have encouraged teachers to set up a simple carbon arc and the books describing this activity are still available in many schools. The important features of any method of doing it safely are:

- never to make connections with 4 mm plugs and sockets or by twisting wires;

- to make connections with standard 13 A plugs and sockets or with terminal blocks with shielded conductors which are further enclosed but in a way

[12] ASE (1996, updated) *Safety reprints*.
[13] SSERC Bulletin 158 (1987) *Ring main models*.
[14] CLEAPSS *Laboratory Handbook*, Chapter 6. Available to members of CLEAPSS.
[15] Such plugs and sockets are available from MK Electric (available only through distributors such as Edmundson Electrical Ltd, Newey & Eyre, RS Components, Senate Electrical Wholesalers Ltd, etc.) and Arena Walsall Ltd.

which allows an insulated screwdriver or instrument probe to make contact;

- to make use of standard electrical connection boxes so far as possible.

Instructions for making a single box which can be used to make the connections for this demonstration and for the conductivity of glass can be found in *Safety reprints* or the CLEAPSS *Laboratory Handbook*. These allow the connection to the carbon rods to be made by **insulated** crocodile clips and the connection to an insulated electric radiant heater (as a resistor, safe for use at mains voltages) to be made with a standard 13 A plug and socket.

An opaque non-conducting screen is used both to prevent contact with the carbon rods and to shield the eyes from direct radiation from the arc. A lens is used to project the arc onto a wall or small screen.

9.7 Conductivity of glass

Again, this is a demonstration which has appeared in a number of published courses and it can be done provided the precautions are appropriate. Instructions for making a single box which can be used to make the connections for this demonstration and for the carbon arc can be found in *Safety reprints* or the CLEAPSS *Laboratory Handbook*. It is important to remember that the transparent safety screen is to protect the demonstrator from accidentally touching live components as much as to protect the class.

9.8 Radiant heaters

No electric fire or mains-operated radiant heater with an exposed element is now considered sufficiently safe for use in schools. Types where the element is surrounded by a silica sheath are suitable. In some applications, high-wattage lamp bulbs can be used in place of heating elements with exposed conductors. Further information can be found in the CLEAPSS Position Statement PS28 *Radiant heaters in physics*.

10 Repairs by staff

Students must not repair mains-operated equipment; staff should do so only if permitted by their employer. However, simple repairs such as the replacement of broken terminals or sockets are usually permitted.

10.1 Simple repairs

Even the simplest repairs usually require the case of the appliance to be opened, and it is important to check that the equipment has been disconnected from the supply before opening it. Output terminals can be replaced or their connections repaired and the cover must then be replaced before testing the unit.

10.2 Repairs to the input or mains connections

In this case, obvious faults can be dealt with provided repairers are confident in their ability to do the job correctly but, after the repair, the equipment should be tested for earth-bonding and insulation with a proper test set. Then the functioning of the equipment can be confirmed.

10.3 Repairs involving live testing

Colleges and very large schools may have staff qualified to find more obscure faults which require taking meter or oscilloscope readings while the equipment is live and exposed. If this is to be done a special area must be prepared. This requires the use of a separate supply via an isolating transformer so that it is not earth referenced. The work bench should also be earth-free and an insulating mat should be provided for the repairer to stand on.

When the repairs have been completed, the equipment should be subjected to a full electrical safety test before being returned to use.

Appendix 1 A checklist for formal inspections and tests on portable appliances

Note: This checklist includes all the items which should be considered for a full inspection and test. Item 4 will be omitted if only an inspection is called for and item 6 will often be irrelevant.

Item	Test	Pass condition
1a Mains lead	visual inspection	two layers of insulation and BS colours no damage
1b Mains plug	visual inspection	correctly connected outer sheath gripped by cable clamp, correct fuse fitted
Either		
2a Mains-lead, instrument connector (if lead detachable)	a) attempt to open connector without using tools b) attempt to pull cable from connector	unopenable no movement
Or		
2b Grommet/clamp (if lead attached)	a) inspection of grommet b) sharp pull or push on cable c) rotation of cable	cable insulation protected no appreciable movement no appreciable movement
3 Mains on/off switch	a) visual inspection b) attempt to pull out of panel or attempt to rotate	no damage visible no appreciable movement
Either		
4a Conducting case	a) visual inspection (if marked with this symbol proceed to 4b) b) use earth-bond tester which passes a maximum current of at least twice the fuse rating c) apply 500 V ac to insulation with commercial tester	no damage which allows access to internal wiring resistance of earth circuit 0.1 Ω or less *or* 0.5 Ω or less if plug fused at 3 A or less no fault indicated after 5 s
Or		
4b Insulating case	visual inspection	maker's double-insulation mark visible and case completely undamaged
5 Accessible fuse	visual inspection	no damage
6 Exposed output connections (mains outputs to be shuttered)	a) visual inspection b) visual inspection c) for outputs greater than 40 V, check specified short-circuit current	no appreciable movement no output greater than 40 V short-circuit current limited to 5 mA or less *or* marked 'unsuitable for use by children'

Note: No attempt should be made to pass large currents through either:

■ moving parts such as the pans of balances (consult supplier) or pick-up arms

or

■ earth terminals on the panels of instruments which are placed there to provide earths for experiments. (Some suppliers mark these ⏚ ; terminals marked ⏚ can be tested).

Appendix 2 A suggested form of record card or log of formal testing

Record card of formal testing

SCHOOL NAME: ....

EQUIPMENT...........................SUPPLIER...........................CATALOGUE NUMBER...........................

DATE OF ACQUISITION...........................SERIAL NUMBER...........................

Date	Initials	Test 1	Test 2	Test 3	Test 4	Test 5	Test 6	Action

Appendix 3 Notes on GS 23, *Electrical safety in schools*

This guidance was first issued by the Health and Safety Executive in September 1983 after questions in the House of Commons about the level of electrical protection really necessary in school laboratories. It was revised after the publication of the Electricity at Work Regulations 1989 to provide guidance on the preventive maintenance recommended to meet those Regulations. The following is a summary of the most significant points from this guidance.

It reminds school management that the electrical installation should be inspected and tested by a competent person at least every 5 years and that all electrical equipment, including socket outlets, are likely to be meddled with. Consequently, electrical equipment should be selected with this in mind. Stage lighting should be inspected and tested annually with any temporary wiring inspected and tested before being energised.

Portable electrical appliances which are made to current or recent standards should be safe in normal use provided they are properly maintained. Obsolete, redundant or defective apparatus should be removed from service or stores and modified, repaired or disposed of. Any modification work should be made by a competent person working to the manufacturer's instructions.

All portable electrical appliances should be routinely inspected and tested.

All such apparatus should be visually inspected each term, with some items having a more frequent inspection. (Later guidance indicates that items which are used infrequently should be inspected before use and items which are rarely moved could be inspected only once every two, three or even five years.)

All Class I (earthed) equipment should be subject to a detailed inspection and test at least once every year. The earth continuity test should be made with proprietary test equipment at not less than twice the current rating of the fuse protecting the equipment.

All Class II (double-insulated) equipment should be visually inspected by a teacher or technician before use and subject to a detailed inspection and test based upon experience and use.

Flexible cables should be selected, maintained and used so that there is adequate protection against foreseeable mechanical damage.

There is special guidance for **school laboratories and other practical areas**.

Standard socket outlets, suitably positioned and used in conjunction with properly maintained mains equipment, are generally acceptable for use in school laboratories.

Where water outlets are in close proximity to electrical socket outlets, the provision of a high standard of electrical protection is important. This can be achieved through the use of residual-current devices (RCDs), isolating transformers or earth-free areas. If RCDs are used, they should be tested frequently using the test button on the unit. When the installation is being routinely tested, the tripping current and timing of the RCDs should also be checked.

If an isolating transformer is used with a centre-tapped secondary connected to earth through an impedance of 12 000 Ω and an RCD is fitted with a nominal tripping current of no more than 5 mA, standard plugs and sockets may be used.

Where mains voltage outlets are needed in areas with wash-down facilities or out-of-doors, waterproof connectors should be used.

There is also guidance on **live working**.

When there is a possibility of a person coming into contact with conductors live at more than 25 V, the staff involved should be electrically competent. Students in schools must not be exposed to such voltages unless the apparatus is incapable of inflicting a dangerous electric shock. Where hazardous activities are part of the learning process:

- the risks must be assessed
- written instructions must draw attention to the risks and the precautions to be taken to limit them
- the teacher should be satisfied that there is no danger when the supply is connected
- connection to the supply should be made only by the teacher using a safe system
- the student should need to change connections while the system is live
- interconnecting leads having plugs with retractable shrouds should be used where the voltage exceeds 50 V.

LASERS, INFRARED, ULTRAVIOLET AND VISIBLE RADIATION

This topic updates and expands items to be found in the second edition of Topics in safety, *particularly Chapter 2 'Eye protection', Chapter 3 'Electricity' (Appendix 5) and Chapter 5A 'Microbiology'. It also includes new material not included in previous editions.*

1 Lasers

Low-power lasers sold for teaching purposes are an excellent way of demonstrating various wave-optic effects because the beam is highly monochromatic, highly intense, coherent and hardly diverges at all over the distances used in school laboratories.

Many of the demonstrations traditionally done, with difficulty, using conventional light sources are more easily and convincingly done with a laser, including those involving geometrical optics. However, a monochromatic beam will not create a continuous spectrum.

Diffraction at a single slit between two razor blades, at a pinhole, round a ball bearing, through a grating, and any resulting interference, can all be shown relatively easily. Refraction at boundaries is simply shown; a little milk added to water aids visibility. An 'optical fibre' made up from a polythene tube filled with milky water shows multiple internal reflections when a laser beam enters one end.

1.1 Hazards, risks and control measures

The intensity of the laser due to its lack of divergence may allow the narrow beam to enter the pupil of the eye and be focused on to the retina with damaging effect. Since there are no pain receptors in the retina, an injury may pass unnoticed until a blind spot is identified in the person's field of vision. Lasers emitting infrared radiation (IRR) are also known to promote cataract formation.

The risk of damage depends on the radiant power, wavelength, exposure time and the size of the image formed on the retina.

The natural aversion responses of blinking and turning the head away, which take about 0.25 s, are the main forms of protection from low-power lasers producing visible radiation. This response is most effective in the clearly visible red to green wavelengths, less effective in the deep red wavelength of an inexpensive laser pointer and ineffective where the laser radiation is ultraviolet or infrared.

Lasers must be placed so that beams cannot fall on the eyes of those present, either directly or by reflection. Keeping students well back from the apparatus should avoid direct viewing although there is no reason why older students, under close supervision, should not be allowed to work with Class 2 lasers. Keeping background lighting at a high level ensures that the pupils of the eye are very small but some effects are not best viewed in this way, which means the risk may be greater. Clamping the laser securely avoids sudden changes in direction of the beam.

The original DES (now DfEE) advice on laser goggles, contained in AM 7/70, has now been withdrawn. If school-based work adheres to the advice given in this Topic, laser goggles are unnecessary. Although essential for high-power laser work, they are useless with low-power lasers because, when the goggles are worn, the demonstrator can neither see the beam clearly nor see where it may be going![1, 2, 3]

1.2 Classification of lasers

A laser of unknown or doubtful classification should never be used. Classification is based upon the laser's power rating, wavelength, beam divergence, likely exposure and the use to which it may be put.

Class 1
The laser found inside laser printers, etc., where the beam is hidden from view, may be high-powered but enclosure ensures no hazardous radiation escapes. No attempt should be made to expose, remove or utilise the actual user device.

Class 2
Low-power devices emitting only visible radiation with the output power limited to 1 mW. A deliberate attempt to stare

¹ CLEAPSS (1992) *Laboratory Handbook*, Section 12.12.
² SOEID (now SEED) Circular 7/95, *Guidance on the use of lasers in laboratory work in schools and colleges of education, and in non-advanced work in further education establishments.* (SOEID = Scottish Office Education and Industry Department; SEED = Scottish Executive Education Department.)
³ SSERC Bulletin 188 (1996) *SOEID Circular 7/95 on lasers – a commentary.*

into the beam might produce retinal damage but the period for safe viewing, 0.25 s, is about the same as the natural aversion response. The older helium-neon (He-Ne) educational lasers and the newer diode lasers designed for educational use fall into this class.

Class 3A

This includes higher power lasers with larger beam diameters where the natural blink avoidance mechanism should be able to prevent retinal damage from visible radiation. This aversion response would however be inadequate if the radiation was to be concentrated by a lens. A Class 3A laser emitting non-visible radiation, for which there is no natural protection, would be unsuitable for use in schools.

Class 3B

These are never to be used without laser goggles and are **not** recommended for schools.

Class 4

Such high-powered lasers must **never** be used in schools. This accords with DfEE advice[4].

1.3   Laser pointers

Small battery-powered laser pointers are freely available from both reputable suppliers and dubious traders – who often sell them as 'toys'. Some pointers may be safe to use in schools but past experience has shown that others may be wrongly classified, indicating they are of a lower power than they really are. As they can be picked up and switched on very easily they need to be mounted so as to reduce the risk of this happening. Prevention of theft is vitally important because of the damage they might do in the wrong hands.

A Class 2 laser pointer, securely anchored in a clamp, could justifiably be used in a science laboratory for demonstration purposes. The use of these devices simply as 'pointers' or the use of more powerful ones for demonstrations is unlikely to be justified by a risk assessment.

1.4   DIY and secondhand lasers

Embedded lasers marked as being Class 1 (if of sufficiently low power) or Class 2 may be removed from obsolete equipment and could be used in schools. They should be securely boxed and mounted with a key switch similar to that used on commercial types. The output must be less that 1 mW and the unit must pass the regular portable appliance test of electrical safety (see Topic 17). If the output is unknown or uncertain, calibration is required (see below).

Lasers from commercial sources obtained by donation must be checked to ensure that they are suitable for use in schools. If their class is not known or unclear they should not be used until proved to be suitable. Again, the portable appliance test applies.

Constructing a laser is not difficult but, as the classification process requires a calibrated power meter

and it is not likely that school staff would have access to this, such home-made lasers are not recommended for use in schools.

1.5   Light-emitting diodes (LEDs)

Currently there is no agreement on how LED products should be classified. The hazards are minimal with low-powered LEDs.

High-power LED products, often described as 'ultrabright' or 'superluminescent' should be treated as one would treat a laser. High-intensity LED products utilising infrared radiation should not be used.

1.6   Exposure to laser radiation

Exposure to low-power Class 1 and Class 2 laser radiation should only ever be momentary and easily alleviated by the blink-aversion response. Any exposure over and above this threshold may require medical attention, especially as the person exposed may not be aware of any loss of vision until some time after the event. Medical staff treating the patient may require exact details of the incident, which should be readily available.

2 Infrared radiation (IRR)

A common source of artificially produced IRR is the beam from the remote-control units for TV and audio systems. These are generally considered to present little hazard and can show simple reflection – a task not beyond the agility of the most hardened couch potato!

IRR lamps and heaters are more commonly used in the laboratory either as driers or to show the heating properties of the radiation.

2.1   Hazards, risks and control measures

Short-term exposure to IRR may cause the skin to redden or produce a blister if the skin burns. Long-term exposure of the eyes to IRR is associated with cataract formation rather than retinal damage.

IRR lamps and heaters will quickly char paper and set it on fire. They can also damage bench tops and the insulation on electrical cables. Keep a clear area around these IRR sources when in use.

Laboratory IRR sources are only intended for use over short time periods. If used for extended time periods, because of their intensity, it would be best to warn those present to limit skin exposure within, say, one metre of the source and not to view the source directly at all within this distance.

---

[4] DfEE (1996) *Safety in science education*. Note that advice in the earlier DES AM 7/70 (1970) and its equivalent in Scotland is now obsolete.

Mains-powered (230 V ac) carbon filament and glass- or silica-envelope IRR heaters are those most commonly used in laboratories. However, the use of mains heaters with exposed elements, which were common in schools, presents too high a risk of electric shock no matter how fine the protective mesh and is considered too hazardous by the HSE and DfEE. **This includes use by staff for demonstration purposes**. Such heaters should be withdrawn from use and replaced by low-voltage models or the newer mains-powered versions, which no longer rely on a protective mesh but instead have a silica sheath. See also CLEAPSS[5].

Glass and silica envelopes may fracture explosively if splashed with water when at working temperature. Carbon filament lamps are vacuum devices and so they implode if the glass envelope fails. However, this very rarely happens and the risk can be considered minimal in terms of requiring eye protection to be worn.

2.2   Detection of IRR

Using the cheek as an IRR detector should be avoided with younger students or in cases where students may come into contact with the radiant device. In such cases the back of the hand is preferred but even so the susceptibility and sensitivity of young skin varies considerably and great care is necessary to avoid burns.

The trigeminal nerves in the cheeks are highly sensitive to IRR and older students may usefully experience this fact by momentary exposure to IRR under close supervision.

3 Ultraviolet radiation (UVR)

Many fluorescent effects are enhanced with UVR, some photochemical reactions require it for initiation; it may induce mutations in micro-organisms and it can be used to produce ozone. The effect of UVR on photographic film may be part of some work on the spectrum and UVR is needed in practical work on photo-electrons and the Planck constant as well as work on plant growth and germicidal sterilisation. UVR is produced by electric arcs, used for both lighting and welding and sun beds, but the Sun itself is by far the major source of our personal exposure.

3.1   Classification

Ultraviolet radiation is classified by wavelength into:

UVA	315–400 nm
UVB	280–315 nm
UVC	100–280 nm

Visible blue light has a wavelength range of approximately 400–500 nm. 'Black lights' are mercury discharge tubes fitted with filters which block visible light, UVB and UVC, so that only UVA is emitted. They present minimal hazard, as do the UVR emissions from standard fluorescent lamps.

3.2   Hazards, risks and control measures

UVB is considered to be carcinogenic and UVA, which penetrates more deeply into the skin, may also contribute to the induction of cancers. UVC from artificial sources is unlikely to penetrate the skin sufficiently to be a hazard, while UVC from the Sun is absorbed by the atmosphere.

The dangers of UVR producing skin cancer should now be widely known both by the users of sun beds and those who fail to protect their skin from the Sun. Many LEAs now advise staff to minimise the risk to children on school trips and when working out of doors by insisting on the use of sun-screen lotions as well as covering up exposed skin.

In the laboratory, skin exposure to all kinds of artificial UVR should be kept to a minimum with experimental arrangements designed to make it so.

The eyes should be well protected from all laboratory sources of UVB. Although UVB is considerably more damaging than UVA, many sources produce both types, so avoiding eye contact is by far the best protection whether the source is UVA or UVB. Ordinary glass does not transmit UVB and so makes an effective shield.

Prolonged exposure of the eyes to a source of UVA/UVB may cause painful inflammation lasting for two or three days and will require medical attention.

Electric arcs between, say, carbon rods produce a great deal of UVR and require a thick glass shield for setting up. Thereafter they should only be viewed indirectly.

Ozone is formed around UVR lamps and the gas may cause headaches and irritate the eyes and upper respiratory tract. Ventilation should be adequate to disperse the gas.

4 Visible light

4.1   Laboratory hazards

Apart from the hazards of sunlight detailed above, there is a particular hazard associated with the use of daylight reflected by the mirror of a microscope. If the mirror should catch the Sun, a ray of intense sunlight could pass through the eye to the retina and permanent damage may result.

---

[5] CLEAPSS Position Statement PS28 (1997) *Radiant heaters in physics*.

For this reason, microscopes utilising daylight for illumination must never be sited on a bench near a window where direct sunlight may enter.

Overhead projectors should not be left on windowsills, and nor should glass containers of liquids. Any one of them may focus the Sun's rays to start a fire.

4.2 Viewing the Sun

Since there are no pain receptors in the retina, those viewing the Sun without protection will initially be unaware of any retinal damage.

In 1999, with the advent of the total solar eclipse in part of the UK, much was written about how to view the Sun and its eclipse. The two basic rules are, firstly, only view it with the naked eye through a special dense solar filter and, secondly, never to view it directly via an optical instrument no matter how dense a filter is used.

The safest view of the Sun is probably by way of an image projected on to a screen. Optical instruments allowing direct viewing require specialised filters designed to attenuate both the visible and the invisible components of sunlight. Home-made filters are most unlikely to be effective at doing so. If solar eclipse spectacle filters are used, bear in mind that the filter material may be damaged or ineffective since it has a short shelf life.

This is a new Topic which was not included in the first or second editions of Topics in Safety.

1 Introduction

At the time of writing, the rules governing ionising radiations for schools and colleges are undergoing change and review. However, it is not likely that there will be much, if any, change in what happens in the laboratory even if the administration becomes different.

Radioactivity can be an emotive issue. There are likely to be a range of audiences for whom this Topic will be relevant. This includes those working in a variety of schools and colleges, education authority staff (e.g. science or health and safety advisers), as well as members of the public (e.g. on school governing bodies or school boards) or those involved in the nuclear industry. We therefore felt it prudent to set the Topic in its historical context. It may in any case be some time before some of the legislation and guidance changes, at least in parts of the UK. However, there is more in this Topic than the average science teacher will need on a day-to-day basis.

2 Practical work with ionising radiations

2.1 Why carry out practical work with radioactive materials?

Ionising radiations are studied in schools because it was the investigation of their properties that led to the enormous improvement in understanding of atoms in the previous century. A student at a grammar school in 1900 could well have used a chemistry textbook which included the warning: '*The student should not be led into the error of thinking that atoms are real: they are merely a convenient model for understanding the way in which the elements combine in particular proportions.*'

Even in 1900, that book was not completely up-to-date because evidence for the reality of atoms was already being collected; but whenever did school texts reflect the latest research?

The study of this subject is therefore of vital importance to the structure of science as a whole but there is a strong temptation to teach it by 'secondhand evidence',

using books, videos, computer simulations, etc. There are several reasons for using practical work, including demonstrations, where possible. These are:

■ to achieve an understanding of the supreme patience and determination of the early researchers who had to work with insensitive apparatus;

■ to experience the thrill of detecting something so incredibly small as the behaviour of an individual atom;

■ to see the evidence for the different types of ionising radiation and the tracks of ion pairs left by the passage of the radiation;

■ to get to grips with randomness in a physical situation (since this is almost the only place in school physics where anything is less than completely predictable);

■ to show that hazardous substances and agents can be handled safely with appropriate control measures, and so develop public understanding of hazard, risk and risk assessment;

■ to reduce the apprehension which many members of the public have developed towards this subject as a result of exaggeration in the media, and

■ to enhance the understanding of radioactivity, so that members of a democratic society are better able to make informed judgements and decisions.

The activities which are used to do this are described briefly below.

2.2 Understanding history

Simple work with gold-leaf electroscopes or dental X-ray film and slightly radioactive rocks can be done with quite junior students to show how tedious the early experiments were.

2.3 Detecting individual atoms

A spark counter can be used to demonstrate, as separate sparks, the individual alpha particles from a source of low activity. Each alpha particle comes from the decay of one atom. Less direct evidence could be obtained using a GM tube and scaler. Every other experiment in school science requires millions of atoms to be involved if any effect is to be observed.

2.4 Properties of different radiations

Simple demonstrations with sources of the three common types of ionising radiation allow them to be distinguished by their differing abilities to penetrate matter. This is more convincing when the detectors used are specific to the types of radiation.

alpha radiation	spark counter or solid-state detector
beta radiation	end-window Geiger-Müller tube
gamma radiation	specially-designed G-M tube, G-M tube with filter over window or G-M tube used sideways on

Ideally, scintillation counters would be best for gamma radiation but they are too expensive for most schools. Another difficulty with these demonstrations is that school sources are rarely quite as simple as one would like. (See Table 1.)

It is difficult to demonstrate the differences in the cloud-chamber tracks due to α, β and γ radiation but after the class has seen the α tracks they could be shown pictures of the other two.

2.5 Understanding randomness

The unpredictability of when a nuclide will decay, but the probability that the event will occur within a known time span, leads to what Einstein called 'the spookiness of nature'. Demonstrations with weak sources show the randomness of the decay but, in order to gain a feel for it, it is necessary to use analogues as well. Many schools use dice, ideally dice with a variety of numbers of faces, but there are other analogues which have been used to great effect, such as that devised by Professor Lowarch which used phosphor-bronze balls rolling down an inclined surface with holes in it. This is one aspect where the additional use of computer simulations is justified. However, it can be difficult for learners to realise the strange behaviour of nuclei with excess energy: that these nuclei can remain in a 'metastable' state for very long periods before achieving greater stability by ejecting radiation.

2.6 Reduction of apprehension

While the legislation on the use of sources of ionising radiation must be complied with, it is important not to over-emphasise the hazards of using those approved for use in education. For every child to see a teacher handling radioactive sources safely but simply must be a valuable part of their education and can serve to reduce the apprehension of the public at large.

3 Legislation governing use of radioactive substances

The use of radioactive substances has been controlled since 1960 by statutes, regulations, orders, circulars and memoranda. Table 2 attempts to explain the current significance of these pieces of legislation. At the time of writing, all of the Exemption Orders are being revised but we believe that the changes will be unlikely to have much effect on what schools actually do.

It was the *Ionising Radiations Regulations* 1985 which included a 'legal' definition of a radioactive substance and required (among other things) that each employer who uses ionising radiations shall appoint a Radiation Protection Adviser if any employee is exposed to moderately high dose rates and nominate one or more Radiation Protection Supervisors in each place of work.

4 The Schools Exemption Orders

4.1 Why Schools Exemption Orders?

A main purpose of the *Radioactive Substances Act* is to prevent persons (or employers) from acquiring and using radioactive materials unless they have a legitimate, justifiable purpose. Other points relate to the need for the safe and secure holding of radioactive substances and their safe and legitimate disposal. To undertake any of these activities, the employer would incur expensive licence fees and would be subject to regular inspections by government environmental agencies.

The *Radioactive Substances (Schools, etc.) Exemption Orders* 1963 (of which there are separate versions for England and Wales, Scotland and Northern Ireland) facilitate the use of radioactive materials in schools through a simplified set of rules which are not subject to a licence fee. The exemption orders give schools the right to purchase certain strictly-specified types of radioactive material for laboratory use. Government education departments control these purchases by issuing the school with a letter of approval to make a purchase (but see section 5.2).

Table 1 Sources used in schools.

Source type	Nuclide used	Actual emission	Half life	Particle energies/MeV
alpha source	Americium-241	alpha + gamma	458 y	5 (α); 0.06 (γ)
beta source	Strontium-90	betas of two energies from Sr-90 and Y-90	28 y (Sr, β); 64.2 h (Y, β)	0.5 (Sr, β); 2 (Y, β)
gamma source	Cobalt-60	gamma + beta	5.26 y	1.3 (γ); 0.3 (β)

Table 2 Legislation to do with radioactive substances.

Legislation	Function	Application and relevance to schools	Status as of November 2000
Radioactive Substances Act 1960	Protection of the environment and national security by controlling the acquisition, holding, use and disposal of radioactive materials.	All users to register.	Replaced by 1993 Act
Radioactive Substances (Uranium and Thorium) Exemption Order 1962	Gives exemption from some of the 1960 Act (and now the 1993 Act).	Users of natural radioactive materials. Covers use of rocks.	In force but likely to change soon.
Radioactive Substances (Prepared Uranium and Thorium Compounds) Exemption Order 1962	Gives exemption from some of the 1960 Act (and 1993 Act), e.g. as regards disposal.	Users of these purified compounds. Covers disposal of these compounds.	In force but likely to change soon.
Radioactive Substances (Schools, etc.) Exemption Order 1963	Gives exemption from some of the 1960 and 1993 Acts **on certain conditions** (see section 4).	Those types of schools and colleges existing in 1963. Different Order for England and Wales, Scotland and N. Ireland.	In force but likely to change soon.
Administrative Memoranda 1/65 (1965) and 2/76 (1976) (England and Wales)	Interpret legislation for schools and colleges and make extra rules (e.g. on X-rays).	All establishments in England and Wales including independent schools 'recognised as efficient'.	Replaced by AM 1/92, but the replacement did not cover independent schools.
Education (Scotland) (Amendment) Act 1984	Gives the Scottish Executive power to control work with radioactive materials. See section 5.1.	All educational establishments in Scotland.	In force.
The Dangerous Materials and Apparatus (Educational Establishments) (Scotland) Regulations 1984	Applies to radioactive material with an activity of more than $100 \, Bq \, g^{-1}$ and apparatus in which electrons are accelerated to more than 5 kV (not television sets).	All educational establishments in Scotland.	In force.
Ionising Radiations Regulations 1985 (under HSW Act)	Protection of persons at work who may be harmed by ionising radiations.	All employers using ionising radiations. Separate but very similar Regulations in Northern Ireland.	Replaced by 1999 Regulations but not in Northern Ireland at time of writing.
The Use of Ionising Radiations in Educational Establishments (1986) (Northern Ireland)	Interpret legislation for schools and colleges and make extra rules (e.g. on X-rays).	All educational establishments in Northern Ireland. Despite the publication date does not take account of the 1985 Regulations.	In force.
Circular 1166 and accompanying Explanatory Notes (1988) (Scotland)	Interprets legislation for schools and colleges and makes extra rules. See section 5.1.	All educational establishments in Scotland.	Partly out of date because of 1999 Regulations.
Education (Schools and Higher Education) Regulations 1989 (England and Wales)	Gives the government power to control work with radioactive materials. See section 5.1.	All educational establishments in England and Wales.	In force.
Administrative Memorandum 1/92 (England and Wales)	Interprets legislation for schools and colleges and makes extra rules. See section 5.1.	Maintained schools (England and Wales) but not independent ones or incorporated colleges.	In force but likely to change when Exemption Orders are changed.

(continued)

Legislation	Function	Application and relevance to schools	Status as of November 2000
Radioactive Substances Act 1993	Almost identical to 1960 Act: uses modern units, updates where to register.	All users to register unless exempt.	In force but under review.
The Radioactive Material (Road Transport) (Great Britain) Regulations 1996	Covers transport of any radioactive material by road (not Northern Ireland).	Minimum conditions apply in certain situations. Relevant only if schools need to move sources between sites.	In force.
Ionising Radiations Regulations 1999 (under HSW Act)	See section 6 and Appendix 1. At the time of writing the Northern Ireland version is not in place.	All employers using ionising radiations, which are now defined as 'radiation employers'.	In force.

Other legislation gives government education departments the legal right to control work in schools and this is done through administrative memoranda (in England and Wales), in Scotland through education department circulars and in Northern Ireland through DENI safety publications. In practice, these education department publications have been far more restrictive than the exemption orders, although one consequence of the impending revision may be to bring them more into line. The need for the involvement of government education departments has also been questioned, as the operation of the exemption orders is overseen by the Environment Agency (in England and Wales), the Scottish Environmental Protection Agency (SEPA) and the Environment and Heritage Service (in Northern Ireland). These are collectively referred to as the environmental agencies.

4.2 Who is exempt?

The effect of the exemption orders is to exclude from the need to register under the 1960 (later 1993) *Radioactive Substances Act* provided certain conditions are met. The original orders applied to:

- maintained schools (as defined in the 1944 *Education Act*, England and Wales);

- independent schools recognised as efficient (in England and Wales);

- all schools in Scotland (as defined in the *Education (Scotland) Act* 1962);

- all schools in Northern Ireland;

- teacher training colleges or colleges of education;

- further education colleges.

Subsequent education legislation has in some cases changed the status of these establishments but the orders have not been amended. Hence one need for revision.

4.3 Conditions of exemption

The conditions apply to all schools and colleges claiming exemption from registration, i.e. maintained and independent establishments. However, maintained schools in England and Wales are subject to the further restrictions of AM 1/92, all schools in Scotland to the further restrictions of Circular 1166 and all schools in Northern Ireland to the further restrictions of *The Use of Ionising Radiations in Educational Establishments* (DENI 86) (see section 5). Any school wishing to claim exemption must comply with the following conditions.

- *Limit on the total activity of sources held.* This is the same as a school approved under category B of AM 1/92 or Circular 1166 or categories B1 and B2 of DENI 86 (see section 5.2).

- *Mutilation.* No closed source must be mutilated or active material removed.

- *Action on theft or damage.* The police and the minister to be informed.

- *Records.* The history of the sources, including a record of disposal (if relevant).

5 Guidance from government education departments

5.1 Current guidance

Government education departments in various parts of the UK have produced guidance for the use of radioactive materials, etc. in schools and colleges. This is generally much more restrictive than the exemption orders, but it clearly must be compatible with the relevant orders. The *Education (Schools and Higher Education) Regulations 1989* apply in England and Wales to the use of 'any radioactive substance which has an activity in excess of 0.002 μCi g^{-1}' (and to apparatus producing X-rays). Article 7(2) of the Regulations states that:

No such substance or apparatus shall be used for the purpose of instruction at a school or further or higher education institution unless that use is for the time being approved by the Secretary of State …

The limit of 0.002 μCi g^{-1} equates to 74 Bq g^{-1}, but equivalent regulations in Scotland place the limit at 100 Bq g^{-1}. It is these regulations which require sources used in schools to be of a type approved by the DfEE or SEED and that schools may only use sources with their approval in accordance with conditions they set down.

When the Ionising Radiations Regulations 1985 were implemented, the then Scottish Office Education Department quickly issued its own guidance, as Circular 1166 (1988). This was supplemented by the *Explanatory Notes* produced by SSERC. The Department of Education and Science, in conjunction with the Welsh Office, issued Administrative Memorandum 1/92: *The Use of Ionising Radiations in Education Establishments in England and Wales* as its last act in 1992 before it became the DfE and later the DfEE.

The equivalent publication from the Department of Education (Northern Ireland) is *The Use of Ionising Radiations in Education Establishments;* but despite publication in 1986 this does not take account of the 1985 Regulations and so it is rather dated.

5.2 AM 1/92 (England and Wales), Circular 1166 and Explanatory Notes (Scotland), DENI guidance (Northern Ireland)

AM 1/92 currently applies to maintained schools (i.e. community, voluntary controlled, voluntary aided and foundation schools, and their special equivalents) in England and Wales. In Scotland, Circular 1166 and the Explanatory Notes apply to all schools. There are a few other differences between these guidance documents. As both are based on the 1985 Regulations, which have now been replaced by the 1999 Regulations, there are some discrepancies which have not yet been fully resolved. Both are likely to be revised when the exemption orders are revised and so the information in this section is likely to become out of date at some stage, possibly, but not necessarily, soon. In Northern Ireland *The Use of Ionising Radiations in Education Establishments* (DENI, 1986) applies to all schools but does not take account of either the 1985 or 1999 Regulations and so there are further discrepancies.

Significant features of the guidance may be summarised as follows.

1 Maintained schools (in Scotland and Northern Ireland, all schools) must seek approval from the appropriate education department before they can obtain, store or use certain radioactive sources or machines producing X-rays.

2 Compounds of uranium and (in England, Wales and Northern Ireland) thorium may be held under certain conditions and must be included in lists of sources reported to the relevant education department, but specific approval for their future purchase will not be required.

3 There are three categories of approval, A, B and C (in Northern Ireland, six categories, A1, A2, A3, B1, B2, and B3).

4 Three distinct kinds of records must be kept (see section 5.6).

5 Employers (in England, Wales and Scotland) are reminded of the need to appoint a Radiation Protection Adviser (RPA) (see section 9) and to appoint a Radiation Protection Supervisor (RPS) in each school (see section 8).

6 No student under the age of 16 may handle a sealed source. After older students have done so, the source must be examined to ensure that it is undamaged.

7 The area of any spill must be monitored and decontaminated as necessary (see section 5.7).

5.3 Categories of approval

Schools in Category C (Category B3 in Northern Ireland) are allowed to hold:

- up to 1.1 MBq (or 30 μCi) as approved sealed sources (i.e. up to six at '5 μCi') so long as no single source has an activity greater than 370 kBq (10 μCi);

- up to 100 g of uranium compounds (in Scotland, for the sole purpose of making a protactinium generator);

- protactinium generators for half-life experiments (either commercial or school-made);

- except in Scotland, thoron generators for half-life experiments;

- no thorium compounds as chemicals, except in Northern Ireland;

- low-level radioactive artefacts such as protected luminous dials, cloud chamber sources and spinthariscopes;

- radioactive rocks.

In Scotland, following consultation locally with the HSE, sealed sources are considered to have a limited working life. Old sources will therefore need to be disposed of in a safe and legitimate way and replaced with new sources. However, investigations in England and Wales by the CLEAPSS School Science Service of some old sources showed no evidence of physical deterioration.

Despite the terms of DENI 86, in Northern Ireland, uranium compounds were removed from some schools in 1999. The legal basis for this was not clear at the time of writing.

The qualifications required for using radioactive sources in category C (category B3 in Northern Ireland) are those of teachers appointed to permanent positions on the science staff, while trainee teachers (and, presumably, others) must be supervised (continuously, in Scotland) by teachers so qualified. It is understood (but not stated explicitly) that only 'standard experiments' will be done under this Category.

Categories A and B (and, in Northern Ireland, all categories except B3) include, amongst other things, the use of X-ray equipment, open sources and greater quantities of sealed sources than category C (B3 in Northern Ireland). In practice, virtually all schools and most colleges are in category C (or B3), which has the least demanding requirements. Therefore, these other categories are not considered further here. Those using sources which would place them outside category C (or B3) will need to seek specialist advice, e.g. from their RPA, or, for members, from CLEAPSS or SSERC.

5.4 Independent schools and incorporated colleges (in England and Wales)

While foundation schools, voluntary-aided schools, independent schools covered by the *Education (Special Educational Needs) (Approval of Independent Schools) Regulations 1991* and non-incorporated colleges in England and Wales are subject to AM1/92 and are required to register with the DfEE, fully independent schools may not (according to the AM). In principle, these independent schools have to register with the Environment Agency before purchasing new radioactive materials or X-ray equipment. In a few test cases, the Environment Agency (in England and Wales) has tried to require independent schools to register and pay for the privilege. However, the *Radioactive Substances (Schools, etc.) Exemption Order 1963* may be regarded as giving the exemption mentioned above and no school needs to hold sources beyond its limits. While not formally accepting the validity of the Exemption Order (since no independent schools in England and Wales are now recognised as being 'efficient'), the Agency has not pursued the registration. (Presumably, the Agency is waiting for the position to be clarified by a revised Order.)

Where an independent school is already authorised under the old arrangements as provided in AM 2/76, it may continue to use the radioactive materials but it would probably be wise for the school to inform the Environment Agency that this is happening and that exemption is claimed under the 1963 Order. Although not directly sanctioned by the legislation, at the moment, any independent school in England and Wales wishing to buy sources for the first time may apply to the DfEE and obtain a letter of approval as though it is a maintained school. Following this route may make life a little easier for such schools.

5.5 Storage

One of the conditions of exemption refers to the actions required if a source is lost or stolen. AM 1/92 and SOED Circular 1166 and accompanying Explanatory Notes, and, to some extent DENI 86, give guidance on how to prevent this, and on how to minimise the doses received by staff and the emergency services in the event of a fire or other calamity. The principles are simple.

■ The sources are to be in a metal container which should be recognisable after a fire. (A lead box or a lead-lined wooden box is therefore inadequate.) The outer containers of the sources may be destroyed or melted but the metal box or tray is there to collect the remains for easy identification and disposal.

■ The sources are to be behind a lock to prevent unauthorised access (including unqualified staff). This lock could be on the metal container, on a wooden cupboard in which the container is kept or on the door of the room. The key must be secure and not left on a hook where anyone can gain access it.

■ The cupboard containing the sources must not be in the same room as a container used for highly flammable liquids. The fire officer does not want fire fighters to worry about radioactive substances while dealing with a flammables fire.

■ The sources must not be stored 'close' to a place where any one person works habitually. This is usually interpreted as 'not within 2–3 m of a desk, bench or sink where anyone works for more than half the week' or 'not within 1 m of a bench where a student works'. The distance is measured in a straight line ignoring walls.

5.6 Record keeping

There are three kinds of records which must be kept and 'kept' means what it says: the records cannot be disposed of when the sources are disposed of. If the school closes, the records must be kept by the education authority or the Health and Safety Executive, ideally until 40 years after the last use. The three kinds of records are:

■ the history of the sources, i.e. a record showing when and how each source was acquired, anything dramatic that happened to it and where it went when it was disposed of (if relevant);

■ the use log showing when each source was removed from its place of storage, by whom, which class used it or watched it being used, when it was returned; and

■ the record of any tests made to confirm that sources are not leaking.

Only the first of these is required in Northern Ireland by DENI 86 but the other two could be considered good practice.

The last one has been interpreted differently in different parts of the UK. The 1985 Regulations required testing but in England and Wales, guidance from the HSE indicated that (apart from radium sources) this was only necessary when there was reason to suspect that a source might be leaking. The radium sources always release a little radon-222 which then decays and contaminates the surroundings of the source with the decay products. Radium sources should therefore be checked regularly for this contamination and cleaned whenever necessary. The 1999 regulations also require regular (usually every two years) leak testing of all sources, 'where appropriate', and this is likely to include school sources, although HSE might be prepared to give exemption as before. In any case, in Scotland, guidance has long indicated that leak testing should be done once every two years on all sources. However, some consider it unlikely that schools will remember to carry out any action unless it is at least annual, although this would obviously be more onerous.

5.7 Radioactive contamination

Work of the type conducted in most schools (i.e. category C, or B3 in Northern Ireland) is unlikely to, but conceivably might, give rise to a liquid spillage from a protactinium generator, or the release of a dust cloud from a thoron generator. Protoactinium (and thorium) generators are in fact open sources even although their containers may never be opened and should be so labelled.

Dropping a sealed source also needs to be considered a 'spill' for the following reason. The sources most commonly used in schools have a nickel-plated brass cup which contains the active material. In many cases, the active material is prepared as a long strip of foil from which circles are punched to fit the cup. When the punch becomes slightly worn, instead of producing a clean-cut circular disc, it sometimes produces a circular arc of active foil as well. It is possible that a fragment of such an arc could be carried into the cup with the foil during manufacture to be shaken out onto the bench if the source is dropped. For this reason, the exemption order in England and Wales requires that, when a source is dropped, the area onto which it fell must be checked for activity. This is done by passing a school G-M tube

slowly over the area and looking for a marked increase in count rate. If this is found, the decontamination procedure below must be used.

Whenever an area of bench or floor may be contaminated, the same procedure is used. While wearing disposable plastic gloves, the area is wiped with damp tissues which are placed in a plastic bag for disposal. The area should be monitored with school counting equipment and the operation repeated until the count-rate is less than 30% above the normal background as determined with a five minute count.

Where a surface has been contaminated by an alpha source, it is advisable to dispose of the surface, where possible, rather than attempt to clean it. This is because the radiation from alpha-emitting nuclides lodged on a surface can be severely attenuated by the micro-structures on the surface. Thus a relatively primitive search by school staff with crude instruments would be unlikely to find the true extent of any contamination.

6 Ionising Radiations Regulations 1999 (IRR99)

One of the main reasons for revising the 1985 *Ionising Radiations Regulations* was the obligation to meet, by 13 May 2000, a European Directive dated May 1996. The Directive was based on international recommendations on radiological protection, published in 1990, to which the UK was a signatory. Other reasons included the need to bring legislation which had been in operation for 14 years up to date and the need to tie in the regulations to the implementation of other health and safety legislation (e.g. the *Management of Health and Safety at Work Regulations* 1992 and 1999). In particular, risk assessment has become an important concept in much health and safety legislation and IRR99 has now extended this into the use of radioactive materials. Schools will already be familiar with the concept and practice of risk assessment and the use, for example, of model (general) risk assessments (see various Topics, especially Topic 10).

The objective of this legislation is to protect employees working with ionising radiation, and any other persons who might be at risk, from the effects of exposure to that radiation. The underlying assumption on which the legislation is based is that all ionising radiation presents a hazard, i.e. it has the potential to cause harm. However, it is more contentious as to whether exposure to low levels of such radiation presents a significant risk, i.e. a likelihood of significant harm being caused. Because the human body cannot detect the radiation directly, these Regulations are very detailed when compared with almost all other health and safety legislation.

There are three key principles of radiological protection:

- *justification*, the process of showing that the benefits outweigh the detriment that the radiation might cause;

- *optimisation*, the process of keeping all exposures as low as reasonably achievable, taking into account economic and social factors; and

- *dose limitation*, the process of keeping the total relevant dose for workers and the public within specified limits.

The justification principle has much wider implications than just the use of ionising radiations, and the UK Government has decided not to implement this as part of IRR99 but the legislation which will incorporate this principle into UK law has not yet been announced. However, since it is regarded as fundamental and the Health and Safety at Work Act (HSW Act) itself is under review, it could be that justification will be incorporated into a revised HSW Act.

The other two principles form the foundation of IRR99 as they did of IRR85. In education, we try to design activities with ionising radiation to achieve the educational objectives while keeping the exposures of students and staff to the lowest practicable levels. Estimates made by CLEAPSS and SSERC of the doses likely to be received by school staff indicate that these doses are certainly less than 10 μSv per experiment and probably very much less, depending on how the work is done. In the context of radiological protection, the risk from such exposure would be considered trivial.

IRR99 does not define a radioactive source as one with a particular specific activity. Any source for which emissions cannot be neglected from a radiation protection standpoint is to be regarded as 'radioactive'.

Even though the risks from radiation exposure from a properly conducted school experiment are very low, it is a requirement of IRR99 that the experimenter minimises the exposure to her or himself and to others. This is the main effect of the legislation.

The rules about RPAs, RPSs and local rules have changed. These are discussed in sections 8 and 9 and a summary of the significant features of the Regulations relevant to school science are given in Appendix 1.

7 Hazards and risks from ionising radiations

7.1 Hazards

The principal effect which ionising radiation has on human tissue is, not surprisingly, the creation of ion pairs. Since the greater part of any animal cell is cytoplasm which is largely water, the most common

ions are formed from water: hydrogen ions and hydroxide ions. An increase in the concentration of these ions simply increases the recombination rate and neutral water is rapidly reformed. If the rate of ionisation is very high, then these ions (particularly the hydroxide ions) may react with some of the molecules present in the cell before they can recombine with hydrogen ions.

Of course, there will be occasions when the radiation will ionise a molecule other than water and then, instead of forming simple ions as above, the molecule will be split almost at random to form a variety of parts, often including 'free radicals'. These electrically-charged fragments of molecules are very reactive chemically. They can upset the normal functioning of the cell in which they are formed or totally destroy it. Fortunately, the human body has one or more defence mechanisms against the attack of free radicals. The precise mechanisms are complex but involve vitamins C and E mopping up the free radicals and converting them to innocuous molecules.

Sometimes the defence mechanisms fail and the cell is unable to repair itself. Even this is not a serious problem because cells are dying and being replaced all the time, unless the death rate is greater than that at which the organism can replace the lost cells.

This shows why there is a 'threshold' for non-carcinogenic radiation damage. Small doses of radiation have no serious effect, they are 'below the threshold' for damage. However, if the dose to a person is sufficiently large, then the damage is sufficiently serious for the threshold to be exceeded and that person suffers from 'radiation sickness' the nature of which depends on which parts of the body received the dose.

This is not the whole story because the ionisation sometimes occurs within the nucleus of the cell, where the DNA is stored. When the DNA of a common cell is damaged, it can cause a cancer. If the cell is involved in the reproduction of the whole organism, then the genetic code could be altered and there is a possibility of mutated offspring.

The carcinogenic effect which has been studied the most is that which gives rise to various forms of leukaemia. There is considerable evidence that ionisation giving rise to one defect in the DNA is not sufficient to cause a cancer and it may be that a very specific gene responsible for the production of one enzyme must be damaged for the cell to grow out of control and form a cancer. In spite of many years of research, there is no hard and fast evidence for a threshold in this effect but it has recently been pointed out that the cancer rate from radon in our homes would be very much higher than it is if there were no threshold. It may be that the body has a defence against this sort of cell damage too, but this is contentious.

Whereas spontaneously-arising or chemically-induced DNA damage may be chemically simple, mainly in single DNA strands, damage produced by ionisation is usually not chemically simple. It can cause both strands of the DNA molecule to break. Therefore, DNA damage caused by ionisation may be less easy to repair than if caused spontaneously or by a chemical agent. Radiological protection is still founded on the assumption that any ionising radiation, at no matter how low a dose level, is dangerous. Thus there is no threshold below which one need take no further preventive action (in so far as reasonably practicable).

The genetic effect is very difficult to pin down. It has been studied in plants, of course, and in fruit flies and even in mice but, naturally, there aren't many volunteers among the human population. Research is therefore mainly based on accidental or incidental exposure, in particular, the nuclear weapons that had been dropped on Japan and the Chernobyl disaster. Despite considerable efforts it has proved very difficult to identify genetic effects resulting from these events. It would be very strange if there were no genetic effect from ionising radiation in humans but it has not yet been observed quantifiably.

7.2 Minimising the risks

The three general principles of justification, optimisation and dose limitation have been discussed briefly above. Although justification has yet to be incorporated into UK health and safety legislation, section 2 of this Topic amply justifies the use of sources of ionising radiation in education.

The choice of radioactive nuclide for each school use has been optimised bearing in mind the energy of the radiation emitted, the half life and the initial cost. The initial activities were chosen to give a reasonably useful life without an excessive initial dose rate. Perhaps the time has come to review the different nuclides to see if there are other nuclides now available which are equally suitable. One of the traditional sources, radium-226, is now too expensive to supply but, for those establishments which hold one, it remains a very useful source.

All of the guidance from government education departments dealing with ionising radiation have required education establishments to have 'local rules' for the use of sources. The *Ionising Radiations Regulations* 1999 do not require such local rules for establishments working in category C (or B3 in Northern Ireland) because the annual doses which staff and students receive are so very low. Nevertheless, AM 1/92 requires maintained schools in England and Wales and Circular 1166 requires all schools in Scotland to have local rules. Other schools still need control measures, which implies written procedures and the provision of information and instructions. It is a moot

point as to whether these should continue to be called 'local rules'. It is a term widely used and understood and would show continuity with the past. On the other hand, continuing to use the term may cause confusion by implying that schools are legally obliged to have local rules. A better term might be 'local procedures for using radioactive materials' but this may be clarified if revised exemption orders address this issue. The purpose of stating such rules or procedures is to ensure that the doses of ionising radiations are kept as low as reasonably practicable. One example is that the user of the radioactive sources should be at least 0.5 m from the source during the experiment and that anyone observing should be 2 m away from it.

There should also be a statement of the conditions under which exemption is granted from registration under the *Radioactive Substances Act* (see section 4).

8 Supervising the use of radioactive materials in schools

The *Ionising Radiations Regulations* 1985 required one or more members of staff of an establishment to be appointed as Radiation Protection Supervisor (RPS) and this is reiterated in both AM 1/92 (in England and Wales) and Circular 1166 (in Scotland), neither of which has yet been withdrawn. DENI 86 (in Northern Ireland) required a Radiological Officer, who, to all intents and purposes, would have the same functions. The 1999 Regulations no longer require ordinary schools to have an RPS because the annual doses which staff and students receive are so very low. However, someone has to be 'in charge' of the radioactive sources and, even if they are given a different title, the functions will be the same. This person would normally be head of a department (who would delegate immediate supervision to the teacher using the radioactive substances). In a school approved to work in category C (or B3 in Northern Ireland), such a person is not required to have any qualifications beyond those which would be appropriate for teaching science at secondary level. However, some training would be advantageous and both CLEAPSS and SSERC provide this for their members.

It is important to stress that the individual who takes on this role must actively manage the situation. He or she should provide information and instruction for colleagues. Induction of new staff is particularly important. There should be regular monitoring to ensure that agreed procedures or local rules are being followed. Human failings are all too common. Any problems (particularly the loss of or damage to a source) should be reported to the RPA and/or the employer. It is therefore advantageous for this person to be a member of staff with a sufficiently senior position for other members of the team to obey his or her instructions without question; the wrong choice could create unnecessary friction.

9 The Radiation Protection Adviser

9.1 The need for a Radiation Protection Adviser (RPA)

Under the 1985 Regulations the employer was required to appoint a Radiation Protection Adviser (RPA) because, when handling a school source, an employee could be exposed to an instantaneous dose rate of more than 7.5 µSv h^{-1}. It appears that RPAs may not have been appointed formally in Northern Ireland. The 1999 Regulations introduce a number of changes, but at the time of writing the interpretation of some of these in the schools context is under discussion with the HSE.

Any employer using ionising radiations (a 'radiation employer') is required to consult an RPA to see whether or not an RPA needs to be appointed. The Regulations contain a list of innocuous activities for which an RPA is not required but school sources are not covered by any of them. It would therefore be wise to consider that employers in the education sector (i.e. education authorities, governing bodies, school boards and proprietors as appropriate) are radiation employers and therefore need to consult an RPA.

9.2 Qualifications

Anyone appointed as an RPA since the new Regulations came into force (on 1 January 2000, except in Northern Ireland) must meet criteria of competence as laid down by the HSE. However, anyone, whatever his or her qualifications and experience, who was appointed as an RPA before that date, may be re-appointed to act as RPA until the end of 2004. It is likely that there will be similar requirements when equivalent regulations are implemented in Northern Ireland.

Independent schools and colleges have sometimes appointed a member of staff to be RPA. Education authorities have usually nominated the science adviser or inspector to fulfil this role. Clearly an existing officer appointed as RPA before 1 January 2000 may continue to act (but, strictly speaking, needs to be re-appointed). However, if that person leaves, the authority will have to appoint a replacement meeting the HSE criteria. The published criteria lay down core criteria of competence to be met by all RPAs with additional topics which relate to the scope of advice needed.

One way of meeting the core criteria is to obtain an S/NVQ in Radiation Protection Practice, level 4. Alternatively, the potential RPA can obtain a certificate of core competence from an organisation recognised as an Assessing Body by the HSE for the purpose of granting such certificates. This requires:

- evidence of training knowledge and experience meeting a syllabus specified by the EU which includes, among 13 major topics, both basic biology as well as atomic and nuclear physics: a combination which is hard to meet with the UK's highly specialised school science of a generation ago;

- a degree in a physical science or the equivalent in qualifications and experience;

- three years full-time experience in a post directly concerned with radiation protection practice;

- sound knowledge of methods of dealing with operational problems for work involving potential for significant exposure to radiation; and

- the ability to advise management on the implementation of regulatory requirements and radiation protection practices.

A certificate awarded to an RPA by satisfying the above criteria is valid for only five years, after which renewal must be applied for. This application must be supported by evidence that the RPA has kept up-to-date with current practice, for example, by participating in a scheme of continuing professional development. The RPA working in education is, of course, also expected to keep up-to-date in the additional topics listed above.

The guidance on IRR99 also makes it clear that an RPA should possess knowledge and experience relevant to the employer's type of work. Many of those with apparently appropriate qualifications to be RPA may lack relevant experience in the school sector, whereas those with relevant experience may lack the formal qualifications. At the time of writing, both CLEAPSS and SSERC are discussing with the HSE how the apparently demanding requirements for RPAs can be met without undue costs to education authorities or schools, arguing that the cost should be broadly commensurate with the risk. There is concern that if the requirements are over-demanding, schools may simply abandon practical work with radioactive materials.

9.2 The position of independent establishments

All schools and colleges independent of local authorities should have made suitable arrangements for advice on radiation protection in order to comply with the 1985 Regulations. This may have been done shortly after the implementation of these Regulations or later if the establishment became independent of the education authority (e.g. GM and now foundation schools).

If the RPA is still in post, whatever his or her qualifications and experience, she or he may continue to act as RPA until the end of 2004 (but, strictly speaking, needs to be re-appointed). If the original RPA is no longer in post and was not replaced before 1st January

2000, the radiation employer has three options.

- Employ an RPA who holds a certificate of competence and has experience relevant to the work done in the school or college.

- Find an RPA working for a similar radiation employer and appoint her or him for the transitional period up to the end of 2004.

- Anyone having a letter of appointment as an RPA under IRR85 from any employer, but who does not hold a certificate of competence, may be appointed now to be an RPA by any other employer for the transitional period up to the end of 2004. However the scope of that person's work experience and knowledge should be considered in judging whether he or she is fit for the office.

9.3 Duties of the RPA

The prime duty of the RPA is to advise the radiation employer on matters of radiation protection and, in order that he or she shall be able to do this, she or he must know what the employees are doing with the sources. In the case of an education authority, where the use of radioactive sources has been closely controlled for years, she or he should therefore have access to existing records and be in a position to confirm their accuracy or bring them up-to-date as necessary.

In practice, the RPA fulfils these duties by helping the radiation employer to draw up local rules or agreed procedures for the use of ionising radiations (and the radioactive sources which emit them) and is available for consultation over any other matters when they arise.

10 Disposal

10.1 Reasons for disposal

Schools may need to dispose of:

- chemicals surplus to requirements;

- low-level radioactive waste such as plastic gloves or tissues which have been used to clear up a spill;

- sealed sources surplus to requirements.

The disposal of active material from schools and colleges is governed by the various Exemption Orders of 1962 and 1963. The rules for uranium and thorium compounds are different from those for other materials. When the exemption orders are revised, the rules on disposal are certainly candidates for change, particularly as the regulations governing waste disposal are also changing. Again, there are differing practices in different parts of the UK.

In Northern Ireland, all sources may be disposed of via the Northern Ireland Radiation Protection Service[1], at no charge to schools, but prior permission must be obtained from DENI.

10.2 Uranium and thorium

In England and Wales, schools are permitted under Article 7(1)(d) of the *Radioactive Substances (Prepared Uranium and Thorium Compounds) Exemption Order 1962* to dispose of up to 100 g per day of compounds of these elements. The preferred method of disposal is as a solution into the 'foul-water drain', i.e. down a lavatory connected to the main sewer. It is expected that this amount will not be disposed of every day but very rarely! Where a school is not connected to mains drainage, it should consult the RPA, the ASE or CLEAPSS, as appropriate.

Schools in Northern Ireland should use the Northern Ireland Radiation Protection Service. Those in Scotland should consult SSERC.

10.3 Other open sources

In England and Wales, Articles 9(2) and 9(3) of the *Radioactive Substances (Schools, etc.) Exemption Order 1963* allow schools to dispose of up to 10 µCi (370 kBq) of solid waste and 500 µCi (18.5 MBq) of liquid waste in one week (subject to other conditions). The conditions are that:

- the waste arises from normal school activities (not from Bloggs Chemicals in the next street nor the extraction of radium compounds from uranium ores in the school labs);

- in the case of solid waste, not more than 1 µCi is contained in one article and each batch of waste must be of minimum volume 3 cu. ft. (if still permitted, these units will be metricated when the exemption orders are revised!);

- the liquid waste must pass into the 'foul-water drain'.

Schools in Scotland should consult SSERC. Those in Northern Ireland should use the Northern Ireland Radiation Protection Service.

10.4 Low-level waste

Tissues, paper towels, plastic gloves, bench coverings, empty bottles, etc., which may be contaminated with small amounts of radioactive material, should be sealed into a plastic bag (with a wire twist) and placed in the ordinary solid refuse. Schools in Northern Ireland should use the Northern Ireland Radiation Protection Service.

---

[1] c/o Medical Physics Department, Foster Green Hospital, 110 Saintfield Road, Belfast BT8 4HD; telephone: 028 9079 3681.

10.5 Sealed sources

The first point to make is that sealed sources are expensive resources which should not be disposed of lightly. Some officers of the environmental agencies have advised that surplus school sources can be disposed of via the refuse collection, if it is known that this will go to landfill (as opposed to incineration). However, this is disputed and will in any case not be possible everywhere and further strategies are listed below. In every case, the records must be amended and, even though a school has no sources remaining, the records must be kept.

- Transfer the source to another establishment which can use it.

- Persuade a major school apparatus supplier to take it for eventual disposal (but no supplier currently offers this service).

- In England and Wales, call in the professionals, i.e. Safeguard International[2] or Nycomed Amersham[3]. This is likely to be expensive and not all sources may be accepted. Schools in Northern Ireland should use the Northern Ireland Radiation Protection Service. Those in Scotland should consult SSERC

- Amalgamate many sources into one collection, i.e. collaboration between adjacent schools (whether or not organised by an education authority). This may reduce the cost per source significantly.

- (In Scotland) transfer the source to SSERC for disposal. There is a small charge for this service. In England and Wales, members may consult CLEAPSS.

11 Special items

There are a number of particular items of equipment which generate questions and these are dealt with below.

11.1 Protactinium generators

The half-life of protactinium (a grand-daughter of uranium-238) is a convenient one to measure. As a liquid source it has the advantage that in the event of a spill it is much better contained (e.g. by using it over a drip tray) than a solid would be. Another advantage is that its source material, uranyl nitrate, has a coarse, crystalline nature which, were it to spill, is unlikely to cause widespread contamination and is fairly easily recovered.

Although protactinium generators have previously been offered for sale in the catalogues of the major suppliers, they are currently unavailable. Schools in category C are permitted to keep up to 100 g of uranium compounds specifically so that protactinium generators can be made. Uranium salts were withdrawn from some Northern Ireland schools in 1999.

Doing it oneself is very much cheaper than buying ready-made generators. There are sometimes unwanted chemical side effects (including deterioration of cheaper plastic bottles) which may mean that it is best to dispose of the generator annually (the manufactured versions attempt to suppress these side effects giving a ten-year life). Some believe that there is considerable educational advantage in preparing the generator in front of the class: for the students to see the teacher handling radioactive uranyl nitrate safely with only the most elementary precautions is a lesson in itself. It teaches 'proportionality', the principle of matching the precautions to the level of risk. However, making the generator in front of a class is not permitted in Scotland.

Protactinium generators (and the uranium compounds from which they are made) should be handled over a tray, if necessary lined with absorbent paper. They should be stored upright, standing in an outer container, e.g. a glass beaker.

11.2 Thoron generators

Schools have used radon-220 (thoron) for many years in experiments on half-life because it has a half-life which is convenient to measure.

The *Ionising Radiations Regulations* 1985 listed thorium compounds (which release thoron as a decay product from thorium-232) as particularly hazardous with a requirement to clear up any spill very thoroughly. There have been instances of the plastic thoron generator bottles splitting and spilling their contents in school laboratories. These led the Scottish Education Department to ban the use of thoron generators in their guidance to schools dated 1987.

In England, the same problem led to two studies: one sponsored by HMI into the frequency with which the bottles actually split (1980, but unpublished) and another study into the consequences of such a spill sponsored by the Department for Education and Science in 1988. These two studies showed that bottles split very rarely, when they do split normally no powder is released and when thorium compounds are spilt, despite the small particle size of the precipitated material, the density prevents the powder from being dispersed from the spill site. However, these findings are disputed by some people who believe that particles could reach the breathing zone, although using the bottle inside a strong plastic bag would reduce the likelihood even further.

---

2 Safeguard International, Building 392, Harwell Business Park, Harwell, Didcot, Oxon OX11 0RA; telephone: 01235 464046; FAX: 01235 434408; e-mail: safeguard@aeat.co.uk.
3 Nycomed Amersham, Amersham Laboratories, White Lion Road, Amersham, Bucks HP7 9LL; telephone: 01494 543313; FAX: 01494 545028.

AM 1/92 permits the use of thoron generators in England and Wales although it does require schools in Category C not to hold thorium compounds as chemicals. In Northern Ireland, DENI 86 does not even have this restriction. Independent schools and colleges in England and Wales, which are not subject to AM 1/92 but only to the 1963 exemption order, have to make their own decision anyway.

If used, such sources should be handled over a tray. During storage the source can be stood in a strong outer plastic bag and may be used within this, with only the tubing projecting.

11.3 Elution sources

A third alternative for half-life investigation is the Cs-137/Ba-137m isotope generator where Ba-137m is eluted out of Cs-137. Although this and similar systems have been on offer for many years, they have not received formal approval from government education departments as being suitable for use in UK schools. Until this approval is granted, they cannot be used in an institution covered by AM1/92 (England and Wales), Circular 1166 (Scotland) or category B3 of DENI 86 (Northern Ireland). If they were to be used, extreme care would be necessary to ensure that the correct solution was used for elution.

11.4 Non-approved sources

Many schools have acquired sources which are not strictly approved for use in education. Some of these are relatively trivial while others present a problem. Schools are advised never to accept sources unless they are of a type approved for educational use.

Sealed but non-approved educational sources

Sealed sources which have been approved by government education departments are currently only available from Philip Harris and Griffin Education. In the past, suppliers of approved sources have also included Irwin, Nicolson, Panax and Labgear. Sources from Labgear had been available through Griffin only. Sources supplied by the US company Pasco and the Aktivlab sources from AEA Technology and formerly from Amersham have not, so far, been approved for UK use, although they could be used by independent schools and colleges in England and Wales.

Uranium metal

In the past, some GCE A-level examining boards have supplied schools with small pieces of uranium metal for use in practical examinations. These are not particularly hazardous, as the decay of uranium is slow so the build-up of radium and other decay products is small. Nevertheless, there is detectable beta and gamma radiation from the decay products as well as the alpha emission from the parent uranium. These sources must be treated with respect but may be retained so long as the total mass does not cause the establishment to exceed its permitted holding of uranium.

Other establishments have acquired relatively large pieces of uranium from the nuclear industry. These should be disposed of because they are probably over 25 years old and the build up of decay products may make them difficult to store and handle safely.

Calibration sources

Schools have acquired second-hand ratemeters from a variety of original owners and these were sometimes supplied with small calibration sources. Although the activities are often trivial, these sources have not been approved by government education departments.

Colleges may have a need to teach about the calibration of dose-rate meters and therefore may have a justifiable need to retain the sources. This raises questions over the application of the exemption order and could lead to the college having to register under the Radioactive Substances Act. This could be economically unviable. Each case should be discussed with the RPA.

Civil defence training sources

When local authorities closed down their centres for providing civil defence in the event of nuclear war, they had to dispose of the small radioactive sources which they used for training purposes. Since the officers involved were often physics teachers, these sources (which often look like metal buttons about the size of milk-bottle tops) often ended up in schools. Again, these sources are not very hazardous and probably contain a uranium compound so one could argue that they are covered by the uranium provision. However, they are not approved for use in schools and strictly should not be there (except in independent schools and colleges in England and Wales), so they too should be disposed of.

11.5 Items bearing radium-based luminous paint

Many items have been made in the past with dials or pointers coated with radium-based luminous paint so that they can be seen in the dark. These range from old alarm clocks and wrist watches to prismatic compasses and wartime aircraft instruments. The amount of radium used was so large that these items can be quite strong sources. The main hazard arises when the luminous paint is knocked off the dial or pointer and then one does not know where it will end up. Even quite a small particle, picked on a pen tip and ingested when someone sucks the top of the pen, carries a significant risk of causing a cancer in the gastrointestinal tract.

Any such item not covered by a glass front should be transferred to a substantial plastic bag as soon as possible. The former container should then be checked for contamination with school counting equipment. If contamination is heavy, the RPA should be consulted over its disposal, otherwise it can be handled as discussed above.

If the luminous item is flaking or simply not used, it too should be disposed of but strictly speaking it can no longer be put into the solid waste – it must be handled as a radioactive source (see section 10). However, it is unlikely that any enforcement action would be taken against a school that disposed of an old alarm clock, securely wrapped in a substantial plastic bag, in the refuse collection.

12   Crystal ball gazing

Since the *Radioactive Substances Act* 1993 is currently under review and all the (older) exemption orders have been recently reviewed, it is possible that there could be many changes.

Experience indicates that there will not be substantial changes to the Act: users of radioactive substances will still have to be registered with someone. It is possible that those users currently covered by exemption orders may be exempted by redrafting the Act itself. In this case, the conditions could change. They could be more vague, perhaps 'subject to conditions which may from time to time be laid down by the minister . . . '. On the other hand, they could become much tighter in that the total holding which may be exempted could be reduced or discharges of waste radioactive material could be much more restricted.

However the details change, it is hoped that the position of independent schools and incorporated colleges in England and Wales will be clarified so that there is no argument over their right to claim exemption.

Appendix 1: Significant features of IRR99

This Appendix is not intended to be a comprehensive summary of the *Ionising Radiations Regulations* 1999 (IRR99). It focuses only on those areas where there is a significant change and that change is likely to be relevant to school science. The interpretation and implications of some changes are currently under discussion with the relevant authorities and some matters may be clarified by the revised exemption orders.

The definition of a 'radioactive substance'

IRR85 defined a radioactive substance as one with a specific activity of more than 100 Bq g^{-1}. This is more open in IRR99, where a radioactive substance is defined as one containing one or more radionuclides the activity of which cannot be disregarded for the purposes of radiation protection.

We can still regard potassium compounds as presenting a negligible radiation risk in an educational science laboratory. However, the more open definition of radioactive substance may remove the requirement to store certain small rock samples as radioactive materials. For example, a rock sample giving rise to a dose rate of less than 1 μSv h^{-1} at a distance of 10 cm, could be stored in a glass-fronted, locked display cabinet which prevents an approach closer than this distance.

Attitude to 'trainees'

Normally, a trainee below the age of 18 is distinguished from employees in health and safety legislation. In IRR99 a trainee (between the ages of 16 and 18) is to be considered as an employee for purposes of radiation protection.

This gives the trainee as much protection as an employee and also requires the trainee to behave as responsibly as an employee would be expected to, for example, by following the local rules carefully. In particular:

- a female trainee now has the duty to inform the radiation employer if she becomes pregnant or is breast feeding,

- it has become a criminal offence for a trainee knowingly to ignore the local rules (but schools would not normally need to have local rules in the sense intended here).

Dose limits in pregnancy

The dose limit for a pregnant female is lower than that for any other radiation worker but the only activity in schools or colleges which might be affected would be the use of an electron microscope (which would require special approval anyway). It would also be unwise for a female who is breast feeding to use any open radioactive source which might give rise to skin contamination. For example, it would, therefore, be better for the preparation of a thoron or protactinium generator to be done by someone else.

Prior authorisation and risk assessment

IRR99 introduces a requirement for 'prior authorisation' before certain practices are begun. This will not apply to the standard procedures followed in ordinary schools and colleges. However, there is a requirement to make a 'prior risk assessment' which goes a little beyond that required by the Management Regulations. This risk assessment must:

- demonstrate that all hazards with the potential to cause a radiation accident have been identified;

- show that the risks from those hazards have been evaluated;

- enable the radiation employer to take all reasonably practicable steps to prevent such an accident and limit its consequences; and

- ensure that the employees have been given adequate information, instruction, training and the equipment necessary to restrict exposure to the radiation.

AM 1/92 and various CLEAPSS publications and, in Scotland, SOED Circular 1166 and SSERC Explanatory Notes provide documentation which show that the hazards have been identified and the risks evaluated. For example, there are lists of sources and their radiation hazards and calculations of doses for standard experiments. These would constitute model (general) risk assessments (see Topic 10) and the existence of local 'rules' or procedures agreed with the RPA would show that the model assessment had been customised to meet the specific situation in a particular establishment.

In particular, local rules or some other document must remind the staff what to do in the event of predictable incidents. These are:

- a sealed source being dropped;

- a radioactive material being spilt (e.g. from a protactinium generator) or a radioactive rock sample being broken or crushed;

- a 'thoron generator' splitting;

- a radioactive source or sample being stolen.

It would therefore be wise for whoever is in charge of radioactive sources in each school (previously known as the RPS) to confirm that the local rules do indeed cover these four eventualities.

Dose limitation

There is a need to repeat the calculations of typical doses received by users and observers in education to confirm that no new limit is approached. Such calculations have been carried out for the normal school activities by CLEAPSS and SSERC and no problem has been identified.

Radiation Protection Adviser

The most significant change introduced by IRR99 is the definition of a Radiation Protection Adviser (RPA):

> *Radiation Protection Adviser means an individual who, or body which, meets such criteria of competence as may from time to time be specified in writing by the Executive (HSE).*

These criteria of competence have now been published; they are discussed in section 9. Any RPA who was appointed before 1 January 2000 shall be deemed to meet these criteria until 31 Dec 2004 but does, technically, need to be formally re-appointed. After that date every RPA will have to meet the published criteria. Since RPAs will have to take steps to prove their competence, the effect of this could be to make the services of an RPA much more expensive to individual establishments and to local education authorities.

Work for which an RPA is *not* needed

The schedule of work which is of sufficiently low risk not to require the appointment of an RPA has been revised. However, most educational use would not be covered by the exceptions for the following reasons.

Where the specific activities of the substances used are very low. The specified levels are so low that such substances would be useless for teaching about radioactivity.

Where the quantities of radioactive substances used are very low. The quantities used in education are also above the specified limits.

Where the above limits are exceeded but the materials are all in sealed sources of approved type and the dose rate at a distance of 0.1 m is less than 1 $\mu Sv\ h^{-1}$. The dose rates at this distance from educational sources is usually much greater than this limit.

Where the dose rate from X-rays is less than a similar limit. Educational X-ray systems do keep within this limit.

Where the use of high-voltage equipment (e.g. CRTs) does not generate X-rays beyond that limit. Some very old demonstration CRTs (30 cm diameter) may do so but it is unlikely that such old equipment is still working.

Where the work only involves contaminated materials which have been 'declared not to be subject to further control'. This is very unlikely in education.

Consequently, we conclude that, where any work is done in education with radioactive sources, these Regulations continue to require the radiation employer to appoint a suitable Radiation Protection Adviser. Where work is restricted to the use of an educational X-ray set such as the Tel-x-ometer, an RPA is not needed but, unless the exemption orders are changed, special approval is required for this work anyway.

Conclusions

A prime requirement of the Regulations is that the radiation employer must take all necessary steps to restrict exposure as much as is reasonably practicable. Equally, an employee has a duty not knowingly to expose him- or herself, or other people, to ionising radiation to any extent greater than reasonably necessary. However, over many years, use of radioactive materials has been tightly controlled in schools. Therefore, the *Ionising Radiations Regulations* 1999 will have little effect on day-to-day practice. As explained in section 5.6, leak testing of all sources is likely to be necessary at least every two years but as schools will already be familiar with testing radium sources this will not add a significant burden.

There is no need for extensive retraining of those teaching about radioactivity or supervising the use of sources in schools. However, the provision of information on radiation safety and refresher training is valuable in promoting health and safety. Induction training should be given to new teachers, especially since science, or even physics, graduates may not have been trained as undergraduates to work with radioactive substances.

Guidance accompanying the *Approved Code of Practice* (but without the same statutory force) defines the competency of RPAs which may then affect radiation employers in education. Revised exemption orders (giving exemption from registration under the *Radioactive Substances Act*) should clarify the position of independent schools and could have a more profound effect on school activities.

INDEX